PSYCHOSOMATICS

Howard R. and Martha E. Lewis

PSYCHOSOMATICS

How Your Emotions Can Damage Your Health

FOREWORD BY *Lawrence E. Lamb, M.D.*

NEW YORK / THE VIKING PRESS

TO OUR PARENTS

FOREWORD

Perhaps no other subject interests man more than himself. As man's knowledge of himself has grown, superstitions have been discarded, fact has replaced myth, and tolerance has replaced intolerance. It is natural that many different approaches have been used in an effort to explain the complexities of the human body, its normal function, and its malfunction. It is natural too that proponents of one discipline tend to disregard other disciplines and fabricate a simplistic concept of man and what happens to man. With increasing knowledge it becomes apparent that many different mechanisms all play a part in man's life and state of being, and no one mechanism excludes the others.

Man really is a product of his heredity, his physical environment, and his emotional environment, and each of these influences the other. A physical response or a physical characteristic can be caused in many different ways.

With a wealth of case histories, this book reports on a major finding of medical science that there is no doubt that the psyche is closely related to the function of the soma, or body. Hypnosis, for example, can be used in some people to induce sufficient anesthesia to permit a radical breast operation. In a larger number of people it can be used to make minor surgery easier—for example, common dental procedures. It can also be used to relieve pain or obscure signs of structural illness, such as seen in advanced stages of cancer.

The physical environment includes many causes for illness, including bacteria. Respiratory infections are much more common in schoolchildren in part because of increased exposure to infectious agents. The parents of school-age children have many more respiratory infections than people without children, for the same reason. Insufficient humidity, another environmental factor, leading to drying out of the normal protective lining of the nose and throat, increases the likelihood of a respiratory infection when one is exposed to the germs. In addition to bacteria, there are such factors as nutrition, physical activity, drugs (including coffee, alcohol, tobacco, pep pills, and tranquilizers), radiation, pollution, decreased oxygen, and even the weightlessness of space flight, which affect the physical well-being of the human body.

It is a mistake to assume that because a bodily disorder can be produced by one mechanism it cannot also be caused by another mechanism. A good example is the sensation of body heat and sweating. It is true that emotion and psychic stress can cause some people to feel warm and finally even to begin sweating. Sweating is one of the mechanisms by which the body is cooled. The body's complex heating and cooling mechanisms are controlled by its thermostat—the temperature center located in the hypothalamus of the brain. In this same region many of man's most complex emotional responses are integrated. Hence, during emotional episodes the body's thermostat may be affected by the adjacent mechanisms, and the message goes out from the thermostat to start the mechanisms used to cool the body. Blood flow is increased in the skin to carry hot blood to the surface, and sweating ensues, cooling the body by evaporation.

This well-established observation, however, does not prove that sweating is on a "psychosomatic basis" all the time. Another simple reason for sweating is that the body is hot, or the external environment is so hot that the only remaining way for the body to cool itself is through evaporation, hence sweating. The body temperature may be raised because of an infection. Or it can even be raised following the ingestion of spicy foods.

The whole concept of feeling hot or cold is made even more

complex because we sense temperature by nerve endings located only in the skin. The feeling that the skin is hot or cold may have very little to do with the internal body temperature. The skin may be cold in sunstroke from overexposure to the sun because there is little blood flow through the skin, and yet the body temperature may be 108 degrees Fahrenheit. This simple example demonstrates how complex the many factors that relate to a bodily response can be, and why no one factor alone provides an all-inclusive explanation of bodily reactions.

The frequent problem of impotence is another illustration of the multiplicity of factors that can produce a common effect. Often impotence is caused by emotional factors. However, it can also be caused by disease of the artery to the penis, limiting the amount of blood flow to the penis and making erection mechanically impossible. Impotence is also caused by diabetes, sometimes in relatively young men.

One example of the problem of overemphasis on one factor as the cause of abnormal body function was a case of a man who was receiving psychotherapy for intermittent periods of impotence. As the therapy progressed, the man became totally impotent, and he was so distressed by the deterioration of his condition that he shot and killed his psychiatrist. On examination at the time of his arrest, the man was found to have diabetes, the real cause for his impotence.

The converse may also be true: a person who has diabetes may have an impotence problem totally unrelated to his being diabetic, based solely on psychological factors. Regardless of whether impotence is caused by diabetes or psychological factors, the end result is the same, creating equal amounts of distress. Impotence is no less important when it is caused by psychological factors.

In some illnesses caused by anatomical changes, such as coronary-artery disease, the course of the illness may be affected by emotional and psychic factors. The common changes in the arteries that lead to heart attacks have been shown to be present in over 70 per cent of young men with an average age of 22 years, killed in the Korean War. Similar changes are almost universal in middle-aged American men. The frequency is so high in the American culture as to include almost all personality types and individuals with all known varieties of emotional backgrounds, psychic stress, and personalities. When the disease progresses to the point at which it causes recurring chest pain (angina pectoris) the pain may be precipitated by physical exertion or by emotional factors. Emotions may increase the work of the heart. An exciting football game may raise the heart rate and the blood pressure of the football enthusiast, and if the response is excessive the increased work of the sick heart may cause chest pain not greatly different from the effect of the increased heart rate caused by walking uphill.

A physician's early description of chest pain from heart disease included the comment that "the man who can make me angry holds my life in his hand." And indeed, one day, in a fit of anger, he died. Without the pre-existing structural changes in the heart, he could have easily tolerated the increased work the emotional stress imposed upon his heart.

Anxiety is a normal and expected reaction in many instances of illness. A person may develop cancer, for reasons that still defy medical science, and if the cancer is not curable it is to be expected that the person will be worried, depressed, and anxious. Those aspects of treatment which deal with these problems and the patient's immediate comfort are a major consideration in total treatment of the total patient and his total problem.

As this book shows, psychosomatic medicine, the name given to the study of the interrelations of the psyche and soma in disease, is an important and inescapable aspect of medicine. The psyche can be the main cause for malfunction, or malfunction can cause disturbance of the psyche. There is no such thing as mind *or* body. The mind is a function of the brain, which is part of the body; hence they are one.

LAWRENCE E. LAMB, M.D.

A NOTE FROM THE AUTHORS

As we wrote this book, we became more and more aware of the role psychosomatics plays in our own lives.

Sometimes our minor psychogenic afflictions were very obvious. Recently one of us (Howard) was writing a newspaper column. It was a feather in his cap and paid well, but it was taking up too much time and was increasingly a drag. The result was conflict.

Determined to quit, Howard phoned his editor. Suddenly a frog the size of an elephant clogged his throat. "Water," he croaked, and it was only with a constantly replenished supply that he managed to deliver his resignation. After the call, of course, his voice was just fine.

In a more serious vein, some months ago Howard became involved in a round of political activism. For the time being he forgot about writing this book, though it and a number of other obligations were growing more and more pressing. At last, one evening after a big dinner, he was stricken with sharp pains across his chest.

The diagnosis was a peptic ulcer. Getting back to work helped it heal. Thus, we experienced in personal terms that you can put something out of your mind but not necessarily out of your stomach (or some other part of your body). Our doctor thinks it ironic that, while doing a book on psychosomatic illnesses, Howard developed one.

As a youngster Martha was plagued by acne and allergies. In the course of researching this book it became clear that these ailments were linked to Martha's taking pride in her "common sense" and emotional control. Specialists we've gotten to know speculate that her expressions of anger were forced into these physiological forms. All in all, our research has led us to see ourselves as minds and bodies inseparably integrated.

This book is based on the work of professionals in the fields relating to psychosomatics. We extend to them our thanks. Except in Freud's classic case histories, we've made it a rule to disguise the identity of patients; any similarity to an actual name is sheer coincidence. A word of special appreciation is due our editor, Beatrice Rosenfeld, whose search for an up-to-date, readable book on psychosomatics led to this project.

HOWARD R. and MARTHA E. LEWIS

Shady, New York

CONTENTS

Part III: The Uses of the Body

Part IV: Protective Illnesses

Part V: Gut Reactions

Part VI: Closets in Your Skeleton

Part VII: Sex Problems

Part VIII: Breath, Skin, and the Supernatural

Part IX: Heart Disease and Cancer

Part X: Overcoming Resistance

In order to cure the human body it is necessary to have a knowledge of the whole of things.

—HIPPOCRATES

The av'rage unmarried female, basic'lly insecure
Due to some long frustration, may react
With psychosomatic symptoms, difficult to endure
Affecting the upper respiratory tract.
In other words, just from waiting around
For that plain little band of gold
A person . . . can develop a cold.*

—MISS ADELAIDE in *Guys and Dolls*

PROLOGUE

The Stunted Children

The doctor examining Eddie guessed he was about a year old. Actually he was four. Another boy, Steve, at eleven and a half, was smaller than most children half his age.

Physicians at Johns Hopkins Hospital saw thirteen such youngsters who were severely undersized and grossly immature in their speech and behavior. At some point early in their lives, their total development—physical as well as emotional—had been stunted.

How come? Food was no problem, the doctors found—there'd been plenty. Nor had the children inherited any physical disorders.

But emotionally the youngsters were deprived. All were from broken homes. Their fathers neglected them. Their mothers tended to be unstable. One mother was an alcoholic and psychotic. Another said of her son: "I hate him."

When the children were sheltered in a warm, accepting setting, they immediately began to thrive. In less than a year Steve grew more than six inches and gained a whopping thirty-nine pounds. Every child placed in a foster home or orphanage continued to flourish.

But children who returned to their own homes stopped growing and lost weight.

The effect of your emotions on your health is what this book is about.

PART I

Mind and Body Are One

Most illness hinges on emotional as well as

bodily factors. You are a mind-body unity. Your emotions

are physical phenomena, and every physiological

change has an emotional counterpart.

CHAPTER 1

Body, Mind, and Illness

Most sickness has an emotional component

• Chris has mixed feelings about becoming a father. He produces sperm normally during and just after his wife's period. But during the times of the month she is likely to conceive, he has no live sperm in his semen.

• A fifty-three-year-old suburbanite watches in horror as a car jumps a curb and races across his lawn toward him. The car misses him, leaving him unscratched but badly shaken. Within an hour he is dead of a heart attack.

• A man's leg is amputated because of gangrene. He soon begins to feel excruciating pain in the missing limb.

• A woman with cancer of the lymph glands enjoys a remission for three years. Her youngest son goes into the Army. She has a relapse. Another son is called back into service. Again the cancer flares up.

• An infant—the child of a cold, inconsistent mother—develops a peptic ulcer.

• A devout Catholic spontaneously bleeds from his hands, feet, and side. His wounds correspond to those of Christ on the cross.

• A rheumatoid arthritis condition is diagnosed purely on the basis of the patient's personality. The doctor does not know any physical findings, only the patient's traits and mannerisms.

3

This sampling of cases from this book illustrates aspects of psychosomatic medicine, or psychosomatics, the study of the relationship between emotions and bodily illness. "Psychosomatic" (from the Greek *psyche* = soul, *soma* = body) describes a total approach to health that is gaining increasing recognition among physicians. You are viewed as a mind-body unity, and your whole way of life is the context in which your health is considered.

The aspect of psychosomatics of most interest to laymen is that concerned with psychogenic disorders, those in which the emotional state plays a direct role in the production of a bodily illness. "We cannot weigh guilt or calculate the infective dose of fear," observes Dr. Bernard L. Mallett, an English psychiatrist, "yet these may be as productive of disease as the staphylococcus or the virus." The first four parts of this book deal largely with the general mechanisms of psychosomatics, the latter parts in the main with specific psychogenic disorders.

Such illnesses are extremely common. At the private outpatient service at Johns Hopkins Hospital in Baltimore, Dr. Bernard I. Lewis took a detailed survey of 163 patients, most between the ages of 20 and 60 and from upper- and middle-income brackets. Lewis found that 49 per cent had psychogenic disorders with no physical findings to account for their symptoms, and 27 per cent represented a combination of psychic and somatic illnesses.

In other words, 3 out of 4 patients in this study were suffering wholly or in part from emotionally originated disease.

Strong Passions

The word "psychosomatics" is relatively new. It was first used in German medical literature in 1922 but didn't come into common English usage until the early 1930s, when Dr. Helen Flanders Dunbar of the Columbia University College of Physicians and Surgeons used it as her term of choice in her monumental book *Emotions and Bodily Change*. This encyclopedic thousand-page "survey of psychosomatic interrelationships" quickly became a standard, and so along with it did "psychosomatic," the word Dr. Dunbar preferred to describe a concept that had been around for a long, long time.

The realization that mind and body are interrelated can be traced back at least 4500 years. Huang Ti, the Yellow Emperor of China and author of a classic on internal medicine, observed that frustration can make people become physically ill. "Their wishes and ideas should be [investigated and] followed," he prescribed, "and then . . . those who have attained spirit and energy [will be] flourishing and prosperous, while [others who have not] will perish."

Five centuries before the birth of Christ, Hippocrates postulated that to effect cures it was necessary for doctors to "have a knowledge of the whole of things." Socrates came back from army service to admonish his Greek countrymen that in one respect the barbarian Thracians were ahead of them: They knew that the body could not be cured without the mind. In Rome the physicians Soranus and Caelius Aurelianus practiced psychotherapy in order to alleviate their patients' bodily suffering.

During the Middle Ages both physical and mental illnesses were treated by ministering to the whole person, through that part of him that theology called his soul. Early in the sixteenth century Martin Luther declared, "Heavy thoughts bring on physical maladies; when the soul is oppressed so is the body." Luther was morbidly preoccupied with his health. He suffered throughout his adult life from constipation, which is frequently pychogenic. His agonizing inner struggles over his fealty to the church and his spiritual dissent he often likened to his torments on the toilet.

For centuries it was taken for granted that people could die of grief, that unrequited love could cause illness, that fear and anger could make men ill. At the beginning of the nineteenth century, a French physician named Pierre Cabanis expounded on the concept that "strong passions" could have pathological consequences on the body. This was during the French Revolution, and Cabanis called for the total adoption of a psychosomatic approach as a means of reforming medicine.

But with the flowering of the germ theory of disease in the second half of the nineteenth century, and with medicine's increasing interest in discovering specific microorganisms as causes of specific diseases, much of this earlier understanding of human nature and the role of emotion in disease was tossed aside.

Your Emotions and Your Health

Chances are you are used to thinking of some aspects of yourself as physical and others as mental. But the distinction is merely one of language. For your "mind" and your "body" are actually integrated parts of your whole being. And it is impossible for one part of you to change without effecting a change in other parts.

Every emotion you feel is a physical event. When you have a strong emotional reaction, even one generated by watching a movie, hormones are secreted and your body chemistry is altered. When the feelings are particularly strong, the physical reactions are likely to be equally extreme. Emotion can alter your endocrine balance and your blood supply and pressure, inhibit your digestion, and change your breathing and the temperature of your skin. A sustained state of emotional upset may cause changes that lead to disease. Your psyche may trigger the overreaction of hormones, which may produce a disease process.

Your body tries continually to be in a state of equilibrium, maintaining a precarious balance between too much of a substance and too little. If stress or other factors upset this seesaw, the body will seek to adapt by altering its chemistry. This alteration can be damaging to the rest of the organism, causing so-called diseases of adaptation.

One source of stress is external change. Big events, good or bad, in your private life may make you vulnerable to illness. Social change, war pressures, job tensions are accompanied by sharp rises in disease. The chronic stresses of fast-paced everyday life are taking their toll.

What makes a person develop one disease rather than another? To some degree, his personality make-up. Researchers are finding that people with certain character traits are likely to suffer from certain illnesses. For example, people with neurodermatitis—a type of skin affliction—usually have a craving for close physical contact. A hereditary vulnerability, or one acquired through illness or injury, may combine with emotional factors to produce a disease. Thus someone with an inherited predisposition to diabetes may develop symptoms of the disease during a stressful period.

Virtually all illness has emotional components. Excluded from most discussions of psychosomatics, however, are such strictly inherited conditions as hemophilia and sickle-cell anemia. Also not considered in the realm of psychosomatics are diseases caused by environmental factors, such as food poisonings, occupational diseases, and poisoning from pollutants. On the other hand, it is possible that in such cases the level of impairment may be increased by psychic stress—once a condition is present, the emotional state of the victim often helps determine the course of the illness.

Your susceptibility to microorganisms of disease—the virus of the common cold, for example; the bacilli of tuberculosis—may fluctuate with your state of mind. Gastrointestinal conditions, sexual disturbances, heart disease, and countless other ailments have been found by investigators to have strong psychological factors.

Even cancer has recently been linked to emotion. Researchers are finding that cancer victims are often people who have long felt hopeless, who have believed that their lives are doomed to despair. The onset of the disease in many cases is associated with a series of overwhelming losses that makes the person finally give up entirely.

Treatment of psychosomatic conditions is hampered by the fact that, despite growing recognition of the importance of emotional factors in bodily illness, many physicians remain unaware of psychosomatic principles. Trained to hunt for single causes and specific remedies, they tend to think of some problems as "mental" and others as "physical." They may overlook the complex interrelationship of a patient's emotions, physiology, and environment. Often physicians are hostile to psychiatry. In ignoring emotional problems which contribute to illness, they may inadvertently worsen the patient's condition.

Medicine can come to its fullest flowering only when the medical profession takes into account the integrated nature of the human being, and learns to treat psyche and soma as the inseparable phenomena they are.

CHAPTER 2

The Unity of You

Your emotions and your body are inseparable

The twenty volunteers urinated into specimen jars, then gathered to see a movie. Afterward Dr. Lennart Levi of the Caroline Institute in Stockholm had them give follow-up urine samples.

The film they saw, a routine travelogue, evoked little emotional response. Urinalyses showed that while the volunteers were watching the movie, their glands reduced the production of the hormones adrenalin and noradrenalin.

By contrast, over successive days the volunteers saw a war tragedy, *Paths of Glory;* a comedy, *Charley's Aunt;* and a horror film, *The Devil's Mask.* These spurred strong reactions—sorrow, joy, fear. Urinalyses disclosed correspondingly sharp rises in the volunteers' production of these hormones.

Emotion alone (and experienced through a movie, at that) had caused profound changes in their body chemistry.

Mind and Body Are One

Mental and physical phenomena are always so interrelated. Your body and your mind are inseparable parts of a single biochemical unity, the sum total of which is you. There is but one process going on within you. You may be aware of some of its

9

manifestations in your tissues and organs. Other outcroppings you may discern as thought or emotion.

Because of language and custom, you may call one type of manifestation "body," the other "mind." But in actual operation they are as intermixed as the yolk and the white in a scrambled egg.

"It is not possible in biology to set up a partition between mind and body," observed Henry Maudsley, a distinguished English psychiatrist. "Mind does not merely affect the body, it permeates its constitution. . . . On the other hand, there is not a function of any organ of the body which does not enter into the constitution of the mind."

To divide human functioning into the mental and the physical is to make an artificial distinction. You are in fact one integrated being functioning as a whole. Every mental response, whether an emotional reaction or an intellectual activity, is part and parcel of a physical process. By the same token, every physical state —be it comfort or disease—has emotional components.

"The question 'Physical *or* psychic?' . . . is in most cases wrongly put," Swiss psychiatrist Eugen Bleuler pointed out. Rather, you need always to consider, "What of this is mental, and what is physical?" The two invariably go together.

You may find this hard to accept because language can work against you. Words are rife to distinguish between "mind" and "body," "mental" and "physical," "psychic" and "somatic"—and this distinction is made official by dictionaries which define such couplets as antonyms, when actually they're functionally inseparable.

Dr. David T. Graham of the University of Wisconsin Medical School calls such mind-versus-body terminology "linguistic dualism." For many day-to-day purposes it is convenient to conceive of, say, doing a multiplication problem as "mental" and catching a cold as "physical." But it is important to remember that this is nothing more than a linguistic convenience—it is in direct opposition to the way you actually work.

" 'Psychological' and 'physical' [and their synonyms] refer to different ways of talking about the *same* event, and not to different events," says Dr. Graham. "The difference between 'mental' and 'physical' . . . is not in the event observed, but rather in the language in which [it is] discussed."

In Mental Ways

You already know from your own experience that your body chemistry is interwoven with your emotional state.

Merely recall the last time you had a bad cold. Chances are you were gloomy and short-tempered, and you lost your usual enjoyment of food and reading and company. These mental effects were as much a part of your cold as your runny nose.

Indeed, during influenza epidemics some companies urge employees to stay home at the first sign of illness. Not only might they spread infection, but also, mentally befogged by flu, they are likely to commit costly errors on the job.

The most prominent symptoms of some serious physical ailments are seemingly emotional in origin.

Tuberculosis is sometimes marked by lassitude, fatigue, and vague aches and pains. These symptoms are so nonphysical in the traditional sense that doctors sometimes label such sufferers "crocks" and overlook TB in its early stages. A similar problem is posed by pyelonephritis, a kidney infection. Victims of this disease may be dismissed as "depressed" or "bored" before their physical condition is recognized.

In the last century members of the British army and navy in the Mediterranean were falling ill with what seemed to be a species of madness. Patients were extremely irritable and depressed. They suffered from fatigue and insomnia, and literally shook from nervousness. Their problem proved to be a bacterial infection caught from drinking raw milk. Labeled "brucellosis" (after Sir David Bruce, an early investigator), the disease remains fairly common in agricultural areas. Dr. Wesley W. Spink of the University of Minnesota Medical School warns that patients with chronic brucellosis must be carefully differentiated from patients with personality aberrations or neurological disorders.

Some types of cancer have a similar tendency to simulate psychiatric illness. Dr. Z. J. Lipowski of the psychiatric faculty of McGill University tells of having three patients referred to him over a brief period, each supposedly a psychotic suffering from depression. In each case Dr. Lipowski found the depressive psychosis was a result of undetected cancer of the pancreas.

Nutritional disorders also may affect behavior in bizarre ways. Pellagra results from a dietary deficiency in niacin, a compound of the vitamin B complex. The first cases in the United States were found in institutions for the insane. The patients were psychotic, disoriented, and suffering from hallucinations and delirium. Once niacin was added to their diet, their symptoms disappeared.

It is a commonplace that any interference with the physical function of the brain can directly affect emotion and intellect. Dr. William B. Abrams of Jefferson Medical College describes an intelligent and personable executive in his sixties who took pride in his neatness and dress. During a period of a few months he became slovenly and antisocial. His language became profane, and he grew more and more suspicious and depressed. This profound personality change was due to a series of "little strokes," destruction of small areas of brain cells resulting from the hardening and blockage of local arteries.

An abscess within the brain can likewise lead to psychiatric illness, usually attacks of depression or anxiety accompanied by vague headaches. Brain abscesses most frequently occur after infections of the ears or sinuses.

The most prevalent infection of the brain arises from untreated syphilis, generally from ten to twenty-five years after the original illness. One syphilitic state of mental deterioration— termed general paresis or paretic neurosyphilis—often is marked by paranoia. Some paretics have manic symptoms.

Winston Churchill's father, Lord Randolph Churchill, was a dazzling orator who seemed certain to cap a brilliant political career by one day becoming Prime Minister. Alas, he had contracted syphilis in his youth—and the disease progressed unchecked so that, as his friend Lord Rosebery observed, "he died by inches in public." Irrationality born of paresis led to a number of rash judgments, including abruptly resigning from the Cabinet. Ravaged by the illness, he made his last speech before Parliament. It was so garbled that members of the House of Commons fled into the lobby out of pity and shame. With a terrible, mad look, Churchill screamed after them, "You damned fools!"

It's All Physical

All activities of your body—"mental" as well as "physical"—depend on alterations in your body tissues.

Even doing a multiplication problem, ordinarily thought of as a mental operation, entails a great number of physical changes. Quick. Multiply 2×3.

Now let's see how you've been physically affected by the process of arriving at the answer.

First, the characters 2×3 flash onto the rear wall of your eye, your retina, as dark shapes on a white field, activating individual nerve cells. These "sensors" are excited by the energy of light. From surrounding fluid they draw in electrically charged chemical particles called ions.

This puts the cell into an abnormal electrical state. The ions travel through the cell to an "end branch." There they combine with a compound, forming a "transmitter substance." The transmitter is instantly discharged from the end branch into the space between nerve cells (termed the "synapse"). This restores the cell's normal electrical balance and readies it to receive and transmit the next impulse from the eye.

The transmitter substance crosses a gap and touches the next cell. Excess ions now flow into the second cell, triggering a like reaction. Again a transmitter is formed and ejected, activating a third cell. And so on, through the fibers of your optic nerve. About a thousandth of a second after you first see 2×3 on the printed page, it chemically registers in the rear of your brain.

Within this flickering of time, more switching and signaling have gone on than takes place in all the telephone exchanges on this planet. The precise message that is conveyed depends on which branch of a cell is activated and exactly what transmitter substance is produced. A nerve fiber is made up of a multitude of cells whose branchlike ends are intertwined by the thousands. An astronomical number of routes is thus possible, and each of these routes—with subtly varying chemistry—can accommodate a different message.

What the shapes 2, ×, and 3 signify and what you should do with them are largely matters of memory. You have in your brain some ten billion interconnected nerve cells. When a cell receives a stimulus, it produces a molecule of a substance called ribonucleic acid (RNA). This molecule causes the cell on receiving a given impulse to respond in a particular way: varying its chemical make-up, releasing special compounds, taking part in an electrochemical circuit. Such responses constitute your mental activity.

RNA may prove to be the essential unit of memory. James V. McConnell of the University of Michigan extracted RNA from trained flatworms and injected it into untrained ones. The training appeared to be transferred along with the chemical. Merely from the injection, the untrained worms performed as well as the trained ones had.

In your brain the RNA of innumerable cells is implicated in your interpreting the symbols 2 × 3 and coming up with the answer 6. All of which points out that your ability to multiply exists as a physical fact. It's not off in the blue somewhere as "mental"; it exists in your body cells.

Charley Horses and Orgasms

Proprioception (from the Latin for "taking one's own") is the term for your ability to perceive sensations originating within your body. A Charley horse is a proprioceptive sensation. So is a stomach-ache. So for that matter is an orgasm, or a general sense of well-being.

Such feelings are largely the product of proprioceptors, specialized nerve endings that are sensitive to changes within your muscles, tendons, joints. Proprioceptors may make you aware of pressures inside your abdomen or legs or genitals, in much the same way that nerve endings in your skin can alert you to outside changes in temperature or texture.

Your emotions are proprioceptive sensations. If this surprises you, where do you feel this surprise? In the back of your neck? In your belly?

The precise spots vary from person to person. But every emotion you feel, you do just that: you *feel* it. Physically. In specific locations.

Like your intellectual ability to multiply 2 × 3, emotions exist in your body cells. Tune into yourself the next time you feel in a particular way—happy, sad, whatever. You'll find that essentially the same set of proprioceptive sensations constitute the feeling you've come to label "happiness" or "sadness." Happiness may in part be a lightness in your chest, sadness a leaden weight there. From such proprioceptive locations come the figures of speech "lighthearted" and "heavyhearted."

Painful feelings like anxiety and depression are literally pains: hurtful proprioceptive sensations. When you say, "My feelings are hurt," you mean exactly that. The ache of rejection is no less an ache than the ache of a crushed finger.

Against Common Sense

From where in your body do such feelings spring?

In a book-lined study at Harvard, William James—brother of the novelist Henry James and a pioneer in psychology—speculated on the dynamics of proprioceptive sensations. With C. G. Lange, a Danish physiologist, James advanced a theory which forms the basis of most contemporary work on emotion, though it flies in the face of what most people believe is the normal course of events.

Common sense suggests that first you have an emotional experience and then your bodily expression follows. Presumably you are sad, therefore you cry. You're afraid, and so your heart beats faster. You become enraged, and in response to your rage your adrenal glands pump the hormone adrenalin into your bloodstream. According to popular belief, a stimulus (S) produces an emotion (E), which leads to physiological responses (PR), such as tears or an increased heartbeat or adrenalin in your bloodstream. The common-sense sequence can be represented by:

$$S \rightarrow E \rightarrow PR$$

But, argued James and Lange, this puts the cart before the horse. They contended that the stimulus leads to physiological responses, and it is these bodily phenomena that you experience as emotion. The sequence they suggest is:

$$S \rightarrow PR \rightarrow E$$

According to the James-Lange theory, you feel sad *because* you cry. You feel fear *because* your heart beats faster. You are enraged *because* adrenalin is pouring into your blood. The resulting proprioceptive changes are what you subjectively interpret as emotion.

The $S \rightarrow PR \rightarrow E$ sequence proposed by James and Lange is now widely accepted. There's little doubt that your bodily expression can help determine your mood. From your own experience, you know that if you smile when sad you can feel happier. In the recent phenomenon of encounter groups, a favorite technique is to ask you to punch a pillow. Participants are often astonished at how the physical act of hitting can bring forth long bottled-up feelings of anger, which may be dispelled through the punching.

At the same time, the physiological basis of the James-Lange theory has undergone considerable refining. As critics have pointed out, you feel afraid a moment or so *before* your heart starts pumping faster. Your increased heartbeat may prolong and intensify your initial feelings of fear. But your internal organs react too slowly to account for the immediate emotional reaction.

Subsequent studies have also shown that adrenalin pours into your bloodstream in dozens of situations besides those provoking rage. Can the same amount of adrenalin in one situation be experienced as rage, in another as excitement, in a third as ecstasy? Not by itself, it can't. Such a bodily reaction alone is too indiscriminate to account for the subtle range of emotion.

Finally, experiments have demonstrated that there is a component to emotion over and beyond outpourings of hormones. Subjects were injected with fear-related hormones. In a detached way many felt "as if" they were afraid. But few experienced the actual feeling of fear.

Thus, James and Lange recognized the physical origins of emotion. It took more recent investigators to explain how you correlate your conscious experience of emotion and your subtle bodily sensations.

A Brain for Emotion

A current view of emotion holds that it is largely a function of the limbic system. "Limbic" means "border," and the structures comprising the system extend from the fringe of the brain to its center.

Paul D. MacLean of the Yale University School of Medicine has developed a theory that the limbic system serves as a "visceral brain." It interprets experience in terms of feeling—i.e., nonverbal sensations—rather than in terms of intellectualized symbols: words, conclusions, ideas.

The limbic system is a primitive part of the brain. Its counterpart is found in the brains of lower animals, in contrast to the cerebral cortex which is found only high up on the evolutionary scale. Intellectual activity is centered in the cerebral cortex, whereas emotional experience is achieved through the limbic system, which generates "organ language" instead of words.

Alterations to the limbic system directly cause emotional changes. Experimenters have found that lesions in some areas make shy monkeys fearless, turn mountain lions into docile pets, and convert tame laboratory rats into snarling aggressors. Specific centers of the limbic system have been stimulated with electrodes, with dramatic emotional effects. (The presence of such an electrical connection does not pain or discommode an animal.) Fear and fearlessness, hunger and satiety, rages and sexual urges have all been induced by sending a tiny current to a given area. Sometimes completely opposite effects have resulted from moving an electrode from one group of cells to another a mere fiftieth of an inch away.

A notable series of experiments in electrical stimulation of the brain came about by accident. James Olds of McGill University was placing an electrode in the brain of a rat. Olds intended to shock the animal when it reached a certain corner of an experimental box.

However, in placing the electrode he was somewhat off his mark. When the rat reached the proper corner, Olds gave it a small shot of current, expecting it to withdraw due to the shock. To his surprise, the rat enjoyed the experience. Instead of avoiding the corner, it kept returning to it.

Olds and his colleague Peter Milner discovered that a portion of the brain functions as a "pleasure center." They rigged up a treadle, which a rat could press to receive a dosage of current to this portion of its brain. Some rats with electrodes in the pleasure center of their limbic system would press the treadle at the rate of 200 times an hour. Nearby groups of cells are evidently centers of absolute ecstasy. Rats with electrodes there pressed the treadle as often as 5000 times an hour until they dropped from exhaustion.

Amalgam of Perceptions

The limbic system has a strategic relationship with other areas of your brain, providing clues to the interplay between your conscious awareness and your bodily feelings.

Tracings show that through circuitry from your sense organs, the limbic system can receive external stimuli—sights, sounds, tastes, smells, and touches that can evoke emotion. Through other nerve connections the limbic system can respond to your body sensations and can work in close association with centers of consciousness in your cerebral cortex.

The emotion that a proprioceptive feeling develops into depends a great deal on your conscious interpretation. In one experiment a group of volunteers were given injections of adrenalin, which causes a nonspecific internal arousal—you feel "funny." One by one, some of the volunteers were put into a room with an actor who pretended to be euphoric. He spoke in a wild, exultant way and acted with unrestrained hilarity. The volunteers caught his high mood. They joined in his antics and added their own. For them, the adrenalin opened the door to euphoria.

Other volunteers were asked to fill out a long, excruciating questionnaire. This time the actor who was placed in the room with each of them exploded with pretended anger. "I'm not going to waste any more time on this," he yelled. He tore up the questionnaire and stomped out of the room. The subjects caught the feeling he generated, and their adrenalin reaction developed into anger.

Still other subjects who received adrenalin were told at the outset what to expect in the way of physical symptoms. Able to account for the effects of the adrenalin, they stared incredulously at the antics of the "euphoric" actor and remained calm despite the "angry" one. A final group of subjects received dummy injections. Having no unusual internal sensations, they likewise tended to remain unaffected by the actor.

Thus a complete emotional experience is an amalgam of your perception of external events combined with your perception of internal bodily sensations. To the uninformed subjects, the physical effects of the adrenalin could become either euphoria or anger, depending on the influence of the actor. In cases where there were no physical sensations or where the sensations were nullified by information, the emotional effects were similarly diminished.

Your Other Nervous System

The limbic system evidently translates both conscious and bodily stimuli to the hypothalamus. This structure is near the base of your brain, under (*hypo* in Greek) the thalamus, a sensory relay center. The hypothalamus mediates such basic drives as hunger, thirst, and sex. It determines the internal environment of your body through control of your autonomic nervous system.

If you diagramed your entire network of nerve fibers as an electrician might chart the circuits of a building, you'd find two major branches. One—the one you're most aware of—is the cerebrospinal system. It carries sensory impulses to your brain, and from your brain transmits impulses regulating the voluntary movement of your muscles.

The other system—the autonomic—works below your conscious level (it's autonomous, hence its name) and is far more important to sustaining life. Respiration, circulation, metabolism are all within the purview of the autonomic system.

The system keeps your body in a perpetual state of adjustment. Your blood pressure rises and falls. Your oxygen consumption changes. Minute passages in your lungs dilate and contract. The number and type of cells in your blood are in flux. Your blood-sugar content increases and decreases. The movement of food in your digestive tract speeds up and slows down. Your secretion of hormones trickles, then floods, then stops altogether.

This activity is accomplished through two opposing subsystems—the sympathetic and the parasympathetic—which enable the organs to work smoothly yet adapt quickly to change. The sympathetic nerve system generally tenses and constricts involuntary muscles and blood vessels, and steps up the activity of glands. The parasympathetic does the reverse, producing expansion and relaxation.

Your autonomic nervous system generates many of the bodily sensations you recognize as emotion. These manifestations figure in popular speech. People have "cold feet" and are "frozen with terror"—products of contraction caused by the sympathetic subsystem. Conversely, "bursting with enthusiasm," "warmhearted" and "swollen with pride" are derived from the parasympathetic expansion.

Your emotions, then, are physical phenomena, existing within your body as proprioceptive sensations. They are products of a complex interplay between portions of your brain—particularly the cerebral cortex, the center of conscious interpretation; the limbic system, which serves as a clearinghouse; and the hypothalamus, which regulates the autonomic nervous system.

All these mechanisms can play a part in the development of psychosomatic disease.

CHAPTER 3

Your Emotional Chemistry

Your psyche can trigger your glands

It's after dinner. You're alone, relaxing, reading a newspaper.

Suddenly, from the next room, there's a noise. The sound of a window slowly being raised.

You look up from your paper.

More noises. Someone is climbing in.

You get up.

A door flings open.

From out of the darkness a stranger rushes toward you. . . .

Fight or Flight

If this episode occurred in real life, you'd undergo sharp physical changes that would help to prepare you for vigorous effort and the results of injury. You may even now feel a twinge of this reaction just from reading the foregoing account. Let's see what happens inside you as you go from relaxation to a state of stress.

When you're relaxed, your parasympathetic nervous system predominates. Your brain functions at a moderate level of arousal. After a meal you're likely to be somewhat drowsy as blood is shunted from your brain and muscles to your digestive tract. You breathe easily. Your heart beats regularly and slowly. Your skin is warm and dry.

Then come the menacing sounds in the next room. As if alerted by a siren, you mobilize your resources. Abruptly your sympathetic system takes over. Your digestion comes to a halt. Blood shifts to your muscles and brain. Your muscles tense. Your brain becomes highly aroused. You suck in air more deeply. Your blood pressure rises. Your heart pounds faster. As the peripheral blood vessels contract, your skin becomes cold and clammy./

Sugar, a fast-burning fuel, is released into your blood from the liver. Fat gets mobilized for fuel. Additional red corpuscles enrich the circulation. White cells, to combat infection, pour in from your spleen. Increased platelets improve the blood's ability to coagulate.

Physiologist Walter B. Cannon termed this set of responses the "fight or flight" pattern. At Harvard in 1914 Cannon was studying movements of the stomach. He fed a cat a meal laced with salts of the element barium, so the cat's stomach showed up on X-ray film. Cannon found by X ray that as long as the cat was content, its stomach went through wavelike digestive motions: now looking like a smooth sausage, now like an hourglass pinched in two or three places.

The instant the cat was angered or frightened, these motions came to a dead halt. As if paralyzed, the stomach remained smooth or constricted for an hour or more. It stayed frozen even after the cause for fright was removed and the cat made comfortable.

As an explanation, Cannon advanced his "emergency theory" that adrenalin prepares the animal for fight or flight during times of stress. In an emergency the animal suspends nonessential tasks such as digestion and quickly becomes physically capable of meeting its enemy or running away.

In humans, these changes are associated with such elemental emotional experiences as pain, fear, rage. The physical alterations you undergo are holdovers from the distant past, when primitive man daily had to fight savage beasts or run away from them.

"The facts at once have significance if considered in relation to the struggle for existence," Cannon wrote. "If fear always paralyzed it would result only in danger of destruction. But fear and aggressive feeling, as anticipatory responses to critical situations, make ready for action, and thereby they have had great survival value."

Chemicals that Govern

Adrenalin is secreted from the interior (the medulla) of the adrenal gland, a two-inch-long, roughly pyramidal structure straddling one end of each kidney. The adrenal gland is triggered by the sympathetic nervous system, and this nerve-gland system gave experimenters the first clues to the inseparability of mind and body and the causes of psychosomatic ills.

A gland is a collection of cells specialized for the secretion of fluids. The first glands explored by physiologists were the *exocrine* glands, which release secretions through ducts onto a selected body surface. The salivary glands are exocrine. They send saliva into the mouth by means of minute tubes. The sweat glands similarly have ducts connecting with the surface of the skin.

The other major group of glands—*endocrine* or ductless glands such as the adrenal—are far more important in the development of psychosomatic diseases. These glands release their secretions directly into the blood. The secretions, termed "hormones" (from the Greek *horman,* to stir up), are highly potent. Though greatly diluted, a mere drop may stimulate a particular activity.

A few crystals of adrenalin, dissolved in 100,000 parts of water, can be injected into a cat. In less than a minute the cat will arch its back and bare its claws. Its widened pupils gleam. Its whiskers stiffen. It foams at the mouth. Its tail bushes out to many times its normal size. Its heart is racing, breathing rapid, blood overflowing with sugar. All this from the equivalent of a sprinkle of salt in a bathtubful of water.

Sensitive to Emotion

The adrenal gland was discovered in 1563 by an Italian anatomist named Bartolomeo Eustachi (who gave his name to another of his discoveries, the Eustachian tube between the throat and ear). For centuries no one knew what the structure did. Indeed, in 1716 the Academy of Science of France offered a prize to anyone who could explain its functions.

Nearly 200 years later two Englishmen, Dr. George Oliver and Sir Edward Sharpey-Schafer, strained an extract from the medulla and found that it had amazing powers of increasing the heart and raising the blood pressure of the arteries. Soon afterward Dr. John J. Abel of Johns Hopkins University separated the active substance itself and named it adrenalin.

Walter Cannon at Harvard with a colleague, D. de la Paz, discovered the relationship between emotion and the outpouring of adrenalin and its consequences. In 1911 Cannon and de la Paz reported that when a cat, strapped into a holder, was frightened by a barking dog, detectable amounts of adrenalin suddenly appeared in the blood. Cannon further found that adrenalin causes the liver to release amounts of sugar into the blood: A normal cat, when frightened, had abnormal quantities of sugar in its urine—whereas in cats whose adrenalin glands had been removed, the sugar remained the same.

The applicability of this to humans? Cannon took urine samples of Harvard students in the midst of difficult exams. With striking frequency they had excessive amounts of sugar in their urine due to adrenalin released in response to the emotional strain of their tests. Cannon, an indefatigable researcher, went to the Harvard football field and collected urine from players during the most exciting game of the season. Even players on the bench had high sugar concentrations, the product of adrenalin released in the heat of emotion.

Stressful Situations

Almost any type of emotional strain can raise your production of adrenalin. Among stressful situations that have been explored:

Air travel. Investigators found that adrenalin levels among passengers of a military air transport jumped after the plane took off. Even the pilots experienced a marked rise in adrenalin during flight.

In another experiment pilots underwent simulated emergencies in a flight-training machine. In this replica of a cockpit, equipment was made to malfunction, air pressure went out of control, and so forth. The pilots' adrenalin levels rose with each unexpected incident.

Anxious anticipation was felt by a group of volunteers waiting to ride in a centrifuge, a high-speed merry-go-round that immobilized the rider and made him much heavier than normal. The ride has elements of fun—it's found in some amusement parks —but it also can be stressful. Adrenalin levels of the volunteers started rising well before they actually got on the machine.

Harassment. Researchers M. Frankenhaeuser and S. Kareby assigned volunteers a series of tasks. The volunteers set about doing the work diligently. But Frankenhaeuser and Kareby rushed them and criticized them unfairly. This unexplained harassment was part of the experiment. The adrenalin output of the angry, frustrated volunteers skyrocketed.

Laboratory tests have simulated some of the conditions of ordinary employment—and have found that enough harassment is present in day-to-day jobs to cause sharp rises in adrenalin levels. Dr. Lennart Levi of the Caroline Institute in Stockholm, a principal researcher in this field, set up a situation duplicating the tedium and irritation inherent in many factory jobs. He gave volunteers the job of sorting 2000 steel balls close in size to one another. The boredom of the job was worsened by harassment from noise, bright light, criticism, and a tight deadline. Adrenalin levels rose sharply, even among volunteers who'd shown a high tolerance for stress.

In a study of young women performing their everyday work as invoice clerks, Levi found evidence of the strain that can be caused by supposed job incentives. The girls' adrenalin output increased substantially on days when they were on a piecework rather than a salaried basis.

Tiredness. Lack of sleep can greatly increase the emotional stressfulness of a situation and the consequent secretion of adrenalin. In one study volunteers suffered a night of sleep deprivation. This alone caused an increase in adrenalin. When the volunteers tried to perform routine laboratory tasks following a night of sleep loss, their adrenalin response was even more markedly exaggerated.

Fear. Four-year-old Denise was to undergo the extraction of some baby teeth. Some time before, she had had a bad experience with a local anesthetic for stitches in her forehead. Now, screaming, she balked at sitting in the dentist's chair. It was necessary for the dentist to give the struggling child a sedative before he could proceed.

Within minutes of the extraction, Denise had a heart attack. She was rushed to a hospital, but died two days later. The coroner found that her heart had stopped because of the excess of adrenalin in her bloodstream due to fear.

Shell Around a Nut

Many other hormones besides adrenalin are released into the blood during times of stress.

Noradrenalin, discovered in 1946, is also secreted from the adrenal medulla. It serves to increase blood pressure during emergencies. Noradrenalin may help spur you on to vigorous, aggressive behavior. Studies of African mammals show that aggressive animals—lions and the like—have higher concentrations of noradrenalin pumping through their circulatory system than do nonaggressive beasts, such as giraffes and antelopes.

The medulla of the adrenal gland is covered by a barklike cortex, resembling the shell around a nut. The cortex is a gland totally independent of the medulla. In some animals the two are separate glands; in humans the medulla can be scooped out without disturbing the cortex.

Like adrenalin, the hormones of the adrenal cortex ebb and flow with your emotional state. Indeed, the adrenal cortex is the gland that has been most extensively studied in terms of its response to emotional stimuli. Dr. John W. Mason of the Walter Reed Army Institute of Research has credited the massive body of data accumulating from these studies with leading the way to "establishing a solid foundation for a science of psychoendocrinology."

The importance of the adrenal cortex was first reported in 1855 by Thomas Addison, an English physician. Addison happened to see over a brief period a number of patients with the same combination of symptoms: greatly weakened muscles, low blood pressure, nausea with diarrhea and cramps, and bronze patches on the skin. All the patients died a few months after the condition began. On autopsy, Addison found that the adrenal cortex of every one of them had been destroyed.

It was sheer chance that enough patients with this condition came to Addison to arouse his curiosity. Addison's disease is rare —many physicians go through their careers without seeing a single case. After adrenalin was separated from the adrenal medulla, physicians hoped it would cure Addison's disease. When injected into the body, adrenalin *did* temporarily raise the blood pressure—but only for a short time. It at last became clear that the adrenals were made of two distinct glands—the medulla, which produced adrenalin, and the cortex, with altogether different functions.

Subsequent investigators found that the adrenal cortex is essential to maintaining the balance of sodium and potassium in your blood and cells. When the balance is upset because of damage to the cortex, the blood loses water and thickens while the tissues become waterlogged and disabled. Toxic wastes gather in the kidneys, poisoning the body. The body becomes less and less able to withstand infection, cold, and heat. Even a slight illness or injury can cause shock, often death.

In 1927 physiologists separated a substance from the adrenal cortex and injected it into animals whose adrenal glands had been removed. The animals had been suffering all the symptoms of Addison's disease. Now the substance reversed the course of the illness. This, the experimenters concluded, was the hormone of the adrenal cortex that they called "cortin."

To their surprise, later experiments showed that they had separated out not one hormone but about thirty. These hormones are often termed steroids because they contain carbon rings typical of the sterol family of chemicals; they are also termed corticosteroids and adrenocorticosteroids to indicate that they are derived from the adrenal cortex.

Some of the steroids—for example, cortisone and cortisol—raise muscle strength and efficiency and increase blood flow in certain parts of the body. This group (called glucocorticoids) also reduces inflammation and protects the tissues against the effects of injury. Because of their anti-inflammatory properties, these compounds, extracted from animals and synthesized in laboratories, have wide use in the treatment of conditions ranging from poison ivy to rheumatoid arthritis.

Other corticosteroids (the mineralocorticoids) promote proper sodium and potassium balances in the blood and cells and help regulate the functions of the kidneys. DOCA (desoxycorticosterone) was the first corticosteroid to be duplicated in a laboratory. This achievement meant that no one need ever again die of Addison's disease.

Chemical Telegraph

There is a hormone linkage—a sort of chemical telegraph system—between the brain and the adrenal cortex. This method of sending a message from the brain to a gland is wholly different from the nerve system which connects the hypothalamus of the brain to the adrenal medulla. The hypothalamus also connects across a bridge of nerve tissue with the pituitary gland, a pea-sized structure that emits at least ten secretions. The pituitary is called the master gland of the endocrine system because it produces secretions which trigger other glands—"target" glands—to produce, in turn, hormones.

On receiving a certain message from the hypothalamus, the pituitary releases into the bloodstream ACTH (for adrenocorticotropic hormone; the suffix "tropic" means "acting upon"). ACTH acts upon the adrenal cortex, causing it to secrete steroids.

The first hint of this process was found in 1922 by an investigator named T. Uno, who exposed rats to six-hour periods of fighting and other excitement. He then dissected the rats and weighed their pituitary glands against those of control rats. The glands of the excited rats were heavier, suggesting that the pituitary was affected by the excitement.

The pituitary-adrenal cortical system is remarkably sensitive to even subtle psychological factors. Housing conditions, the amount of handling, the degree of social activity with other animals—all are reflected in corticosteroid changes. Marked responses are noted in novel experiences. Transfering a monkey from one cage to another, for example, will send its ACTH response up, as will punishing it or placing it in a restraining chair.

Human corticosteroid responses to stress are similar. One volunteer, on duty at a hospital, tripled his corticosteroid output on being summoned to an emergency call. Other studies—of racing car drivers at the Indianapolis Speedway 500-mile event, of parachute jumpers, of college students taking final exams—show increased corticosteroid activity in response to stressful events.

In a study of stress supervised by Dr. G. W. Thorn of the Harvard Medical School, physiological tests were given to members of the varsity crew during practice sessions, as well as before and after the Harvard-Yale race. Thorn and his colleagues expected that the terrific physical effort of the practice sessions would produce evidence of stress, but the oarsmen's corticosteroid response was not as great as might have been expected.

The morning before the race, however, corticosteroid secretions began to rise, indicating that emotional components such as tension and anticipation are at least as great an influence on secretions as physical stress. In the excitement of the race, these outpourings climbed to extreme heights and the crewmen finished up completely exhausted.

Surprisingly, their coach, who had been watching from the sidelines, showed as much evidence of stress as the crew.

PART II

Emotion Can Cause Disease

Not only does your psyche trigger the release of

hormones, but this response can also cause internal

disturbances leading to disease.

your body. A Charley horse is a proprioceptive sensation. So is a stomach-ache. So for that matter is an orgasm, or a general sense of well-being.

Such feelings are largely the product of proprioceptors, specialized nerve endings that are sensitive to changes within your muscles, tendons, joints. Proprioceptors may make you aware of pressures inside your abdomen or legs or genitals, in much the same way that nerve endings in your skin can alert you to outside changes in temperature or texture.

Your emotions are proprioceptive sensations. If this surprises you, where do you feel this surprise? In the back of your neck? In your belly?

The precise spots vary from person to person. But every emotion you feel, you do just that: you *feel* it. Physically. In specific locations.

Like your intellectual ability to multiply 2×3, emotions exist in your body cells. Tune into yourself the next time you feel in a particular way—happy, sad, whatever. You'll find that essentially the same set of proprioceptive sensations constitute the feeling you've come to label "happiness" or "sadness." Happiness may in part be a lightness in your chest, sadness a leaden weight there. From such proprioceptive locations come the figures of speech "lighthearted" and "heavyhearted."

Painful feelings like anxiety and depression are literally pains: hurtful proprioceptive sensations. When you say, "My feelings are hurt," you mean exactly that. The ache of rejection is no less an ache than the ache of a crushed finger.

Against Common Sense

From where in your body do such feelings spring?

In a book-lined study at Harvard, William James—brother of the novelist Henry James and a pioneer in psychology—speculated on the dynamics of proprioceptive sensations. With C. G. Lange, a Danish physiologist, James advanced a theory which forms the basis of most contemporary work on emotion, though it flies in the face of what most people believe is the normal course of events.

Common sense suggests that first you have an emotional experience and then your bodily expression follows. Presumably you are sad, therefore you cry. You're afraid, and so your heart beats faster. You become enraged, and in response to your rage your adrenal glands pump the hormone adrenalin into your bloodstream. According to popular belief, a stimulus (S) produces an emotion (E), which leads to physiological responses (PR), such as tears or an increased heartbeat or adrenalin in your bloodstream. The common-sense sequence can be represented by:

$$S \rightarrow E \rightarrow PR$$

But, argued James and Lange, this puts the cart before the horse. They contended that the stimulus leads to physiological responses, and it is these bodily phenomena that you experience as emotion. The sequence they suggest is:

$$S \rightarrow PR \rightarrow E$$

According to the James-Lange theory, you feel sad *because* you cry. You feel fear *because* your heart beats faster. You are enraged *because* adrenalin is pouring into your blood. The resulting proprioceptive changes are what you subjectively interpret as emotion.

The $S \rightarrow PR \rightarrow E$ sequence proposed by James and Lange is now widely accepted. There's little doubt that your bodily expression can help determine your mood. From your own experience, you know that if you smile when sad you can feel happier. In the recent phenomenon of encounter groups, a favorite technique is to ask you to punch a pillow. Participants are often astonished at how the physical act of hitting can bring forth long bottled-up feelings of anger, which may be dispelled through the punching.

At the same time, the physiological basis of the James-Lange theory has undergone considerable refining. As critics have pointed out, you feel afraid a moment or so *before* your heart starts pumping faster. Your increased heartbeat may prolong and intensify your initial feelings of fear. But your internal organs react too slowly to account for the immediate emotional reaction.

Subsequent studies have also shown that adrenalin pours into your bloodstream in dozens of situations besides those provoking rage. Can the same amount of adrenalin in one situation be experienced as rage, in another as excitement, in a third as ecstasy? Not by itself, it can't. Such a bodily reaction alone is too indiscriminate to account for the subtle range of emotion.

Finally, experiments have demonstrated that there is a component to emotion over and beyond outpourings of hormones. Subjects were injected with fear-related hormones. In a detached way many felt "as if" they were afraid. But few experienced the actual feeling of fear.

Thus, James and Lange recognized the physical origins of emotion. It took more recent investigators to explain how you correlate your conscious experience of emotion and your subtle bodily sensations.

A Brain for Emotion

A current view of emotion holds that it is largely a function of the limbic system. "Limbic" means "border," and the structures comprising the system extend from the fringe of the brain to its center.

Paul D. MacLean of the Yale University School of Medicine has developed a theory that the limbic system serves as a "visceral brain." It interprets experience in terms of feeling—i.e., nonverbal sensations—rather than in terms of intellectualized symbols: words, conclusions, ideas.

The limbic system is a primitive part of the brain. Its counterpart is found in the brains of lower animals, in contrast to the cerebral cortex which is found only high up on the evolutionary scale. Intellectual activity is centered in the cerebral cortex, whereas emotional experience is achieved through the limbic system, which generates "organ language" instead of words.

Alterations to the limbic system directly cause emotional changes. Experimenters have found that lesions in some areas make shy monkeys fearless, turn mountain lions into docile pets, and convert tame laboratory rats into snarling aggressors. Specific centers of the limbic system have been stimulated with electrodes, with dramatic emotional effects. (The presence of such an electrical connection does not pain or discommode an animal.) Fear and fearlessness, hunger and satiety, rages and sexual urges have all been induced by sending a tiny current to a given area. Sometimes completely opposite effects have resulted from moving an electrode from one group of cells to another a mere fiftieth of an inch away.

A notable series of experiments in electrical stimulation of the brain came about by accident. James Olds of McGill University was placing an electrode in the brain of a rat. Olds intended to shock the animal when it reached a certain corner of an experimental box.

However, in placing the electrode he was somewhat off his mark. When the rat reached the proper corner, Olds gave it a small shot of current, expecting it to withdraw due to the shock. To his surprise, the rat enjoyed the experience. Instead of avoiding the corner, it kept returning to it.

Olds and his colleague Peter Milner discovered that a portion of the brain functions as a "pleasure center." They rigged up a treadle, which a rat could press to receive a dosage of current to this portion of its brain. Some rats with electrodes in the pleasure center of their limbic system would press the treadle at the rate of 200 times an hour. Nearby groups of cells are evidently centers of absolute ecstasy. Rats with electrodes there pressed the treadle as often as 5000 times an hour until they dropped from exhaustion.

Adults whose thyroids are severely underactive from iodine deficiency won't ordinarily become cretins, but they may develop myxedema, a disease in which the victim becomes cold, dull, and listless. "Myxedema" comes from "mucus," a phlegmlike secretion, plus "edema," a swelling of the skin; in myxedema the skin is swollen with mucus, and the victim looks bloated and puffy. The condition occurs most often in mountain regions and other areas far from the sea where diet and drinking water lack iodine. Most cases can be reversed by adding iodine to the diet, as by means of iodized salt.

Hyperthyroidism, the product of a revved-up thyroid, is the opposite of myxedema and is potentially more dangerous. Studies suggest that hyperthyroidism is usually due to an overactivity of the pituitary gland. Normally when thyroxin in the blood falls below a certain level, the pituitary secretes TSH (thyroid-stimulating hormone), which spurs the thyroid to produce more thyroxin. When the thyroxin content of the blood rises to the proper level, the pituitary shuts off the TSH, to start up again only when the thyroxin level once again declines.

In hyperthyroidism, it is thought, the pituitary overproduces TSH, causing the thyroid to pour forth thyroxin. Evidence abounds that the thyroid responds to emotional stimuli, though there's a curious inconclusiveness in laboratory tests. Generally, in association with emotional disturbances, small animals such as mice and rabbits show a decrease in thyroid activity, while larger animals, including man, show an increase.

One study found thyroid activity climbing in soldiers recalling painful war experiences. In another experiment, Dr. Eric D. Wittkower, now of the McGill University Medical School, hypnotized volunteers and induced in them unpleasant emotional reactions. Nearly all the subjects had a rise in thyroid activity, some as much as 20 per cent.

Another study showed that family problems can cause thyroid levels to climb. One young man underwent an hour-long interview in which he discussed his painful relationship with his father. His thyroid activity climbed until it was about 20 per cent above normal. It remained elevated for at least three hours.

Even a distressing movie can cause sharp, sustained rises in thyroid activity. Dr. Franz Alexander and his associates at the Chicago Institute for Psychoanalysis showed volunteers a film depicting fear and pain. All the subjects responded with a rise in thyroid action. Normal subjects tended to have an initial decline, followed by a marked elevation. Volunteers already suffering from overactive thyroids intensified their conditions. Their thyroid secretions jumped by 100 per cent and remained so for at least two hours after the film.

"Exciting Causes"

About the beginning of the 1800s, an English doctor named Caleb Hillier Parry examined a young woman showing symptoms of hyperthyroidism. The disease had developed just after an accident in which the woman was badly frightened but suffered little physical injury.

The concept that a sharp emotional disturbance may influence the thyroid gland can be traced back to Parry's classic description of this case, published in 1825. Ten years later, R. J. Graves, another English physician, reported evidence of a relationship between psychological trauma and the disease which now often bears his name.

Since these early reports, the frequent occurrence of severe emotional distress just prior to the onset of hyperthyroidism has been widely reported. One researcher found evidence of psychic trauma in 94 per cent of 200 hyperthyroid cases he investigated.

Another investigator reported a "clear history of psychic trauma as the exciting cause" in 85 per cent of 3343 cases. Eleven per cent of the total cases involved reactions to surgery or to the delivery of a baby. An additional 13 per cent had had severe, life-threatening crises, such as fires, earthquakes, shipwrecks, combat experiences, or narrow escapes from accidents. By far the largest category—61 per cent of the patients—had sustained long periods of emotional disturbance, such as worry, disappointment, or grief.

Shortly after World War II a researcher named P. A. Bastenie went back over Norwegian and Danish medical records to learn the incidence of hyperthyroidism during the German occupation. In this stressful time there was a five- to sixfold increase in the disease. After liberation the illness fell to peacetime levels.

"When I see a patient with Graves' disease I just wait until the patient describes the precipitating situation," says Harvard surgeon Oliver Cope. "The event or sequence of events is usually vivid and tormenting."

Cope believes that psychotherapy is the most effective treatment for hyperthyroidism, more so than traditional measures, such as surgery, radioactive iodine, and antithyroid drugs which attack only the thyroid gland. "They leave the emotional component unattended to, and this may go on to produce . . . some other bodily disturbance."

A Matter of Personality

Different personality types tend to get different diseases.

This conclusion, one of the most provocative in psychosomatic medicine, is strongly supported by studies of hyperthyroid patients. The hyperthyroid sufferer often starts out in life like thirteen-year-old Betty, whose mother describes her as a "little old lady" because she is so prematurely grown-up, obedient, and responsible.

Betty learned to cook when she was six and has cooked and helped with the housework ever since. Whenever her mother gets ill, Betty cleans the house and takes care of the whole family. She acts like a second mother to Bobby, her younger brother. The pattern doggedly continues, despite her eruption of hyperthyroidism.

Like Betty, the typical hyperthyroid patient was prematurely self-sufficient. As an adult, he may appear unusually calm and independent. This role is hard to let go of. Dr. Glenn W. Flagg, a Los Angeles psychiatrist, tells of patients in the throes of hyperthyroidism making "desperate attempts" to impress him with their good health and self-reliance.

Hyperthyroid victims often suffered grave threats to their security in early childhood. Many lost their mother early in life. Many others were brought up by parents who were unhappily married, or they felt rejected by one or both parents, or displaced by a brother or sister. Commonly, the hyperthyroid victim was the oldest child in a family that was deprived both economically and emotionally.

In such situations the child may be left with feelings of being deserted. This can lead to pronounced fears of death from violence or neglect. The child may perceive an actual threat to his physical being.

A child in such a family cannot turn to parents or loved ones for help. Thus he is constantly frustrated in his "dependency needs"—the vital needs of a child for mothering, affection, protection, warmth. If dependency needs are not satisfied, the child is likely to feel worthless and cast out. The natural consequence is to be desperately anxious over one's safety in a threatening world.

What often characterizes hyperthyroid patients is the way they find of handling this anxiety. Commonly, a person with thwarted dependency needs shows manifestations of regression: He returns to infantile patterns of reacting. The person likely to develop hyperthyroidism takes the opposite tack: He seeks to become excessively mature.

Supermother

In some cases this "maturity" is forced on the patient. The father of Harry Daley (we'll call him) was a puritan, harsh and impersonal. He fondled his children only as long as they were helpless infants. As soon as they were able to walk and talk, he demanded adult behavior.

Mr. Daley kept Harry's mother and older sisters from giving Harry any attention. Mrs. Daley worked in the family store. She was unable to stand up to her husband, who constantly threw in her face the fact that he had married her "out of pity" because she had borne a child out of wedlock.

After Harry entered the first grade, Mr. Daley insisted that no one read him the funny papers any more. "He should learn to read them for himself," declared Mr. Daley.

Harry developed hyperthyroidism by the time he was thirty-five. In such cases the deprived child makes a desperate attempt to identify himself prematurely with his parent, usually his mother. This psychological maneuver might be summed up in one statement: "If I cannot have her, I will become like her and then I will not need her."

Such a precocious attempt to free himself from the need for his parents' love is, of course, beyond the capacity of the child, both psychologically and physically. The child—and subsequently the adult he grows into—is forever seeking to live up to unattainable standards of parentlike responsibility and maturity. Inevitably, as long as he clings to this method of dealing with his anxiety, he is in a vain struggle to relieve his insecurity through self-reliance.

Moreover, in seeking to act like his mother or father, the child tends to idealize the parent role he assumes. The child feels he must become superfather or supermother—*super*loving, *super*responsible, *super*competent. Thus the little girl who wants to be mothered often becomes a mother. She takes care of the house, cooks the meals, and serves as the mother for her brothers and sisters. She usually gets married early and has many children.

The man who wishes to be protected and dependent likewise begins early to take responsibility for his brothers and sisters. He plays the little man in the family and tends to marry early. He is likely to become an extremely conscientious parent. Possibly he will assume other parental roles, such as taking care of orphans or becoming a philanthropist.

Choice of occupation is many times determined by this need, notes Dr. Glenn Flagg. For example, the woman may enter nursing, and the man become a physician.

Dreams, Death, and Pregnancy

Often the hyperthyroid person will assume responsibility for younger brothers and sisters to the point of going out to work to support them through college, then keeping a home for them thereafter.

Protecting younger siblings gives the sufferer vicarious gratification for his own thwarted dependency needs. But almost certainly he resents his servitude to his brothers and sisters. Yet he dare not show his hostility, for such is not the way of the ideal parent. To expiate his guilt over feeling hostile, he may mother them even more, thereby intensifying his problem.

Shortly before the onset of full-blown cases of hyperthyroidism, victims often have dreams of death, caskets, ghosts, and dead persons. "Grandma and Grandpa were lying in their coffins and reached out to drag me in," recalled one patient. Another remembered: "I was making a bed and knew it meant I was going to die."

These are signs of an unconscious conflict that is finally proving intolerable for the victim. Often such dreams spring from his resentment of his siblings. The sufferer may suddenly become desperately concerned with the safety of his family. His conscious fear that they will be injured or killed may well represent his unconscious wish.

Violence and death are extremely common in the memories of hyperthyroid victims. A striking case in point is Doris, who as a child knew extreme poverty. Her parents' marriage broke up, and her mother's second husband treated Doris harshly. When she was four, she saw a woman burned to death. At eight, a friend of hers died. While Doris was standing near the coffin, it tipped over and the corpse fell out. Later she saw her grandfather kill himself. She witnessed her grandmother's death. Her husband died, leaving her to support the family. All these horrors are vivid in her mind and may help account for her hyperthyroidism.

The hyperthyroid woman typically plays supermother by having lots of children. Again, she follows the pattern of seeking responsibility despite deep anxiety. Pregnancy allows her to combat her fear of death by giving life to children. Loss of her own mother is counteracted by becoming a mother herself.

At eighteen Darlene married a childhood friend. In fourteen years she had five children, though she suffered from frigidity. "If my husband hadn't died," she says, "I would have had all the children that medical science could deliver to me. They are hard to have and so painful, but the more it hurts the more you love them."

Since her husband's death, Darlene has carried on two jobs at once to make sure her children are nicely dressed. In addition, she has taken into her home a great-aunt, who does nothing and who has to be taken care of.

The Disease Erupts

Many people, of course, go through life playing the perfect parent and evidently escape any related psychosomatic disease.

When, then, do some become ill? And why in particular do they suffer from hyperthyroidism?

Dr. Franz Alexander of the Chicago Institute for Psychoanalysis, a principal figure in the study of psychosomatics, points to the thyroid gland's function as a stimulant of growth. The person's emotional need to mature at an accelerated rate, he feels, spurs hyperactivity of this gland.

Thyroxin is an accelerator of metabolism and of the whole maturational process. The hormone increases alertness and is called on when the organism faces long-term efforts. Moreover, the close relationship between thyroxin and anxiety has been firmly established.

A woman's hyperthyroidism may be brought on by her urge to have children. In pregnancy there is a normal increase in thyroid secretion. The woman whose thyroid is already overactive may be further pushed over the line into disease as the number of her children increases. Being more and more the nurse—instead of being nursed—is likely to worsen her already frustrated dependency needs.

In a man, the precipitating circumstance tends to be one that causes doubt about his masculinity. His self-reliance and independence may come into question. Perhaps he suffers a setback in realizing work ambitions.

Hyperthyroidism can explode in a person. Shock Basedow (named after the physician who first described it) is the term used for the sudden onset of hyperthyroidism a few hours after a severe emotional jolt, such as a catastrophic loss of a relative or a narrow escape from death. By far the most common precipitant, however, is a series of emotionally stressful events which the patient senses as calamitous to his emotional security. This may be the gradual dissolution of a marriage upon which the person bases his complete emotional security. Another frequent precipitant is the death of an aging mother and father within a short period of time, to which the patient reacts by feeling, "Now I am really alone. I can no longer feel protected."

CHAPTER 5

Diseases of Stress

When your emotional balance upsets

Your total being strives to maintain a precarious balance.

For example, the amount of sugar in the blood must stay at about $\frac{1}{60}$th of an ounce per pint. If the concentration is too high, the blood will draw fluid from the tissues. This will dehydrate the cells and dilute the blood. A person undergoing this change may constantly be thirsty and at the same time be urinating frequently. He is likely to be constantly hungry.

Physicians recognize these as the first symptoms of diabetes. If untreated, the diabetic may suffer impaired circulation. Heart ailments and amputations among diabetics are not uncommon. In rare cases, the blood, which normally is faintly alkaline, becomes acidic, and this condition can kill rapidly.

Conversely, if blood sugar is too low for a long period, the cells get too little food and fuel. The nervous system is affected first, and the victim of hypoglycemia (from the Greek, meaning "low sugar in the blood") may be confused and have hallucinations. Convulsions and ultimately coma may result.

Internal mechanisms maintain your delicate balance of blood sugar, so that the concentration remains essentially the same no matter how much sugar you eat or how much energy you expend. When there is a slight drop in the blood's normal sugar level, a group of cells (the "alpha cells") of the islets of Langerhans in the pancreas secrete the hormone glucagon. This spurs the liver to release stored sugar. To conserve sugar for the nervous system, which absolutely requires it, the pituitary gland secretes STH (somatotropic hormone), which keeps sugar from entering muscle and fat cells. If blood sugar still drops below a critical level, the adrenal medulla secretes adrenalin.

As soon as the blood sugar rises to a point above normal, glucagon, STH, and adrenalin switch off. The liver stops issuing sugar and rapidly starts taking it up. A second group of cells (the "beta cells") in the islets of Langerhans secretes the hormone insulin, which promotes the entry of glucose into muscle, liver, and fat cells. If blood sugar now gets too low, the process again reverses.

The body is thus in a state of perpetual adjustment, and if any hormone goes awry, illness is likely to occur. Insulin is the obvious example in this illustration. If too little is secreted, diabetes develops. If too much, hypoglycemia.

The Sum of Your Parts

The picture is never simple, since no hormone acts alone. For example, the normal response to hypoglycemia is a massive outpouring of adrenalin. Thus, in addition to the symptoms of too little sugar, the victim suffers those of an adrenalin excess: over-rapid heart action, anxiety, sweating, pallor, a rise in blood pressure. Any of these, in turn, can lead to further complications.

The action of one hormone is related to the overall balance of the hormones present. B. C. Houssay, a pioneer in the study of hormonal interaction, has expressed this viewpoint: "In the organism, we have always interaction between hormones, but never is one hormone action completely alone."

Biologists increasingly feel that the fundamental character of the living thing is its *organization*. They hold that the customary methods of studying single parts and processes, even the most thorough analysis, cannot provide a complete explanation of vital phenomena. "This investigation gives us no information

about the co-ordination of the parts and processes in the complicated system of the living whole," argues biologist Ludwig von
Bertalanffy of the University of Alberta. "[This co-ordination]
constitutes the essential 'nature' of the organism, and [distin-
guishes] the reactions in the organism . . . from those in the
test tube."

The interaction of hormones takes place in psychological as
well as physiological phenomena. A large number of hormones
react to emotional stress and also interact with one another.

In one experiment a monkey was strapped in a restraining
chair, a lever within reach. As long as the monkey pressed the
lever, it was comfortable. But if the monkey let the lever go,
within twenty seconds it got a mild electric shock.

Dr. John W. Mason and his colleagues at the Walter Reed
Army Institute of Research conducted these "avoidance sessions" for 72 hours per monkey. Before, during, and after the
sessions, technicians took urine and blood samples and tested
them for a number of hormones.

The great bulk of psychoendocrine research has been devoted
to the secretions of the adrenal and thyroid glands. As Dr. Mason's team expected, these hormones rose in response to the
monkey's stress. Not expected, however, was the fact that *every
other* hormone measured also responded, some, such as insulin
and the sex hormones estrone and testosterone, by falling.

"The findings suggest that the scope of psychoendocrine responses is remarkable," Mason has reported. He concludes that
overall hormone balance is a key to the response to emotional
and physical experiences. An individual hormone responds not
only to outside stimuli but also to all the other hormones present.
And the sum of your health may vary with the total of these
parts.

The Same Position

The relatively stable state that the body strives for through
hormone balance, as in the regulation of blood sugar, is given

the name "homeostasis," from the Greek, meaning "same position."

The word, originating in physiology, has been borrowed by psychologists. The balance and constancy which the body seeks applies not only to physiological forces but to life in general. In terms of your emotions, you seek balance and equalization, away from extremes. Through fluctuations, your range of emotional homeostasis can shift as you and your environment change.

The adolescent girl, for example, seeks homeostasis. Her emotional problems are often symptoms of its opposite, disequilibrium. The poles she balances between are the extremes of childhood and adulthood. Each attracts her, each repels her in ever-changing ratio as she makes her uncertain way from being a child to being a woman. Any force which pushes her forward too rapidly or holds her back too firmly gives rise to some degree of disequilibrium. Comments Dr. Robert E. Nixon: "It appears to matter little whether the force be internal, as, for example, the hormonal onslaught of puberty, or external, such as parental refusal to let an eighteen-year-old date."

The girl's level of emotional homeostasis changes step by step as she passes from puberty through adolescence. The ripening of a new phase of growth requires her to establish a new equilibrium on a more mature level. The onset of menstruation is such a crisis. It demands that she establish a new equilibrium. This change from one phase to another may be accompanied by considerable anxiety, possibly resulting in strange behavior and physical symptoms.

Tugs on the Tightrope

Homeostasis is disturbed by stress. Any tug on your tightrope —emotional or physical—that requires you to adjust your balance constitutes stress.

Man functions best when the stresses of life stimulate him enough to exercise his faculties. A complete withdrawal from the normal stimuli of life can itself be extremely stressful. In sensory-deprivation experiments volunteers are isolated in pitch-black soundproof cells, often wearing gloves to blunt their sense of touch. In some experiments the volunteers are given breathing apparatus and kept under water that is heated to body temperature. They can't sense even their own skins or the pull of gravity.

Almost always the volunteers are disturbed by the experience. Tests during and immediately after confinement indicate that sensory deprivation alters perception in curious ways. Time, instead of seeming longer, is telescoped. Volunteers are more subject to pain. Hallucinations occur, and become more frequent as isolation is prolonged.

After confinement shapes and figures are often seen distorted. Volunteers are unable to do routine tests of manual dexterity, such as holding a rod in a hole without hitting the sides. Memory is warped; word lists that ordinarily are easy prove impossible to remember. A normal volunteer deprived of his senses for four days may require several days to recover.

Conversely, the stresses of life can be extremely injurious. Driving a car through heavy traffic, working at a frustrating job, watching a child struggle with illness, quarreling with your mate —the stresses of life take infinitely varied forms. And they can pose as much of a challenge to your health as bacteria, viruses, malnutrition, or chemical and physical forces.

In a series of experiments the Medical Research Group of the Swedish Army sought to determine whether psychological stimuli can provoke physiological reactions that lead to internal disorders. The Swedish experimenters subjected 31 soldiers to the stress of 75 hours at an electronic shooting range. They were not allowed to sleep, use stimulants, smoke, or go for walks.

Although their average age was only 29, their emotional and biochemical reactions were pronounced. One officer experienced temporary claustrophobia and panic. His adrenalin excretion was very high. He suffered headache, blurred vision, and palpitation. His pulse exceeded 100 beats a minute.

About 25 per cent of the subjects developed abnormal electrocardiographic patterns. Only after several days of rest did their ECG readings return to normal. The experiments prove that relatively brief stints of stress, below the intensity that most people ordinarily experience at some time in their lives, can provoke pathological changes in the body. If they are repeated often or are allowed to persist for long periods, they might cause disease.

Each person meets the challenge of stress in his own way. The family quarrel that triggers a heart attack in one may make another resentful, while for a third it may even serve as a goad to useful and productive work. Whatever the response, it involves the whole individual. Inseparably, body and mind play a part in dealing with the stresses of life.

"Everyone recognizes the influence of emotion upon the flow of tears, the secretion of sweat, the color of the face, the temperature of the hands," says Cornell University internist David P. Barr. "Everyone knows the racing heart of excitement, the gasp of horror, the panting of passion. . . . In a resentful man, the effect of the situation which rouses his resentment will be portrayed in his nose, his stomach, his urinary tract, his posture, and the sour look on his face. The entire organism reacts to an environment which it has interpreted as threatening."

Many of these reactions may be intended to prepare the body for vigorous physical activity. Such effort was common in the early days of mankind. To survive in a hunting society, men had to be always on the move and always alert to defend themselves. The development of agriculture permitted men to establish permanent homes, but still required them to do heavy physical labor. It is only in very recent times that men have been able to live with only a minimum of physical exertion.

In today's urban civilization, some of the biological equipment that was necessary in earlier times may have become obsolete. It may even be a handicap. As psychiatrist David A. Hamburg of Stanford University puts it: "The contemporary human organism frequently gets mobilized for exertion but ends up doing little or nothing—preparation for action, without action."

The late Dr. Harold G. Wolff advanced a theory that the body reacts to stresses, emotional as well as physical, by choosing from a limited repertoire of mechanisms of response: changes in heart rate, respiration, hormone flow, and so forth. Since these responses may be unsuited to the immediate situation, they may disturb homeostasis rather than help restore it. They may even be more damaging than the original threat. Disease is often primarily the manifestation of such an unsuitable response, particularly when this response is prolonged or often repeated.

In one conclusive study Dr. John P. Brady and his colleagues at the University of Pennsylvania set out to determine if stress makes rats more susceptible to illness and death. The researchers used three groups of rats. One group was administered electrical shocks. The second group got shocks preceded by a warning signal. The third group received neither shocks nor signals.

The group that became ill and died earlier had been exposed to shock plus warning signals—double stress, since the signals caused anticipation in addition to the actual pain. In contrast, the group exposed to neither shock nor signals had the lowest rate of illness and death.

G.A.S.

In 1926 Hans Selye was a second-year medical student at the German University in Prague. He wondered why the most diverse diseases produced so many common signs and symptoms.

"I felt sure that the syndrome of just being sick, which is essentially the same no matter what disease we have, could be analyzed and expressed scientifically," Selye recalls. "The possibility fascinated me and, with the enthusiasm of youth, I wanted to start work right away."

His limited training as a medical student, however, didn't reach far enough. He got no further than the formulation of an idea.

Years later Selye was working in the biochemistry department of McGill University, trying to find a new sex hormone in extracts of cattle ovaries. He injected the extracts into rats to see if their organs would show changes that could not be attributed to a known hormone.

Much to his satisfaction, the first and most impure extracts changed the rats in three ways: (1) The adrenal cortex became enlarged; (2) There was a shrinkage in the thymus—a growth-regulating gland in the upper part of the chest—and in the spleen and the lymph nodes, both of which produce white blood cells; and (3) Deep, bleeding ulcers appeared in the stomach and in the upper gut.

At first Selye ascribed all these changes to a new sex hormone in his extract. But he soon found that all injurious substances—extracts of kidney, spleen, or even a toxin not derived from living tissue—produced the *same* collection of symptoms.

"Gradually my classroom concept of the syndrome of just being sick came back to me," Selye remembers. "I realized that the reaction I had produced with my impure extracts and toxic drugs was an experimental replica of just being sick."

Adrenal enlargement, gastrointestinal ulcers, and thymolymphatic shrinkage are the omnipresent signs of damage to the body when under disease attack.

Whatever Selye did to his experimental animals—whether he shot adrenalin or insulin into them, whether he exposed them to extreme cold or to extreme heat or to X rays or physical injuries—they always underwent the same physiological changes, following the same pattern. In addition to the specific reactions—burns, for example, or injuries—this complex sequence of general responses could always be seen.

Selye pointed out that the syndrome could be brought about by *any* stressful situation, from emotional tension as well as by physical distress. Selye's first paper on the syndrome of stress, "A Syndrome Produced by Diverse Nocuous Agents," was published in the British journal *Nature*. In this paper he suggested the term "alarm reaction" for the animal's initial response because he thought that the syndrome probably represented a general call to arms of the body's defensive forces.

But the alarm reaction evidently was only the *beginning* of the entire response. Selye's experiments showed that continuous exposure to any noxious agent capable of setting off this alarm reaction is followed by a second stage, one of adaptation or resistance.

Apparently, he has concluded, disease is not just suffering, but a fight to maintain the homeostatic balance of our tissues when they are damaged. No organism can exist continuously in a state of alarm. An agent so damaging that continuous exposure to it is incompatible with life causes death within hours or days of the alarm reaction. However, if survival is possible, the alarm reaction gives way to the stage of *resistance.*

What happens in the resistance stage is, in many instances, the exact opposite of events in the alarm reaction. For instance, during the alarm reaction, the adrenal cortex discharges hormones into the bloodstream. Consequently the gland depletes its stores. In the resistance stage, the cortex accumulates an abundant reserve. Again, in the alarm reaction, the blood volume diminishes and body weight drops. But during the stage of resistance the blood is less concentrated and body weight returns to normal.

Curiously, after prolonged exposure to any noxious agent, the body loses its ability to resist. It enters the third stage, that of *exhaustion.* This stage always occurs as long as the stress is severe enough and is applied long enough, because the adaptability of a living being is always limited.

Selye called the entire response the "General Adaptation Syndrome" (G.A.S.: *general,* because it is produced only by agents that have a general effect upon large portions of the body; *adaptive,* because it stimulates defense and thereby helps inure the body to hardship; *syndrome,* because its signs are coordinated and partly dependent on each other). This whole syndrome then evolves through three stages: (1) the alarm reaction, (2) the stage of resistance, and (3) the state of exhaustion.

Diseases of Adaptation

An important role in the resistance stage is played by the hormone ACTH, which stimulates the adrenal cortex to produce secretions.

Derangements in the resistance stage lead to "diseases of adaptation." These diseases are caused not by any particular agent but by the body's normal response to the stress induced by such an agent. For example, the excessive production of ACTH in response to some mild local irritation could damage organs far from the original site of an injury. In this sense the body's own reactions seem to encourage various maladies. These could include emotional disturbances, headaches, insomnia, sinus attacks, high blood pressure, gastric and duodenal ulcers, certain rheumatic or allergic afflictions, and cardiovascular and kidney diseases.

With sustained stress the adrenal cortex hormones tend to constrict blood vessels in the kidneys. If the stress is sufficiently prolonged, hypertension and damage to the kidney may result.

Overproduction of ACTH can evidently increase susceptibility to disease. Normal rats injected with human tuberculosis organisms will not ordinarily develop tuberculosis. They appear to have a natural immunity. But if given ACTH and then injected, they succumb to TB.

Selye's work has been largely proved out in laboratory animals, and some specialists question its applicability to humans. However, it is well established that the hormonal balance shifts in relation to diverse factors, among which are emotional stimuli. It is therefore quite possible that—like the rats with TB—your natural immunity to many disease organisms diminishes when you are under stress.

CHAPTER 6

Subject to Change

Social disruptions, family conflicts, and job tensions can make you ill

The Mabaan are a tribe of tall, graceful people living in an inhospitable region of the Sudan.

During half the year their land is parched desert; during the other half it is impassable swamp. Though they are deprived of virtually all medical care, the Mabaan are among the healthiest and longest-lived humans on earth. Nearly all, including the oldest, have perfect vision and superb hearing. In sharp contrast to Americans, whose systolic blood pressure rises on average by more than 30 per cent from childhood to old age, their blood pressure remains essentially the same for life. Psychosomatic illness among the Mabaan is virtually nonexistent.

The explanation lies partly in the Mabaan's very isolation. Good health depends less on medicines than on adaptation to environment—and the Mabaan have come to terms with their surroundings, undisturbed by outside influences. Isolated tribes like the Mabaan are spared psychosomatic disorders in large part because their communities have adopted traditions directed away from stress and toward cohesiveness and calm.

Conversely, peoples with simple ways of life often suffer grievously when thrust into contact with so-called advanced cultures. Observers in India and the Far East have noted that such psychosomatic illnesses as bronchial asthma and peptic ulcer are more common in Westernized urban centers than in rural areas little touched by Western civilization. Peruvian Indians migrating from the Andes to the capital city of Lima develop a high rate of psychosomatic disorders, whereas in their native villages such illnesses are almost unheard of. In North Greenland one group of Eskimos has a primitive life style; a second group, genetically identical, has long had contact with Western (Danish) civilization. Psychosomatic disorders are four to five times more common in the "civilized" group.

In rural Rhodesia, hypertension is rare except in the elderly. "I have yet to see in a primitive person . . . a peptic ulcer or ulcerative colitis," says Dr. J. F. Donaldson, a physician at a rural missionary hospital. "Tolerance of pain is often remarkable, and body carriage, general energy, and buoyancy are often to be envied."

The Westernized African on the other hand, observes Dr. Donaldson, has hypertension as an occupational hazard. It is not at all uncommon among teachers and businessmen. Gastric hyperacidity, a condition leading to ulcers, is likewise common. The Westernized African seems less able to tolerate pain and generally carries himself more sluggishly than his country cousin.

"Civilization as we know it today is a mixed blessing," Dr. Donaldson concludes. "The heightening of development and enjoyments achieved appear to come at certain not insignificant costs to the human system."

Dr. James L. Halliday, a Scottish public health physician, is a pioneer in the field of psychosocial medicine, the study of the relationship between bodily illness and sociological phenomena. Halliday contends that society is sick and exhibits psychosomatic disorders as symptoms of its disorganization. He maintains that the rapid social changes of the past fifty years have increased the incidence of psychosomatic disorders. Halliday's statistics show that among Westerners the prevalence of peptic ulcer, hyperthyroidism, and hypertension is sharply rising.

If Your Spouse Runs Off With a Hippie

If within a year your spouse runs off with a hippie, you're swindled by a favorite aunt, you get jailed for drunken driving, and you lose your house through foreclosure, look out (to paraphrase William N. Jeffers, an editor of *Medical Economics* magazine)! These disasters indicate the imminence of something perhaps even worse. Within twelve months you're almost sure to come down with a major illness.

On the other hand, if in one year you wed a dreamboat, discover a cure for an ill bedeviling mankind, win the Irish sweepstakes, and finally master the glockenspiel—again beware: Such triumphs also point to a serious illness within the twelvemonth.

These examples are exaggerated, of course, but they are not at all improbable as cause and effect. "We have proved conclusively that such correlation does exist," states psychiatrist Thomas H. Holmes of the University of Washington School of Medicine. Dr. Holmes explains that a concentration of events that require significant personal adjustments causes stress, no matter whether the events are bad or good. And, Holmes has found, the stress soon brings about illness.

Holmes gave some 400 people a list of 43 major "life events," such as marriage, personal achievement, change in financial status, son or daughter leaving home, divorce. The 400 subjects were asked to rate the life events as to the relative degree of adjustment called for by each. The top 10 came out in this order: death of a spouse, divorce, marital separation, jail term, death in the family, personal injury or illness, marriage, being fired from job, marital reconciliation, and retirement.

Next the subjects were asked to list by year for the previous 10 years any major life events that had happened in their own lives. Afterward their lists were compared with their medical histories. In case after case, the year in which several major life events occurred was followed by a year in which the person was stricken by serious illness.

Holmes theorizes that the connection between stressful life events and disease is based on the functioning of the body's immunity system. Fear, excitement, strain may well weaken it. Stressful events may also upset emotional balance by affecting hormone production. Either way, big events in your life may mean that you'll be ill.

The death of a spouse is especially likely to bring on illness. A widower, in the first six months following his wife's death, is half again more likely to die of coronary heart disease than are married men of his age. A study in Sydney, Australia, shows that in the year following bereavement 32 per cent of a sampling of widows suffered a marked deterioration of their health. Illness occurred among them 16 times more frequently than among married women of the same age and background. The most common complaints were headache, indigestion, heart palpitation, chest pain, and difficulty in breathing.

Sharp changes can evidently make children, as well as adults, more susceptible to illness. Dr. Arthur Z. Mutter and Dr. Maxwell J. Schleifer of the Boston University School of Medicine compared the recent life experience of ill children with those of well children, all between the ages of 6 and 12. Five of the sick children suffered from rheumatic fever, 10 from kidney and other genitourinary conditions. Some had flare-ups of hereditary disorders, such as hemophilia. Many had infections of various types—hepatitis, meningitis, pneumonia, cat scratch fever.

In the six months before becoming ill, every sick child had experienced at least one major life change. These changes tended to pose a considerable threat to the child's well-being. A family member may have been seriously ill or died. A close friend may have moved away. The child may have been permanently placed in another home. About 5 out of 6 well children also experienced changes in the same period, but these changes were generally only minimally threatening, such as going to a summer camp or living through a family member's minor illness.

The severe changes such as a death, serious illness, or separation tended to be compounded by still further disruptions. The child's school situation may have been radically altered. Under the tension of the change, family members may have related differently to the child. The ill children tended to relate more poorly with their parents to begin with. The families of the sick children were less cohesive than those of the well children, and their mothers provided less warmth and security. The stress of all these changes added up to a physiological vulnerability in the child.

Moving to a new residence is a major life change that sometimes precipitates illness. In slum-clearance projects, when a slum family is moved into public housing, the family members are likely for some time thereafter to get sick more frequently and more seriously than when they were living in squalid surroundings. This has been a puzzle to well-intentioned officials who see only the gleaming walls and good plumbing in the new housing.

Dr. James Halliday, applying findings of psychosocial medicine, blames such a family's decline in health on the "social disintegration" that disrupted its normal pattern of living. While a slum may have been unhygienic and unsafe, at least the family was adapted to its social patterns. Taken from neighbors and familiar surroundings, the family tends to be disoriented. Its stress shows in a significantly greater susceptibility to illness. What is called for, of course, is not an end to slum clearance and public housing, but stronger efforts to integrate displaced families into their new community.

Even for well-off families, moving to a new house may precipitate severe emotional illness, with many psychosomatic symptoms. An English psychiatrist, Dr. Peter Hall, tells of the added stress heaped upon already frail marriages when to pay for the move the husband must work overtime and travel longer to work. Wives may find they can no longer go out to work themselves, since they can no longer leave their children with their mothers. Moreover, the absence of friends and relatives may mean that precarious relationships with their husbands and children, no longer diluted by the presence of other people, now become unbearable.

A number of the husbands seen by Dr. Hall complained of heart palpitations (overrapid heartbeat) and constant tension headaches. The disorder and upheaval of the move, the long-drawn-out legalities, the mortgage payments, competitive feelings toward new neighbors, all were extremely stressful to them. Sexual problems for both men and women became underscored by the move. For some couples, having children had been delayed until the couple had a house. Now with a house, the husband and wife were confronted with the inadequacy of their sexual relations and with the threat of assuming adult, parent roles.

On the Job

Your job can be a continual source of stress.

As everyone knows, executives are subject to considerable on-the-job tension, often with damage to their health. In one dramatic experiment investigators forced monkeys to assume executive responsibilities. Pairs of monkeys were strapped to chairs, where they received electric shocks at intervals. One of the monkeys was made a "manager"—he was put in charge of a turn-off device that would avoid shocks for himself and his partner.

The executive monkeys in the experiment developed ulcers and died. Their partners, who suffered the same degree of discomfort from the shocks, stayed alive and ulcer-free. The sole difference between the monkeys in each pair was that the doomed executives suffered the psychological stress of continual vigilance, while the partner was under no such emotional stress.

It is psychological stress—and stress alone—that evidently causes executives to develop psychosomatic illnesses. Hard work, responsible work, or work demanding long hours is not by itself sufficient to produce stress symptoms. Psychiatrist Jackson A. Smith of the University of Nebraska College of Medicine puts "overwork" in the same category as "being hit on the head while a baby" as a supposed cause of mental illness—neither has any substantiation in medical fact.

14

Elliott Jaques, professor of social sciences at Brunel College in London, observes that work can be stressful because in your work you test in reality your ideas about your personal capabilities. "In our society, by and large, we pick up our social and economic status *via* our capacity as exercised in our work," he comments. For eighteen years Jaques was a consultant to the Glacier Metal Company, an engineering concern employing some 4000 people, in a research project on executive organization and industrial relations.

Jaques has found that health-threatening stress results most often from one of these circumstances: Either (1) you are held accountable for completing a task which is impossible because of inadequate resources or other organizational reasons; or (2) you are held accountable for tasks which are too much beyond your personal capacity. Jaques also has found that stress can result if work is too *easy*.

Of the two major causes of occupational stress, work that is beyond your own capacity is the more troublesome. If difficulties arise through organizational shortcomings, you can always argue for organizational change or increased resources. Your personal reputation is not at stake—the shortcoming is outside you.

But when the cause of difficulty is your own inability to cope with the situation, you are likely to alternate between being anxiously indecisive and being unwise and rash in your decision-making. To do badly in your job is to expose the fact that your abilities are lower than your level of responsibility calls for. "It is your own personal reputation that is now very much at stake," says Jaques. "To try to hang on is to put yourself under strain, and that is where the trouble begins from the point of view of inducing stress."

Jaques tells of Mr. Y, who was promoted to the head of a large department. His authority was clear enough, and no one wanted to see him fail. But he turned out not to be big enough for his job. After three years the strain finally told. He developed severe gastric ulcers requiring surgery. After the operation he was given a lower-level job. Despite the reduced pay and the fact that

ELEGANT!

he works long and hard, he is well satisfied. He feels he is earning his salary and is on top of his job, rather than his job being on top of him.

The Overachievers

Present-day emphasis on intellectual achievement places a particular strain on people with relatively limited intelligence. It may seem incongruous to speak of the limited intelligence of a person with an I.Q. of 110, which is significantly higher than the average of 100. But if this person is a member of a family and a social group in which the I.Q.s range in the 130s and 140s, he is *relatively* mentally retarded. Unless his limitations are recognized, he is likely to have unrealistic expectations of himself. Competitiveness and drive may put him in positions where he is out of his depth in terms of his ability to analyze and logically relate information.

Dr. Harold R. Martin and Dr. Wendell M. Swenson of the Mayo Clinic have found that such "overachievers" often function very close to their maximum capacity. Superficially they may have a lot of success in their work. But psychosomatic symptoms often appear when their advancement takes them or threatens to take them completely beyond their capacity.

Henry was the rising star of the large international corporation for which he worked. He became the youngest district sales manager in the entire United States after he pushed sales in his office from an average of $5000 worth of parts a month to $100,000. In so doing, he became wound up like a top. He practically never ate lunch, preferring to work right through the lunch hour, and rarely took a vacation.

By the time he came to the Mayo Clinic, he was suffering from insomnia and persistent trembling. Pain is another common complaint of overachievers; so are nausea and vomiting, and fainting and dizziness. On an I.Q. test Henry scored between 99 and 103. He had difficulty in abstract reasoning and a limited fund of general information.

These limitations helped explain the events leading up to his anxiety state. He had recently made several business blunders. He had prepared an audit that was not acceptable to his home office, and had used poor judgment in firing a long-time employee. He had bought an expensive piece of property for the company but had overlooked a problem relating to the title. When reprimanded by the company, he went into a tailspin. His need to prove himself had carried him well beyond his capacity to function with any reserve or equanimity. His overachievement made him vulnerable to emotional and physiological symptoms.

In some fields the minimum level of acceptable performance is so high that severe stress, even for gifted people, is almost inevitable. A concert performance demands extreme mental concentration from musicians for a much longer period than most people can sustain. The average span of concentrated attention is 20 to 30 minutes; after an hour of concentrated attention, fatigue often sets in.

The normal two-hour length of a concert therefore places a heavy strain on musicians. Soloists suffer the greatest stress, a University of Vienna team of investigators has found. The stress of musicians in orchestras is only slightly less. They are forced to perform teamwork requiring precise timing, no more than a hundredth of a second off. Moreover, the contribution of an individual orchestra member, though it may be superlative, is generally lost in the overall concert—whereas the slightest fault or wrong reaction is immediately noticed and often sharply criticized.

Constant fear of such failures thus creates extreme stress. Severe anxiety may set in two weeks before a challenging concert. The musicians often suffer extreme tension during the performance, and sleeplessness and fatigue after it. Some have an almost permanent mood of frustration. During concerts musicians commonly suffer from fits of perspiration, trembling, and giddiness in their fear of missing their cues.

Another stressful field is investing. A New York psychiatrist writing under the name of Conrad Sewil describes a condition he

calls "Wall Street sickness." Victims suffer from fatigue, headaches, and gastrointestinal disturbances. Even relatively successful investors may have feelings of self-doubt and indecisive-
ness because they didn't hold on longer to a rising stock or get
rid of another before it bottomed out.

One such was a man whose symptoms were mysterious until
his doctor discovered that the value of his large portfolio had
dropped 30 per cent during a stock market slump. Though he
was still a wealthy man and had played benefactor to many
friends and relatives, he feared they'd consider him a failure if
they learned of his reverses. After confiding this fear to his doctor, he decided to sell his more volatile stocks. His condition improved as he once more felt like a successful investor.

Blue-collar Blues

While laymen often discuss the health problems of executives
and professionals, studies show that lower-level jobs may be
even more subject to stress illnesses. Workers often evaluate
their own worth in terms of the status of their jobs. Investigators
at the Institute for Social Research of the University of Michigan
have found that the lower a jobholder's position, the lower his
self-esteem and the more likely he is to develop peptic ulcers.
The blue-collar worker, it turns out, is more likely to have ulcers
than an executive.

Shift work apparently increases the jobholder's problems. Men
working afternoon and night shifts have greater strain and tension in marriage than do day workers. Men working the night
shift report difficulties with their roles as protectors of their family and as husbands. They are disturbed by sexual incompatibil-
ity with their wives. Shift workers are commonly bothered by
problems of body functions that ordinarily are influenced by the
clock: sleep, appetite, moving the bowels. They also are more
likely to suffer colds, headaches, infectious diseases, ulcers, and
rheumatoid arthritis.

Any substantial change on the job can be similarly threatening. Dr. Jackson Smith tells of seven men who came to his hospital during a short period with a number of bodily complaints. All seven were employees of a railroad that was converting to a new type of equipment. Each of the men, it developed, lacked confidence in his ability to operate the new machinery. It was only after no physiological basis for their illnesses could be discovered that they discussed their concern over their new responsibilities. None had associated his problems on the job with the symptoms that brought him to the hospital.

While employment may be stressful, *un*employment is even more so. When a worker loses his job, his health almost invariably suffers. Saltville, Virginia, is a river town of some 2000 people and for seventy-five years was heavily dependent on its main employer, the Olin Chemical Works. When new water pollution laws were passed by the state, Olin announced it could not economically comply with them and would close its Saltville plant, throwing 650 people out of work. There are few other nearby employers, and most of the plant workers have limited skills and education.

Saltville now is suffering from epidemics of stomach distress and alcoholism. There is a rise in hypertension and other stress ailments, especially among older workers. One fifty-year-old recalls that news of the closing "shook me so it took me three days to get back to normal."

The health effects of unemployment are no different higher up the job ladder. Blaw-Knox is a manufacturer of steel and aluminum mill equipment. It was merged into a conglomerate, White Consolidated. Within a year Blaw-Knox's headquarters staff of 230 people was cut to 40. "Your job and mine will continue as in the past," the B-K president had announced. Within a year he, too, was gone.

A no-man's land was created of stringent economy cuts and directives sent to managers to move out, by discharge or transfer, large numbers of employees. In six months' time equipment orders fell from $55 million to $4 million. And in the months following the merger, one executive developed a bleeding ulcer, another suffered a heart attack, a third had a stroke.

PART III

The Uses of the Body

Unconscious conflicts can burst forth in the form

of physical symptoms. What illness you may get,

and how much pain you may feel, may be foretold

by your personality.

CHAPTER 7

Who Gets What

Does your personality invite disease?

Alan Owens was small, neat, poised. He was obviously intelligent and was open and responsive toward the interviewer, a psychoanalyst we'll call Dr. Jones.

Owens mentioned that his first marriage had "just dissolved itself."

"What went wrong?" Dr. Jones asked. "Who didn't like whom?"

"We were both young," Owens replied. "I was thinking too old for my age, and she was thinking the age she was, and so we didn't have maybe the intelligence to reconcile this difference."

"How did you get to thinking so old?"

Owens laughed. "Now that's a question. I was a boy until I was nineteen, and then I became a man overnight, and I became an older man than I should have become. When I was a boy I was a prankster. Then overnight I accepted the responsibilities of the world."

Owens and Jones were taking part in an experiment at the Chicago Institute for Psychoanalysis. Researchers wanted to see if certain common organic disorders could be diagnosed *without* a medical examination, merely on the basis of the patient's personality. The disorders under study were bronchial asthma, hypertension, hyperthyroidism, neurodermatitis, peptic ulcer, rheumatoid arthritis, and ulcerative colitis.

A transcript of the lengthy interview Owens had with Dr. Jones was sent to an internist, whose job it was to delete any clues that could possibly suggest the medical nature of the disease. "Then the rash appeared," would obviously be censored out of a transcript, for it suggests dermatitis. But so also would such allusions as "I had to be near a bathroom all the time," a particular problem for ulcerative colitis patients, or "Thank God I didn't need surgery," which would focus on conditions often requiring operations.

Copies of the edited transcript then went to psychoanalysts who knew nothing more of Alan Owens and his condition than what they could read in this expurgated interview. From dozens of personality clues coming out of the interview, one analyst offered this interpretation: "He was an acting-out person, early as a prankster, later in 'grinding down' his wife by an indiscriminating imposition of his will and wishes."

The analysts noted that Owens was rigid and self-controlling and wished to control others. At the same time he was a responsible person with a strong desire to care for others. This combination of personality traits matched characteristics they had already observed in large numbers of rheumatoid arthritis victims. They thus concluded that Alan Owens suffered from rheumatoid arthritis.

In Owens' case, the analysts were unanimously correct. He had developed rheumatoid arthritis two years before, following the breakup of his second marriage. Overall, the analysts predicted the correct diagnosis 41 per cent of the time, a remarkable average since the disease could be diagnosed only in terms of the person's behavior patterns and moods.

Personality Portraits

The idea that certain personality types are predisposed to certain diseases is not new to medical thought.

Hippocrates himself formulated a connection between illnesses and temperament. When medicine was based on clinical observations alone, sharp-eyed physicians noted the frequent occurrence of certain diseases in persons of distinct physical and mental types. The observant clinician knew that the long, lean, narrow-chested person was more inclined to tuberculosis than the rotund, robust type—who, on the other hand, was more likely to suffer a cerebral hemorrhage.

Early physicians commented that diabetics are fond of the pleasures of the table, that heart disease often occurs among the anxious, that peptic ulcer sufferers are frequently hard-driving go-getters. Expressions like "melancholia" reveal the intuitive knowledge that many depressed people suffer from gallbladder disturbance. Melancholia, a term for severe depression, is derived from the Greek *melas* ("black") and *chole* ("gall"). Balzac in his *Cousin Pons*, one of the first novels written on a psychosomatic theme, draws a masterful picture of a bachelor who develops first melancholia, later a gallbladder condition.

Relatively new, however, are systematic studies linking personality types with bodily disease. This approach is under debate throughout the field of psychosomatics, and some investigators discount such a search as a wild-goose chase.

One critic, Dr. Lawrence S. Kubie of the New York Psychoanalytic Institute, has examined patients suffering from such psychogenic ailments as migraine, ulcerative colitis, and heart disease, yet has found no consistent personality types. "I have been impressed by the dissimilarities at least as vividly as by the similarities among the individuals in each [disease] group," Kubie reports. "Indeed I could not convince myself that the similarities were greater than those which obtain among any heterogeneous group of neurotic patients."

True, there is no single theory that can account for all psychosomatic disorders, and psychosomatic personality studies are often contradictory: Many kinds of personality can voice the identical complaint. Individuals with the same personality may manifest many kinds of illnesses.

On the other hand, an impressive body of evidence shows that to some degree at least there is a significant correlation between the kind of person you are and the kind of bodily disease you are prone to. For some illnesses more than 80 per cent of the sufferers fall into characteristic personality patterns. By contrast, in some disorders, far fewer than 80 per cent of patients show the *physical* signs characteristic of the disease. "In other words," observes Dr. Helen Flanders Dunbar, "the diagnostic symptoms of a disease may show greater variability than the personality pattern."

One skeptic, Dr. E. F. Gildea of New Haven Hospital, set out to disprove the idea of the personality profile. He evaluated patients in eight different disease groups, then drew up his own personality portraits. To his surprise, each of the distinct pictures he drew of the typical hypertensive, the typical asthmatic, and so on, corresponded with the portraits already drawn by previous investigators.

Acid Test

Of the acid tests to which psychosomatic personality studies have been subjected, few have been more stringent than one devised by psychiatrist Floyd O. Ring of the University of Nebraska College of Medicine.

Dr. Ring found much truth in the concept that patients with a given personality profile could often be matched to a corresponding bodily illness. "But," he cautioned, "with a little imagination one could see almost any profile in almost any patient if one were looking for that profile."

Like many tough-minded investigators, Dr. Ring was disturbed by the fact that if you knew a person had, say, a peptic ulcer, you could easily find evidence of his being a hard-driving executive type—and therefore "prove" the supposed correlation between that physical condition and that personality profile. On the other hand, if you thought he had rheumatoid arthritis, you could equally well select evidence to support your preconceived notion of a presumably different personality pattern. Everyone has many diverse currents of character working simultaneously, and depending on your idea of what a person *should* be like, you can pretty well pick out whichever pattern you choose.

Dr. Ring set out to determine if in a given disease, an individual personality pattern really is predominant and self-evident. He had colleagues refer to him more than 400 patients suffering from any of fourteen ailments: asthma, backache, coronary occlusion, degenerative arthritis, diabetes, dysmenorrhea, glaucoma, hypertension, hyperthyroidism, migraine, neurodermatitis, peptic ulcer, rheumatoid arthritis, and ulcerative colitis. Ring wished to see if an illness could be determined on the basis of a personality interview lasting as little as 15 minutes, no longer than 25.

In order that he and his fellow examiners be given no clue to the patient's precise illness, every patient was instructed to say nothing about symptoms, treatment, disabilities, diet, medical conditions, or anything else in any way associated with his physical self. Furthermore, the patient's body was covered during the interview, so the examiners could get no physical hints to the disease. To keep the sampling airtight, all interviews were conducted with at least two other professionals looking on. If the patient let slip a clue to his illness, or removed even his hand from under cover, he was rejected from the sample.

Dr. Ring's percentage of correct diagnoses on first crack was so far beyond what chance would dictate that it supports his conclusion: "Persons with some illnesses can be picked out . . . with a good percentage of accuracy by personality . . . alone." One hundred per cent of the hyperthyroid cases were detected. Similarly, personality alone uncovered 83 per cent of the patients with peptic ulcer and rheumatoid arthritis, 71 per cent with coronary occlusion, and between 60 and 67 per cent with asthma, diabetes, hypertension, and ulcerative colitis.

In at least one case the personality interview revealed a correct diagnosis where a physical examination report had erred. After talking with a forty-year-old man, Ring concluded that he had rheumatoid arthritis. Because the man's medical chart listed "bleeding peptic ulcer," Ring was about to mark his own impression wrong. He questioned the patient further. It turned out that rheumatoid arthritis *was* the man's main problem now. He had been taking medication for arthritis and had developed the ulcer as a side effect.

From repeated observations, Ring asserted that personality types not only exist but fall into three broad categories. In some diseases the typical sufferer is excessively apprehensive. He readily expresses his thoughts, and freely reacts to his feelings of fear or anger. In nearly all his spheres of living, he is physically and verbally active.

He was asked, among other questions, "If you were sitting on a park bench . . . and [a stranger] just your size, age, and sex . . . walked up . . . and kicked you in the shins, what would you do?" Most such patients, instead of saying they would demand a reasonable explanation, replied: "We'd have a show-down," or "I'd beat the hell out of him." Dr. Ring termed this type of patient the "excessive reactor." He found that in this category fell nearly all the victims of coronary occlusion, degenerative arthritis, and peptic ulcer.

Another type of patient is much the opposite. He tends to suppress his fear and anger, indeed is not even aware he has such feelings. He inhibits his actions and holds back his thoughts.

If kicked in the shins by a stranger, what would such people do? Most of them reply: "Nothing." Nearly all the sufferers of neurodermatitis, rheumatoid arthritis, and ulcerative colitis fall into this group of "deficient reactors."

A final group are the "restrained reactors." They are aware of their fears and anger but rarely act on or express them. A characteristic response to a kick in the shins is: "I'd be pretty mad," or "I might hit him." In this group are most sufferers from asthma, diabetes, hypertension, hyperthyroidism, and migraine.

The Accident Makers

At the age of eight, Mike hitched a ride on the tail bumper of a bus. He lost his hold and suffered a concussion.

At nine, he nearly drowned diving from a high board. At eleven, he broke his coccyx tobogganing. During high school and college he broke an arm, a leg, and a collarbone and smashed up two cars. He took up motorcycling and skidded into a tree, costing him four teeth and wrecking the cycle. Now, friends groan, he's planning to take flying lessons.

One of the most comprehensive psychosomatic personality profiles fits Mike to a T. It came to investigators like a bolt from the blue.

At the Columbia Presbyterian Medical Center in New York, Dr. Helen Flanders Dunbar was exploring the possibility of a relationship between personality patterns and various diseases. She and her associates were interviewing at length all patients admitted for cardiovascular disease, diabetes, and other conditions thought to have a strong psychological component. As is customary in such studies, a large number of normal patients were needed for purposes of comparison.

The most normal individuals arriving at a large hospital seemed to be accident cases. Anyone can have an accident, it was reasoned. And while not all accidents result in broken bones, virtually every broken bone is the product of an accident. Thus several hundred fracture patients were selected as controls.

On reviewing early findings, Dr. Dunbar and her colleagues were surprised to see that on average the fracture cases were psychologically far from normal. In a great many people, it was found, emotional influences were causing repeated accidents. Instead of fractures being normal mishaps, for the "accident-prone" they are a psychosomatic condition. And accident-proneness is one of the most clear-cut personality types.

Dr. Dunbar's cases were no less than fourteen times as likely to have a disabling accident as all the other patients studied. The fracture patients averaged fully four serious accidents apiece. At least 80 per cent of them had had two or more accidents. People who are killed in accidents, Dr. Dunbar found, usually work up to the fatal injury through several lesser ones.

The case for accidents being psychosomatic was bolstered by

the fact that most of the injuries were *self*-inflicted. The accident-prone fracture cases actually were injured less often by someone else than were other groups—they caused the accident themselves and rarely injured other people. About half the injuries resulted from falls in the home, on ice, on the street, in front of cars. In many cases the accidents were repeated with almost monotonous regularity—the same arm or leg being broken over and over, the same joint being hurt again and again.

One paradox of Dr. Dunbar's accident cases was their otherwise good health. A third of them had a perfect health history before their accident tendency. They were much less troubled by colds than the general population. Major illnesses and operations were rare. A large number were actually finicky about health—given to taking vitamins and tonics and going to bed at the first sneeze of a cold.

Another paradox: Patients having fractures were athletic, but only rarely did their injuries come from sports. They were perfectly able to take care of themselves on the playing field. Yet they slipped and fell with amazing regularity at home and at work.

Typically, accident-prone people fit the description "happy-go-lucky." They show little of the nervous tension that characterizes most psychosomatic patients, and would ordinarily be envied for their cheerful outlook on life.

But they have an unstable character. They rarely complete difficult assignments. When the going gets tough or the responsibility heavy, they move on to something easier. Although usually intelligent, the accident-prone person generally has little interest in intellectual values and deep thinking.

He usually likes people, however, and people like him. "Charming" is frequently used to describe accident-prone people. They mix well socially, often exuding a devil-may-care manner that many people find attractive. They like adventure and tend to avoid responsibility and to live from day to day. The average person often envies these tendencies in others, because he cannot normally divorce himself from reality to the same extent.

The accident-prone are quite casual about many things, including marriage and sex. Their marriages tend to be unstable. Extramarital affairs are relatively common with them.

Impulsive behavior is a prime characteristic. The accident-prone make decisions quickly, often without adequate thought. Frequently they take pride in this trait. "I'm pretty fast to make my mind up," Dr. Dunbar was told by a twenty-year-old girl about to undergo major surgery. "Other people would be scared to undergo an operation and I just made up my mind like that."

The same girl was extremely ambitious and bitterly ashamed that her father was a janitor and most of her family worked in factories. Yet she did nothing decisive to change her lot. The psychiatric history of her case summed up much of the shallow thinking of the accident-prone: "She focused upon immediate values rather than long-range goals. Her strong emotional attachments were to people—her family and friends," and also to "concrete experiences of the moment—swimming, tennis, horseback riding. She had no intellectual interests."

A tendency to explosive outbursts of more or less undirected energy seems to be what gets the victim into trouble. These mental processes, which lead to an act of seeming self-destruction, are not in the individual's conscious awareness. He himself feels tension only in terms of working it off by muscular action, and his impulsive burst may do him harm.

A characteristic trait among the accident-prone is their resentment of authority, a hostility the person may not be consciously aware of. This resentment often can be traced to a parent who exercised authority in rigid, severe, overwhelming ways. As the child grows, his resentment of his parent attaches to other authority figures, represented by school, employer, spouse, government, church.

Most accident-prone people are brought up in a strict religious atmosphere by stern, authoritarian parents. A large proportion had neurotic traits in childhood. They walked or talked in their sleep, lied persistently, stole, or were truant. These tendencies eventually disappeared, evidently replaced by the accident habit.

Interestingly, the accident-prone person and many adult criminals share a number of the same traits, especially resentment of authority and a tendency toward impulsive behavior. This tension leads one to break the law, the other to break his bones.

Outwardly the accident-prone person appears to have adjusted to authority satisfactorily. He is busy, athletic, alert: "normal," by most people's measure. Underneath the apparent adjustment, however, he seethes with resentment, especially when disturbed by daily conflicts.

An accident often results when there's a breakdown in the balance between the person's adjustment to authority and his resentment of it. The trigger event is usually a momentary emotional earthquake. Another kind of person might repress his resentment or confront the authority figure directly. The accident-prone individual is likely to respond with impulsive activity. Many are injured taking dares and doing other foolhardy things, in which for the moment they perilously suspend judgment.

An accident may result as a reaction to something the person doesn't want to do. Dr. Dunbar recounts the following cases: A man was afraid to tell his wife he'd been laid off from work; brooding over this confrontation, he slipped on the ice and broke his leg. A young Roman Catholic housewife, ashamed to confess she'd been using contraceptives, and fearing she'd have to promise to give them up, fell down the steps on her way to church. An employee, fuming over having to work on Sunday, fractured a vertebra.

X Factor

In 1932 Franz Alexander and his associates at the Chicago Institute for Psychoanalysis found that, in patients suffering from organic ailments, similar emotional conflicts recurred too frequently to ignore. In such conflicts, they felt, could lie clues to the cause of a specific psychosomatic disease.

The Chicago workers began a series of psychoanalytic studies that continue to this day. Clear patterns of motivation have emerged, among them: Duodenal ulcer patients have a characteristic conflict about dependency needs. Asthma sufferers frequently fear losing their mother and have difficulty crying. Trouble in handling hostile impulses appears again and again in people suffering from hypertension. Neurodermatitis victims intensely crave physical closeness.

Alexander and his colleagues formulated the "specificity hypothesis" as a clue to who gets what disease under what conditions. In essence, the theory goes like this: A person may be born with or develop through illness or injury a physical vulnerability, an "X factor." There is considerable evidence that a predisposition to a specific organic disease is inherited. For example, someone may have as an X factor a vulnerability in his circulatory system. This person may experience a second variable: a basic emotional conflict. His bodily response to this "psychodynamic constellation" may now put a chronic strain on his heart or blood vessels.

As a final variable, this person—his vulnerable organs already under attack by his response to emotional conflict—finds himself in an "onset situation." Such an external life event may trigger a full-blown case of hypertension. Likewise, if the X factor was in the lining of his bronchial tubes, and a severe emotional conflict was present, he might develop asthma.

These variables may well be interrelated. A person born with a vulnerable circulatory system may feel great hostility toward his parents, but never express it because he craves their approval. Unexpressed hostility may affect his internal chemistry, causing a constriction of the arteries and a buildup of cholesterol on the artery walls.

His craving for approval may lead him to an onset situation, perhaps driving him to carry on his work dutifully even under unreasonably difficult conditions; overconscientiousness is a common trait among hypertensives. A "beast of burden" may subtly invite heavier and heavier loads. He then may feel ever greater unexpressed hostility, which in turn can cause further stress to his vulnerable organs and lead to a case of hypertension.

As Alexander notes, individual variations are enormous. Many people are in the same psychological boat as hypertensives but

never develop hypertension. Identical life events may be an onset situation for one person, roll off the back of a second, and be
a blessing to a third. Losing a wife may be a stark tragedy for
Smith, a great relief for Jones.

An inborn bodily defect lies at the root of diabetes. There may
be either an inadequate production of insulin by the pancreas or
an excessive destruction of insulin by the tissues. Either way,
the sugar content of the blood is abnormally high. The condition
is believed to exist from birth, though diabetic symptoms may
show up only later in life. It is thought that prolonged stress,
emotional as well as physiological, may result in a permanent
failure of the person's already strained regulatory mechanisms,
and so the disease becomes apparent.

Before the disease is discovered, Dr. Helen Flanders Dunbar
found, diabetics have a long history of deprivations, fatigue,
weariness, and a sense of depression and hopelessness. The
emotional picture may be the result of the unrecognized disorder
in metabolism. It is thought more likely, however, that these
emotional difficulties represent psychological conflicts boiling
beneath the surface. In at least one case reported by Dunbar,
diabetic symptoms disappeared with psychoanalysis.

Dr. Dunbar found the typical diabetic to be indecisive, frequently letting others make decisions and then bearing his lot
with much grumbling, rarely doing anything to relieve his seeming hard luck. In early childhood most diabetics were torn between resenting their parents and docilely submitting to them.
Many were "spoiled" children. Diabetic men especially were
dominated by their mothers and dependent on them.

Diabetics tend to be passive in a sexual as well as a general
sense. Marriage is often disappointing because the diabetic partner wants to be babied too much for mutual happiness. Dislike
of sex keeps many of the men single.

The diabetic's passivity is widely interpreted to show a strong
desire to return to an early infantile state marked by a craving
for food. Studies at the Chicago Institute for Psychoanalysis suggest that the diabetic has an insatiable wish to be fed. Franz
Alexander theorizes that this craving may cause the release into

the bloodstream of large quantities of sugar. Unable to obtain satisfaction for his infantile oral desires, the diabetic may unconsciously release from his sugar reservoirs the food he wants.

What's the Use?

If you put a wild rat into an absolutely hopeless situation, say in a tank of water from which there is no escape, he will swim around a bit. Then, though he is in no way exhausted or drowned, he will go into shock. His body temperature will fall, his heart will slow down, and he will die. In fights among wild rats, the loser often lies down, weakens, and dies, although he shows no evidence of injury. "A series of bouts may leave an attacked wild rat in a state of collapse," writes zoologist S. A. Barnett, "while the dominant attacker shows no distress. . . . Both rats have leapt wildly about; neither, perhaps, is wounded; yet the effects on the two antagonists are in complete contrast."

There may be a connection between such deaths and the fact noted by Dr. R. S. Fisher, coroner of the City of Baltimore, that a number of Americans die each year after taking poison in doses so small it could not in itself cause death, or after inflicting small, nonlethal wounds on themselves. They evidently die as a result of a belief in their doom. As every doctor knows, one of the most important requirements for recovery in any patient is his will to live.

A group of researchers at the University of Rochester School of Medicine and Dentistry have found that the great majority of patients hospitalized for physical illness experienced a psychological disturbance before they got sick. Most commonly this was not anxiety, fear, or anger—the emotions ordinarily considered to be associated with sickness—but an attitude of "giving up."

"What's the use?" patients would ask. Or they'd report: "It was just too much." "I couldn't take it any more." "I didn't know what to do."

Giving up takes at least two forms: helplessness and hopelessness. In helplessness the victim feels let down or left out. Patients recall experiencing such a feeling as the result of a change or an impending change over which they feel powerless and for which they do not feel themselves responsible.

In hopelessness, on the other hand, the victim has a feeling of futility or despair engendered by what he thinks of as his own failure. He feels incapable of compensating in any way for this failure, and he sees no possibility that anyone can help him.

Certain personality traits appear to be associated with each of these aspects of giving up. For the person most likely to experience helplessness, his first response to a situation is often one of anger and fear. He feels chronically deprived.

In one case, a young woman's fiancé suddenly left town. Gradually she realized he had fled to avoid marrying her. One night while watching a love scene in a movie, she felt a throbbing pain in her right knee. Pain with swelling and stiffness progressed to other joints. The hospital's diagnosis: rheumatoid arthritis. Comments Dr. Arthur H. Schmale, Jr., one of the University of Rochester researchers: "This woman felt helpless in her attempts to give up her desire for the man who deserted her, and she could see no way in which she could get him back."

The person likely to experience hopelessness, on the other hand, often is overactive and selflessly devoted to others. Irrespective of his accomplishments, he has difficulty feeling successful. His feelings of hopelessness are often preceded by feelings of guilt or shame.

A widow fitting this description was informed that her last living sister had died. She bitterly condemned herself for not having visited the sister and helped her, though this was not realistically possible. An hour later she had a stroke.

A giving-up response, in and of itself, does not necessarily lead to physical illness. Some other type of vulnerability must be present—a biological predisposition corresponding to the X factor theorized by Franz Alexander. It matters not only how a person responds to psychological stress but also what predisposition to illness he happens to be carrying with him at the time.

In persons who are biologically disposed to a disease, helplessness and hopelessness may provide the climate suitable for the development of the disease. One woman had in her throat a normal number of streptococcal bacteria kept in check by antibodies. When shame and guilt inhibited her from expressing her wishes for protection and loving, the streptococci increased, evidently because her resistance weakened. Conversely, when she was attempting to resolve such conflicts in a realistic manner and found herself a more worthwhile person, her resistance was restored and the bacterial count dropped significantly.

People who feel "What's the use?" may react to psychological stress by retreating from action into a dependent state. Instead of facing the emergency, their first impulse is to respond as they did when they were helpless children. They withdrew into a state of supposed safety.

Physiologically, they have the reverse of the fight-or-flight reaction, described in Chapter 3. Instead of preparing for war, in part by suspending stomach action, their bodies make ready for a big meal, a state of relaxation.

Franz Alexander tells of a patient we will call Paul who was suffering from a chronic excess flow of stomach acid. Whenever Paul saw a movie in which a hero was acting aggressively or dangerously, he reacted with acute heartburn. Acid poured into his stomach.

Paul identified himself with the hero, speculates Alexander. But this aroused anxiety, and he retreated physiologically from the situation. Just when—in the person of the hero—he would have to fight, his stomach would overfunction and prepare for the intake of food: the opposite of what was needed in terms of the hero role he was playing.

Generally, giving up follows the loss, or threat of the loss, of someone or something close to the patient—a wife or husband, parent, child, home, job, career plan. It is not the loss itself that is significant in the development of illness, but the way the person reacts to the loss. Dr. George L. Engel of the University of Rochester School of Medicine and Dentistry observes: "These patients not only experienced that kind of happening—a loss— but responded to it in this kind of way—by giving up."

At the University of Rochester Dr. Arthur Schmale, Jr., has interviewed 191 patients at random. About 80 per cent recently experienced a loss to which they reacted with feelings of giving up.

Such losses may be actual, threatened, or symbolic. An actual loss includes the death of someone in the family or of a close friend, the loss of a husband or wife by divorce, the loss of money, home, or job. A threatened loss can be the serious illness of someone close, or an indication that someone close—possibly a child—is trying to break away, or an impending operation that is viewed as a threat to life or normal functioning. A symbolic loss may be a reverse, a rejection, a rebuff. Often it seems insignificant to an observer, but is important to the victim because it reawakens feelings of despair stemming from a past threat or unresolved conflict.

Schmale has followed the health consequences following the death of a husband. He located a number of young and middle-aged women whose husbands were fatally ill with cancer. All the women were healthy when the study began.

Schmale observed each of them beginning some months before her husband's death and for a year thereafter. Of the 14 women in the study, 10 experienced feelings of giving up when their husbands died. All these women became ill within six months. Those who did not give up stayed healthy.

Diseases, including cancer, may ebb and flow with situations of loss. A typical case uncovered by Dr. William A. Greene, Jr., of the University of Rochester: For three years a woman with Hodgkin's disease, a cancer of the lymph glands, enjoyed a remission. Her case was well under control. Just before her youngest son was to go into the Army, she suffered a serious relapse. Her condition was again brought under control. Then an older son was called back into the service. She relapsed again.

CHAPTER 8

Choosing Your Symptoms

How your unconscious conflicts can burst forth

Leon feels great guilt about his homosexual tendencies.

He began engaging in homosexual practices at about the age of 13. Shortly thereafter he started seeing zigzag lines and flickerings. Objects shimmered as if seen through a heat wave. This condition, termed scintillating scotomata, resulted from a constriction of blood vessels in the visual center of the brain.

The scotomata became the prelude to attacks of migraine. Leon would suffer monstrous headaches and nausea. He felt as if "an iron bar is being pushed into my eye socket."

At twenty-seven he developed severe sialorrhea, excessive secretion of saliva. He spat all the time to keep his mouth from overflowing.

By the time he was thirty, the scotomata, migraine, and sialorrhea disappeared. He now came down with a peptic ulcer.

At thirty-five he was making a long journey to meet Simon, a man with whom he'd had sexual relations. On the way he had three accidents, in one of which his car overturned. When they finally met, he had the terrifying fantasy that Simon was drunk and would announce to everyone: "Leon is a homosexual."

Leon immediately felt a "terrible fear and something like a freezing cold storm" in his chest. He was having a heart attack.

The Volcanic Unconscious

Leon's succession of symptoms is called a "psychosomatic shift." His physical illnesses are outcroppings of inner turmoil of which he is only dimly aware. A psychoanalyst suggests that Leon's sialorrhea, for example, is a result of his guilt over performing fellatio. It is as though he were seeking to spit out the penis and semen which had been in his mouth.

As in Leon's case, psychosomatic symptoms can move from one body system to another: now migraine, now peptic ulcer, now a heart condition. Underlying all such symptoms is the unconscious, which is like an underground volcano: It can erupt in many places.

Words like "underground" and "submerged" are often used to describe the unconscious. The *conscious* mind is the center of awareness. But it is only a small part of a larger whole, like the fraction of an iceberg that shows above the surface of the sea.

The unconscious is far greater in scope and power. Here lie wishes, hopes, and fears that are unacceptable to your conscious mind. A child senses that his parents' disapproval threatens him with destruction, and so he attempts to cast out impulses and desires that are in conflict with enforced standards of conduct. The process brings relief and stays with him for life. The cast-out thoughts and feelings nonetheless remain part of him. They stay active in his unconscious, along with memories and painful emotions associated with the conflict.

Even though a feeling is unacceptable to your conscious, waking, rational, moral, civilized, disciplined self, it does not mean that the feeling ceases to exist. It goes underground; it is repressed. This process of repression is an unwitting and automatic submersion rather than a deliberate, conscious control.

You may, for example, be in a situation that makes you angry. Anger, however, may be unacceptable to your conscious mind. Without ever consciously being aware of the emotion of anger, you repress the feeling.

"Repression can fool only the mind, not the body," notes psychiatrist Charles William Wahl of the University of California Medical School at Los Angeles. The body responds to unconscious processes. It reacts as if you *were* angry, or afraid, or guilty, or sexually excited.

You may become consciously aware of the pounding of your heart, the sweating of your palms, the twitching of your muscles, the tension of muscular contraction, yet be wholly unable to account for these phenomena. Much neurotic behavior stems from trying to relieve such physical discomfort. One of the goals of psychotherapy is to make conscious that which had previously been unconscious, to enable the patient to resolve his difficulties with the help of his conscious, rational mind.

Wahl offers this analogy: "If one is locked in a dark room with an enemy, [he] can only lash out blindly in the darkness at something he can neither see nor understand. If, on the other hand, light is brought into the room, he can, with his conscious, rational mind, perceive the difficulty and use his rational power to take appropriate steps to solve it."

Anxiety, for example, is a nameless dread. If, through therapy, it becomes identified and labeled, it may be transferred into a specific fear. This is a completely different emotion, which can be handled more directly and realistically than its predecessor, dread.

There is ample experimental evidence for the existence of the unconscious and its powerful effects on behavior. Consider the well-known phenomenon of hypnosis and posthypnotic suggestion. If you've hypnotized someone, you can suggest that he open an umbrella ten minutes after he comes out of the hypnotic state. When he carries out the act he will not be aware of the reason. If pressed, he will give any ready rationalization. One man said, "I thought I'd test the umbrella because it might rain later in the day."

Recent experiments with the tachistoscope yield more sophisticated proof of the existence of the unconscious. In tachistoscope experiments, pictures are flashed on a screen for a fraction of a second and the subject is tested for recall of the picture. Even though he may not recall seeing anything, his dream images and behavior often reveal that the picture was perceived without his conscious awareness.

Symptoms Can Be Symbols

In your unconscious, all your conscious mind's rules of logic, intellect, reason go awry.

The unconscious is not logical, but *paleo*logical (*palaio* = "ancient" in Greek). It is primitive and archaic, reflecting the mental processes of infants and early man. It expresses itself not in rational words and realistic thoughts but in images, fantasy, and physical sensations.

Merely recall the last dream you had, for dreams are windows to the unconscious. A person, thing, situation may have been represented by a symbol, by someone or something similar, even by an opposite. Such is the language of the unconscious.

To relieve the stress placed on it by repressed conflicts, the unconscious may express itself in *physiological* language. This is a form of symbolism and is also an effort to solve a problem or satisfy a need. Unfortunately, since the process is hardly rational, the person's problem often remains unsolved and his need unsatisfied—and the physical changes make him ill.

Dr. Charles William Wahl tells of a woman who complained of severe cramps—a "horrible, sinking tightness" in the pit of her stomach that might take hours to disappear. The woman had a pathological fear of death. Whenever she heard the word "death," her stomach would literally shrink to a mass the size of a grapefruit, causing cramps. She was totally unaware of this contraction. The automatic response was wholly unconscious, evidently a reaction to the repressed conflicts which gave rise to her fear of death.

A specific symptom's symbolic purpose is subject to great variation. One form of symbolism is *pars pro toto* (part for all) in which an individual organ can symbolize the whole conflict. For example, the stomach may be the site of difficulty for a patient with frustrated dependency needs because of its association with the process of being fed and loved by the mother.

Likewise, the symptom may be a concrete expression of an unacceptable idea. A man may vomit because his wife makes him "sick to his stomach." A girl may unconsciously feel that babies grow in the stomach and thus suffer stomach pain throughout her pregnancy. If there is some unpalatable truth which the patient "cannot stomach," he may well be afflicted with nausea, cramps, and vomiting.

Fixing on a Symptom

Symbolism, then, is thought to account in large part for symptom choice. But why one symptom rather than another? The body changes in numerous ways under the influence of emotional stress. For example, when a person is frightened, his heart beats faster, the blood vessels in the skin constrict, the muscles contract, and so on. Yet a psychosomatic disease is mainly characterized by the injurious accentuating of one or two such reactions to the relative neglect of others. Why this reaction or that instead of some other?

For symbolic reasons and also as a matter of chance, it is believed, a part of the total response is reinforced and magnified to the relative exclusion of the remainder. Figures of speech show the natural tendency to focus on just one part of a reaction. A frightened person is said to be "in a sweat," "scared shitless," "scared stiff," "weak in the knees," or "breathless."

The person himself, if chronically frightened, is likely to accentuate only one of these responses, and so may experience such conditions as hyperhidrosis (excessive perspiration) or constipation or muscular rigidity. This may come about because one of these reactions has become a "fixation," an uncontrollable preoccupation. Therein the individual response is magnified and develops into a symptom.

Suppose, for example, a person notices a few lapses in his

heartbeat—a harmless phenomenon. These skipped beats, how-ever, terrify him. He becomes, without wishing to become and without his conscious awareness, "heart-centered." He listens constantly to his heartbeat. As he does so the frequency of missed beats increases.

Evidence shows that such a fixation can affect the function of an organ. Patients with psychosomatic disorders typically are preoccupied with the area of their illness—the hypertensive with his blood pressure; the asthmatic with his breathing. The patient would gladly get rid of the fixation, but finds himself obsessively locked in repetitive rumination which may intensify his symp-toms.

Why fixate on one symptom rather than another? To begin with, a person may identify with a parent who has had similar symptoms. Parents with psychosomatic illnesses tend to produce offspring who have the same problems. A psychosomatic disease thus often "runs in the family."

There are added difficulties if a child is not permitted to ma-ture into the view of himself as a strong, independent person. At some level the child, even after he grows into an adult, may con-tinue to regard his parents in an infantile way: as all-powerful and overwhelming. The offspring of such parents may ask: "If they, with all their strength, are unable to be in good health, how can I?"

Guilt by Dissociation

Guilt, especially over one's feelings toward one's parents, may influence the choice of symptoms.

Physicians attuned to psychosomatics often look for "anniver-saries." Frequently a patient's symptoms appeared on the anni-versary of his parent's death or of the parent's developing a simi-lar condition. These symptoms can be a form of self-punishment for going against one's parents, perhaps for wishing them dead.

Too, someone suffering guilt may use his psychosomatic illness as a way of warding off death. The illness can represent the lesser of two evils. The person believes punishment is called for. He is likely to feel that if he does not suffer from his present illness he will suffer from something worse.

Guilt of another sort can lead to a faulty "body image," i.e., the way you see your body and what you expect of it. If an infant is loved and fondled, and if he has a secure and predictable environment, he can successfully turn his interest from himself. First he turns his attention to his mother, then to the outside world. A child so brought up generally has a satisfactory body image. He takes the good functioning of his body for granted and views it as a basically dependable and sturdy mechanism.

On the other hand, if his body image is deficient, he may never outgrow an aspect of infancy: a preoccupation with his own body, in a pattern of fixation that can intensify a psychosomatic symptom and disturb normal functioning. Dr. Z. J. Lipowski of McGill University recalls a young man who was fixated on his penis and suffered from impotence. Circumcised in infancy, he went from surgeon to surgeon demanding that "my foreskin be replaced by a new one to allow me to have an erection."

Self-exploration of the body is essential to development of an adequate body image. It enables the child to learn where his body leaves off and the world begins. Inevitably the child explores his genitals and his urine and feces. If his parents are outraged by this normal curiosity, the child is likely to feel guilty and frightened. He may extend the taboo to his whole body.

Psychosomatic patients are often ignorant of their body and how it functions. They find thinking about their bodies and its workings distasteful, even frightening. This is usually in marked contrast to the person's sophistication in other areas of knowledge, and is thought to originate in the child's early guilt over self-exploration.

In the Eye of the Beholder

All pathogenic (disease-causing) emotions have one factor in common—psychological stress. But stress, like beauty, is in the eye of the beholder.

In one series of studies, Dr. Lawrence E. Hinkle, Jr., and his group explored the health and illness patterns of nearly 3000 people, some covering a period of more than twenty years. This is considered one of the classic studies showing the connection between emotional factors and physical illness.

Hinkle concluded that illnesses do not occur at random in the life of an individual, but in clusters separated by periods of well being. These clusters commonly correspond to periods of emotional stress in the person's life. But the relationship is not so much to the actual life stresses as to the person's *perception* of difficult life situations. The same type of circumstance can impose greater stress at some times than at other times, and clusters of illness are more likely to occur during these intervals of greater conflict.

The role individual perception plays in forming psychosomatic symptoms is suggested in what surely is one of the most moving studies in psychological literature. The volunteers were 31 parents of children fatally ill with cancer. The youngsters were at the National Cancer Institute in Bethesda, Maryland, undergoing last-ditch experimental treatment. The parents lived at the Institute, their stay essentially a death watch.

While all the parents were enveloped in their tragedy, they had a wide range of responses. Some showed little or no distress, others a great deal. Some could barely function; others seemed unimpaired. Some had exhausted their "defensive reserve"; they were unable to cope with their anxiety, grief, or guilt. Others were still able to mobilize their defenses against such pathogenic emotions.

Investigators brought under scrutiny the parents' defense mechanisms, the unconscious methods the parents used to seek relief from their emotional stress. The researchers found that the more effective a parent's defenses were, the less likely he was to have potentially injurious physiological reactions, as determined by measurements of adrenal cortical activity.

An example of a well-defended, low-reacting parent was Nancy, a thirty-one-year-old mother of three whose eldest son Jerry developed leukemia. Nancy spoke in a controlled and factual manner with only occasional moments of distress. When she talked of the initial diagnosis of Jerry's leukemia or the possibility of his death, she did become sad, but with minimal anxiety, and she seemed able quickly to regain her more typical mood.

Much of the time she seemed to be slightly euphoric, particularly when she discussed the religious significance of Jerry's illness. She declared: "God is in complete control. He is using our family and this disease to bring His message to the world."

Her awareness that Jerry might die was not accompanied by painful feeling since her personal life did not matter, she went on. She rejected the idea that Jerry's death was inevitable. She believed that he might survive, should God so decide.

The interviewer offered this as an illustration of Nancy's effective use of denial, a defense mechanism in which the person becomes blind to a painful reality. Nancy also used as a defense mechanism displacement, focusing on less threatening concerns.

For example, her major concern during the interview was whether she should go home for a weekend, leaving Jerry alone in the hospital. She ruminated about the decision in an unemotional way. She worried that her son might be lonely in her absence, but she did not express concern that a crisis might occur while she was away. Such a crisis was, in fact, a realistic possibility, and she had seen critical episodes of this sort develop suddenly among the other children in the ward.

Throughout Jerry's illness, Nancy used these defenses. For a few days after the diagnosis was made, she felt tense, frightened, and despairing. These feelings suddenly disappeared when she learned that her congregation was praying for Jerry, and she realized that his fate was in God's hands. From that moment she did not experience any similar distress and was able to maintain that what happened to her son ultimately did not matter to her since she was simply fulfilling God's plan.

She felt better about her own worth, she said, since her son's illness dispelled her long-standing sense of being unimportant by giving her an important mission. She suffered no impairment of sleep, appetite, or sexual behavior.

In sharp contrast to Nancy was thirty-four-year-old Arlene, whose older of two adopted children developed a malignant nerve tumor at six. Arlene was warm and sensitive, and she was in considerable distress. While relating the details of her experience, she was able to maintain her composure only with difficulty. Even when talking about neutral subjects she seemed always to be sad. Well-defended parents like Nancy were able to present their experience as if it were a case history. Arlene, however, seemed to be re-experiencing in a painful manner the events she was describing.

Her son had undergone surgical removal of the tumor, and for several months cure was a realistic possibility. Even then, Arlene felt what she called "dread." In her own words: "I just couldn't feel like . . . before. I was living in dread. I just couldn't feel he'd be completely cured of it."

This is a far cry from well-defended parents who, when faced with the same evidence of an apparently well child, were able to deny that a relapse and death were inevitable. Other parents with effective defenses retained an awareness of the impending danger but without the ever-present anxiety described by Arlene. During periods of remission their thoughts and feelings about their children's illnesses became less frequent and intense and their attention returned to some extent to their more ordinary concerns.

Being unable much of the time to defend against distress, Arlene resorted to physical activity in order to dispel her feelings. "I have to keep busy all the time," she said. "I can't sit around just doing nothing. I'm always sewing, doing something to keep my mind occupied." When asked if this helped, she replied, "I don't keep it off my mind but it helps to pass the time away."

Thus physical activity was also ineffective in decreasing her tension.

In addition, Arlene suffered considerable functional impairment. Her relationship with her husband deteriorated. Sexual relations were near zero.

She had difficulty in getting to sleep at night and had anxiety dreams about her son. She was consistently overeating and had gained thirty-five pounds. She had begun to drink heavily.

Arlene was in trouble physiologically as well. Her output of stress hormones was extremely high. Over a prolonged period this biochemical irregularity was likely to cause permanent tissue injury.

CHAPTER 9

The Psychology of Pain

It is highly subjective

A psychotic girl had just torn out her eyeballs. Blood was streaming down her face.

"Didn't it hurt?" asked an appalled observer.

"Not at all," was her calm reply. "They just popped out."

As in this extreme case, pain is highly subjective. Your feelings about an injury can determine to what extent you feel pain from it.

You've noticed this in yourself. Perhaps you've stubbed your toe on the way to answer the phone. You may curse briefly and hobble to find out who's calling. The call is paramount in your mind, and the toe's throbbing soon subsides. But at another time, when you're not preoccupied with something else, the pain from a stubbed toe may seem almost unendurable and endless.

In the same way, a wounded soldier knows that his injury will mean a long vacation from the war. He may thus consider his wound a blessing instead of a horror, something almost to be enjoyed.

During World War II, Dr. Henry Beecher, later professor of research in anesthesia at Harvard, was caring for soldiers wounded on the Anzio beachhead in Italy. He was surprised to find that only one out of four of the severely wounded men felt enough pain to ask for relief. For them the war was over, and they would soon be shipped home.

In civilian life, by contrast, *three* out of four patients recovering from the smaller and less severe wounds of surgery complain of a great deal of pain and ask for pain-killing drugs.

The pure feeling of pain is a warning against a harmful agent. "Yet," note Dr. Roy R. Grinker, Sr., and Dr. Fred P. Robbins, "in the psychic realm it may acquire a completely distorted significance." Grinker and Robbins give as the best example of this the sexual masochist who derives his most intense orgasm only when he is experiencing great pain. "This alone," they say, "should make us aware of the extremes to which life-experiences can alter the response to basic physiological processes."

Wreaking Changes

Pain, and the anxiety it produces, can wreak significant changes in your personality: It can alter your conception of yourself and your relationship to the world.

In a detailed personal account, psychologist Magoroh Maruyama of San Francisco State College has described how his feelings about himself and his future ebbed and flowed during a long siege of severe throat pain. "I had enjoyed an almost perfect health for fourteen years," Maruyama noted. The illness therefore did not seem real to him.

At first he discounted the pain as an ordinary sore throat and went about life as usual. But, as the pain persisted, he became uneasy. His doctor was unable to make a diagnosis and tried one medication after another without success.

The pain rose and fell in intensity. Correspondingly, Maruyama found his outlook on life shifting from discouragement to hopefulness and back.

The pain began to rule his life. Maruyama was on an exciting research trip in Alaska at the time his throat problem erupted. On a day his throat felt well he was able to throw himself into his Alaska work. But the next day, his throat worse, he became preoccupied with returning to California and starting a new project.

The constant mental shifting took its toll. Maruyama lapsed into a sluggish indifference. Finally his condition took a sharp turn for the worse and he returned to California.

In San Francisco a doctor suggested that a biopsy might reveal a tumor or tuberculosis. Weeks of uncertainty followed. On good days Maruyama built up hope. On worse days the hope was destroyed. Also destroyed was his confidence in his judgment. To hope, he believed, was to deceive himself, to open himself to the further pain of disappointment.

As a solution he fell into a deep, overwhelming apathy. Although he used to enjoy Beethoven, for example, the music now "sounded as if it were played for someone else but not for me. It was as if I were a dead man looking at living people from a great distance. . . . At this stage of apathy even death seemed rather neutral . . . and my own old will to live lost emotional meaning just as Beethoven's music lost its meaning to me."

Maruyama at this stage resented anyone who tried to shake him out of his depression. At last the biopsy showed infection but not tumor. "I could again enjoy Beethoven," recalls Maruyama. There had been an ulcer on his vocal chord, and a nerve of his vocal chord had become infected. The pain persisted during the months it took for the nerve to slowly regenerate.

From his experience with fluctuating, prolonged pain and months of waiting for a definite diagnosis, Maruyama has concluded that the *amount* of pain is not as important to your emotional well-being as your *reaction* to the pain: how it is progressing, how it relates to your future, what you can expect in terms of recovery.

The uncertainty may be worst of all. It may have a more adverse effect than an undesirable but definite future. When confronted with the possibility of cancer, Maruyama was sure that the "certainty of death" would have produced in him a response that was emotionally healthier than was his reaction to his uncertain fate.

Pain—Prone People

How much pain you feel depends greatly on what else is occupying your attention.

A musician was tested for his response to pain while he was listening to music. He preferred classics and listened to a Bach fugue intently. His sensitivity to pain was lowered by 26 per cent. A popular dance tune, which he cared for only slightly, lowered his pain threshold by only 8 per cent.

For a young coed, the findings were reversed. She liked pop music much more than Bach.

Boredom and isolation can increase your sensitivity to pain. Patients who are bedridden or housebound for prolonged periods have little sensory stimulation. Their world gets smaller and smaller as the illness continues. They see few people and have few diverting experiences. They become increasingly irritable, restless, and anxious. They may begin to hallucinate.

Having little to do but concentrate on their illnesses, patients with chronic diseases feel pain much more strongly than they would under conditions of normal sensory stimulation. They become increasingly sensitive to every ache and pain. It dominates their attention. They become anxious about the pain, which only intensifies it. The person is thus locked in a spiral of increasing anxiety and pain.

Psychogenic pain is a common symptom of emotionally troubled people. Psychiatrist Frank G. Spear of Middlewood Hospital in Sheffield, England, has found that roughly half of all psychiatric patients in several studies reported physical pain. Patients with anxiety states are particularly apt to have bodily pain. Mental work and emotional strain most commonly precipitated the pains.

Pain of emotional origin tends to be located in the head and trunk and to last continuously for long periods. It remains constant throughout the waking hours, but barely interferes with sleep. This is in contrast to the pains of organic illness, which tend to rise and fall throughout the day, often interfere with sleep, and sporadically diminish for days or weeks.

Patients with chronic psychogenic pain tend to share certain psychological characteristics. Twenty-seven people who suffer from pain in the absence of physical findings have been studied psychiatrically by Dr. Dietrich Blumer of Johns Hopkins.

All but one have a marked tendency to deny emotional conflict; they are blind to its existence. Sixteen are given to relationships of a sadomasochistic nature, deriving pleasure from inflicting or receiving pain. Fourteen suffer pains similar to those they had earlier from an organic illness. Six have pains similar to those of a close relative, twelve of a close relative who was crippled or deformed.

Most are "surgery addicts," averaging a whopping four operations apiece. They look upon surgery as their only possible source of relief.

Dr. Blumer has concluded that for this group "the pain serves as the socially acceptable expression of a sadomasochistic conflict. With the excessive suffering the patient alleviates feelings of guilt and tortures those about him, while at the same time he secures their constant attention and continued care."

A profile of the typical pain-prone individual has been drawn by Dr. George L. Engel of the University of Rochester School of Medicine and Dentistry. Such a person is likely to have a prominence of conscious and unconscious guilt. Pain serves as a means of atonement.

He generally has had a bitterly unhappy early relationship with his parents. Often he has a "masochistic character structure," marked by a history of suffering and defeat and a fear of—or sometimes a panicked flight from—success. He may have a propensity to solicit pain, as evident by the large numbers of painful injuries, operations, and treatments.

Typically he has a strong aggressive drive which is not fulfilled, pain being experienced instead. He develops pain when a relationship is threatened or lost. He has a tendency toward a sadomasochistic type of sexual development, with some episodes of pain occurring in conflict over sexual impulses.

The location of his pain is often determined by unconscious identification with a loved one. The pain is one suffered by the patient himself when in some conflict with the loved one. Or it may be a pain suffered by the loved one, in fact or in the pain-prone person's fantasy.

The Solitary Hunters

"I get real pleasure killing the animal."
"Hunting is man's place in Nature."
"I love to be by myself in the woods."
"I never miss."
The men who made these comments all suffer from unrelievable pain of emotional origin.

Most have severe headaches. The rest have backaches, abdominal pains, or pains in the leg. Half have pain in two or more areas of the body. One says simply, "I hurt all over."

They often describe their pains using metaphors involving violence and aggression. Comments one: "My head feels like someone is hitting me with a hammer." Says another of his abdominal pain: "It's as if someone were sticking a knife in and pulling it out."

Fourteen such men have come to the attention of Dr. David C. Tinling and Dr. Robert F. Klein of the University of Rochester Medical Center. They share a cluster of characteristics which Dr. Tinling and Dr. Klein have labeled the "syndrome of the solitary hunter."

All shared a penchant for solitary hunting. "Some," note Tinling and Klein, "felt that hunting meant as much to them as anything else in life." They all go hunting alone, frequently spending days on end by themselves in the woods.

All the men have major problems coping with aggressive impulses. Half of them suffer from an excessively controlled and obsequious manner coupled with fear that "I'll lose control." Pete, who is subdued and retiring, recalls how his father was sent to prison after going berserk, trying to kill the family and police. As a boy, Pete was frequently knocked unconscious by his father. He always avoids fights, preferring to walk away when angry.

The other men fight frequently, sometimes being literally murderous. Fred's temper is so bad he hasn't worked in years. He's lost nearly all his jobs after explosive arguments and fights with supervisors. Jack has murderous dreams and fears he will kill someone. Phil once threatened to dynamite his landlord's house and shoot a man who had hit him.

Dan has had only two fights in his life, but constantly fears losing control of his temper. The first time, as a teen-ager, he fought his brutal father and then ran away from home. The second time, he recalls, "I almost killed a man with one punch."

In seeking to explain how solitary hunting relates to aggression and pain, Tinling and Klein write: "All the men had difficulties controlling their aggressive impulses, but in the woods they could be murderous without fear of killing someone else or of being injured themselves."

The researchers speculate that the pain developed following actual or fantasied aggressive acts. "The hunting could be considered a defense against murderous wishes, and when such wishes cannot be dealt with appropriately, guilt may supervene, with the need to atone through suffering."

Pain is a logical choice for their suffering, since it is the natural consequence of aggression. Many of the men have settled into a state of chronic depression, defeat, and dependence. Some have quit work and given up entirely.

"These are fragile men who pose as hypermasculine characters," report the investigators. "When they fail, they fall hard. . . . [It's] as if they had been stripped of all their hypermasculine . . . traits and the helpless little boy within is revealed to the world."

These traits are shown in the story of John, a thirty-year-old electronics technician, married and the father of five. John has been suffering from crippling, worsening headaches. He likens the sensation to "having a skullcap on" which is getting tighter and tighter.

He has become irritable, withdrawn, and intolerant of his children. Since the headaches began, he has lost two jobs and has had to sell their property, household furnishings, and automobile. "It wiped out twelve years of progress," he says. He and his family are now living on welfare support.

John is a young, handsome man, with a black patch over his left eye, the result of a hunting accident. He is glib and ingratiating, taking care not to express anger.

John's mother was a hypochondriac, a woman with a violent temper, who was demanding and argumentative and could not be pleased. She derided her husband and sons as inadequate and often declared to John: "You will never be half the man your father was." She dominated the household and held back her husband's plans and business ventures. She frequently meted out physical punishment.

John traces his own short temper to the influence of his mother. He had frequent fights as a child and, as an adult, has a tendency to fight quickly when offended. He was active in school sports but preferred hunting most of all, deriving particular pleasure from solitary hunting.

John's wife relates that he has never seemed able to escape from his mother's attempts to plan his life. "He is always trying to prove his manhood by having intercourse nightly and occasionally attempting to see how many times nightly he can," she says. During their early years of marriage he was unfaithful on two occasions.

When informed of the diagnosis of psychogenic headache, John declined psychiatric therapy, feeling that he would work out a solution by regaining employment. The headaches have continued, but he has become timid about job seeking. Suddenly he is preoccupied with religion. He is jealous and clings to his wife.

Now he feels sad, beaten, and uncertain of his capabilities. He feels guilty over his dependence on his mother and angry that he can't please her. He says, "I keep trying, hoping some day to get a pat on the head."

Phantom Limb

One of the most dramatic examples of largely psychogenic pain is the anguish amputees sometimes feel in an arm or leg that has been amputated.

In most cases an amputee reports feeling a "phantom limb" almost immediately after surgery. At first the phantom limb feels normal in size and shape—so much so that the amputee may reach out for objects with a phantom hand, or try to get out of bed by stepping onto the floor with a phantom foot. Amputees clench missing fists and even try to scratch missing fingers that itch.

As time passes, the limb begins to change shape. The leg or arm becomes shorter, and may fade away altogether, so that the phantom foot or hand feels as if it were hanging in mid-air. Sometimes the limb slowly telescopes into the stump until a phantom hand or foot remains at the stump.

An amputee generally reports a tingling sensation in the phantom limb, but many also report other sensations, such as pins-and-needles, warmth or coldness. About 30 per cent of amputees report pain in phantom limbs. Sometimes local anesthetic in the stump stops the pain for a time, occasionally permanently. A salt solution injected into the tissue around an amputee's spine may also bring some relief.

But in about 5 to 10 per cent of the amputees the pain is severe and may become worse over the years.

Phantom-limb pain is likely to occur in the place where the limb hurt before it was amputated. One patient had a painful bunion the day he lost his foot in an accident: He still felt the bunion afterward.

Although phantom-limb pain usually begins just after surgery, it sometimes doesn't appear for years. Another unusual aspect of this kind of pain is that in some patients it can be triggered by pressure in other parts of the body. So-called trigger zones may develop at distant areas, such as the head and the healthy remaining limb. Even gentle stroking of a trigger zone can evoke severe, prolonged phantom pain. In one case heart pain triggered intense pain in a phantom limb that hadn't been painful for more than twenty-five years.

Neurosurgeons have tried several kinds of operations to relieve phantom-limb pain. The results have been discouraging. One neurosurgical text describes the case of a patient who suffered stabbing pains in phantom fingers. Physicians cut the nerves that carried all sensation from his chest to his brain. He could feel nothing from his shoulders to his navel—except the agonizing pain in his phantom fingers.

What accounts for this strange kind of pain a person can feel in an arm or leg that no longer exists?

Some investigators guess that part of the problem lies in the victim's spinal cord and brain. Nerves extending from the missing limb may be disturbed and form a kind of echo chamber in the spinal cord, a "reverberatory circuit" sending a continuous impulse that the brain interprets as pain.

Dr. Ronald Melzack and his associates at McGill University theorize that normal nerves transmit not only the sensation of pain but also an inhibitor of that sensation, so that the pain will seem to diminish. In an amputation the inhibiting powers of the nerves may be impaired. Thus the message interpreted by the brain as pain may continue unabated for years.

Emotional factors are often critical. Phantom-limb pain can occur when a patient cannot adjust his body image to the loss of a limb. Observe Dr. Roy Grinker and Dr. Fred Robbins: "When a limb is amputated, a patient may not be able to accept its loss and may fantasy its persistence."

One middle-aged man came into the hospital complaining of severe pain in a missing leg. "The personality of this patient was that of an extremely passive man with strong latent homosexual trends," report Grinker and Robbins. "He had spent a great deal of his life as a playboy . . . consorting with many women and having fun in many travels throughout the world."

Shortly before he lost his leg, he married his secretary and settled down for the first time in his life. The amputation of the limb, for a circulatory impairment, was probably the most severe disappointment that he had incurred in his life. He was unable to accept it as a fact in reality. "Therefore," speculate Grinker and Robbins, "he fantasied that the limb was present, and its painfulness was identical to the sensations in the leg when he was suffering from the gangrene that had caused the indications for amputation."

Every nerve block, every possible kind of injection was used. Even spinal cord surgery was performed. Nevertheless the phantom limb remained. It was a "psychological continuation of a limb which he could not give up; he could not face the reality of its nonexistence."

This former playboy ended his life as an addict nursed by his wife.

Relief without Drugs

Physicians have long recognized the potency of placebos—chemically valueless pills, often merely sugar. When patients are given placebos and told that they are powerful pain relievers, the results are often magical.

The word "placebo" means "I shall please" in Latin. It was used in the fifteenth century as a synonym for flattery or a flatterer, and later for a courtesy designed to soothe or gratify. Ever since medicine adopted them, placebos have helped patients feel better. No matter what the placebo or how it is used, it achieves effects in about 35 per cent of cases.

Placebos have relieved organic as well as psychogenic pains, relieving even the severe pains of operative wounds and angina pectoris. Recently experiments have shown that placebos can produce measurable changes in the functioning of the pulmonary, gastrointestinal, and urogenital systems.

In one experiment the warts of a group of New York schoolchildren were painted with chemically inert dyes which they were told were powerful wart medicine. The warts fell off in great numbers.

The most effective placebo of all may be a sympathetic family member, nurse, or doctor. Patients often feel hopeless and helpless, dependent and resentful. The amount of pain they experience is increased by these emotional states.

Patients who complain of pain may not be merely requesting drugs. They may actually be asking for relief from all the different kinds of pain—emotional as well as physiological—they experience attendant to their being ill.

Studies of hospital nurses and patients suggest that pain may be spontaneously reduced if you find out what a patient means by his pain. To what extent is the pain physiological? How does it affect his thoughts and feelings, his ability to cope with his stressful situation?

Mary Ann Bochnak of the Yale School of Nursing has found that when nurses ascertain the meaning of pain to patients, less than a third of the patients require medication for relief. Alas, other studies show that such emotional support is rare. Nurses, and also family members caring for a patient at home, generally see the drug as an adequate solution to his need. There is evidence that patients too share in this stereotyped view of care, and thus, though doped with analgesics, often continue to suffer pain.

Merely inviting a patient to participate in his care may lead to relief of his pain. The human interaction can be that important.

In one nursing experiment patients suffering moderate pain were divided into two groups. In one group the nurse would approach the patient sympathetically, discuss his pain, and recommend a means of relief. In the experimental group the nurses followed the same procedure, but with one important addition: They encouraged the patient to make his own choice about pain-relieving measures.

Thus, in the first group a nurse might say to a patient who complained of leg pain: "Your leg looks twisted and it is off the pillow. I am going to put it in a better position so that some of the strain of the stitches and the cut muscles may be relieved." She would then reposition the leg.

In the experimental group, though, the nurse might say: "It seems that your leg is twisted and has slipped off the pillow.

Perhaps if it was put in a better position some of the strain on the stitches and the cut muscles would be relieved. Would you like to try that?" The patient would thus be involved in his treatment, and the final decision would be his.

The results of the experiment are startling. No patient in the first group obtained relief. In the experimental group all patients except one felt relief of pain.

Other experiments in nursing care suggest that sensitivity to the patient's emotional state can have a great effect on his pain. At one hospital patients in a control group were given pain-relieving medication as a matter of course. As was routine, the nurse spent little time with them, and did not discuss the pain with them. Usually remarks were limited to "This pill will make you feel better" or "Which hip would you like the needle in?"

To test a second nursing approach, the nurses spent more time with the patient. They made sympathetic remarks and involved the patient in some personal small talk, perhaps about his family. "Are these pictures of your children? How cute they are!" The nurses might discuss the patient's pain with him—i.e., how long it had lasted, how intense it was—but, as was typical, they avoided discussing the patient's *feelings* with him. This group of patients was also automatically given medication.

The third group of patients, the experimental group, was given sensitive nursing care. The nurse tried to ascertain what the patient meant by pain. She tried to respond to some of the feelings the patient might have: the loneliness of pain, the sense of helplessness engendered by pain, anxiety about the unknown. She encouraged the patient to talk about how his illness and pain must make him feel. "Sometimes the worst part of it all is just lying in bed, don't you think?" an aware nurse might say. Or "I would imagine knowing you're going to be operated on in a few days would also make it harder for you to relax and for the pain to disappear. Has that been the case?" Typically, comments like these led the patient to elaborate on his feelings. Medication was given only as required.

Just after the nurses had completed their visit with patients in all three groups, the patients were asked if they felt any relief. In addition to requiring less medication than the other groups, only patients in the experimental group experienced *immediate* relief of pain. Since not enough time had elapsed for the medication to take effect, their relief must have been due to the emotional responsiveness of the nursing.

PART IV

Protective Illnesses

Sufferers from anxiety may seek to relieve it by

unconsciously converting it into a bodily condition.

Hypochondriacs often seize on their symptoms in

a desperate need to be cared for.

CHAPTER 10

The Conversion of Anxiety

. . . to a less threatening physical condition

Bruno Walter, the conductor, faced a concert crucial to his career.

Suddenly his arm became paralyzed, making it impossible for him to lead an orchestra. Doctors could find no physical cause. Walter, in Vienna, consulted Sigmund Freud.

Freud recognized that Walter was suffering from a conversion reaction. This condition is symbolic of an underlying anxiety. Instead of experiencing his emotional conflict consciously, Walter was unconsciously converting it into bodily symptoms.

Freud believed in a one-session, intensive treatment for a conversion reaction (also called conversion hysteria and somatic conversion). Walter explored the conflict he was repressing, and the paralysis disappeared in time for his concert.

Afterward Walter wanted to go back to Freud to be psychoanalyzed. But Freud told him, "Psychoanalysis is not for you. You will never have another nervous paralysis as long as you live."

Which is how it turned out.

Anxiety Good and Bad

The most widely accepted definition of anxiety, formulated by the American Psychiatric Association, calls it "apprehension, tension, or uneasiness which stems from the anticipation of danger, the source of which is largely unknown or unrecognized."

Anxiety and fear are accompanied by similar physiological changes. But anxiety is a nameless dread, a looming sense of imminent destruction. Fear, on the other hand, responds to a consciously recognized real-life threat.

Anxiety, while painful, is not necessarily bad for you. It can be useful as a signal keeping you on notice that a threatening situation is afoot.

A study of skydivers, parachutists who jump for sport, reveals how anxiety can be beneficial if respected and treated realistically. Experienced skydivers, the study shows, feel their peak of anxiety on the morning of the jump, when they decide whether or not they'll dive that day. Novice divers feel their greatest anxiety when they're up in the air and getting the signal to wait at the door of the plane. It is at that moment that the novice can either give the go-ahead signal or delay or cancel the jump.

In both cases the healthy anxiety is greatest when it can do some good, by removing the person from the source of danger. Once the commitment to jump is made, anxiety declines. For both experienced jumpers and novices the actual jump is less anxiety-provoking than events that came before.

A number of divers, however, inhibit their anxiety by denying all threat. Such a total defense is likely to break down when the threat becomes immediate, exposing the person to intense and incapacitating anxiety.

Two young women absolutely denied their anxiety. Until they boarded the plane they appeared to be completely relaxed and unconcerned. But as the plane gained altitude they collapsed. One shook uncontrollably. The other was seized with a paroxysm of vomiting. Both girls gave up the idea of jumping and went back down.

Another jumper overcontrolled his anxiety and nearly killed himself. His main chute failed to open. He waited the prescribed time before pulling his reserve chute. Then, "wanting to be sure," he waited a while longer. He waited until it was almost too late.

Some veteran jumpers won't take up a novice who seems too relaxed. Commented one experienced man: "If this fellow does jump and hasn't got this—well, uneasiness . . . he's going to kill himself."

Thus, psychologists Walter D. Fenz and Seymour Epstein of the University of Massachusetts conclude that a properly functioning defense against anxiety does not shut it off completely, but regulates the pace at which it is experienced. Anxiety that does not overwhelm the person enables him gradually to increase his ability to cope with the source of threat.

Anxiety may be extremely harmful, however, when present to such an extent that it interferes with your effectiveness, the achievement of goals or reasonable emotional comfort. The pain of chronic anxiety, and the avoidance thereof, is without doubt the single most common cause of mental illness. Freud called anxiety "the central problem in neurosis." Dr. Roy R. Grinker, Sr., of the Institute for Psychosomatic and Psychiatric Research and Training in Chicago, has observed: "What we call psychiatric disturbances are really the abnormal methods some individuals take to avoid anxiety."

To Placate Anxiety

The conversion reaction is one of the abnormal mechanisms of avoidance. Its physical symptoms serve to lessen conscious anxiety. The symptoms are usually expressed in parts of the body that are under conscious control, in a body system that the patient can employ immediately to placate anxiety.

A conversion reaction is not to be confused with malingering —the deliberate feigning of symptoms for personal gain, usually financial. The malingerer wants to be thought sick, and consciously fakes his supposed illness. One such fraud, claiming a hemorrhaging ulcer, nearly won a sizable disability settlement after doctors witnessed him vomiting blood. A keen-nosed nurse, however, recognized that the blood smelled like tomato juice. The man had trained himself to swallow large quantities of juice, then upchuck it.

The victim of a conversion reaction, by contrast, is utterly sin- cere. Though his impairment occurs in a part of his body that is ordinarily under conscious control, the disability springs from unconscious reasons. It is genuine—and unless the underlying emotional causes are relieved, it generally cannot be reversed.

In a conversion reaction, sensory organs often go awry. The sufferer may feel numb, as if parts of his body were anesthe- tized. Or he may feel extreme, unaccountable pain. One seven- teen-year-old girl suffered from sharp pains in the right side of her abdomen. Doctors removed her appendix, which proved to be normal. The pains continued. Earlier the girl had suffered a hysterical leg paralysis. It was concluded that her abdominal pains too were a conversion reaction.

The victim of a conversion reaction may go completely blind, or suffer from "peephole blindness," a narrowing of the field of vision. He may become stone-deaf. He may lose his sense of smell or his ability to speak.

Dr. Gordon Hoople, an ear, nose, and throat specialist, tells of a woman who suffered from severe tinnitus, a maddening condi- tion in which she was plagued by whistling, ringing, roaring, and other noises in her ears. Dr. Hoople questioned the woman and her husband for an hour about possible sources of anxiety. At last they disclosed that they were devout Catholics but re- cently the wife had not been well, and so they were using contra- ceptives. While spiritually wrong, they felt it was physically right. They had stopped going to church and confession—and now were being bombarded by their priest's and parents' de- mands to know why. Exploring the problem helped relieve the tinnitus.

Imaginary lumps in the throat and stiff necks are common conversion symptoms. So is writer's cramp, a hand impairment that particularly afflicts people who have to express themselves on paper.

Tics, tremors, paralyses, convulsions, the loss of reflex actions —the list of possible conversion symptoms is endless. A West Point cadet suffered from astasia-abasia, a loss of muscular coordination that rendered him unable to stand or walk. The symptoms disappeared after he left the Academy.

There have even been reported cases in which the victim believes he is dead. One elderly woman went about her business in much the usual way, except that she was convinced that she had died. Her doctor tried to reason with her, a futile effort since the anxiety which gives rise to the conversion reaction makes the victim invulnerable to logic.

Finally the doctor said to her: "Let me ask you a question. Do dead people bleed?"

"No," the woman replied. "Of course not."

The doctor pricked her finger with a needle. Pointing to the blood, he asked: "Now doesn't that prove something?"

"Yes." The woman smiled sweetly. "That dead people *do* bleed."

The person's emotional conflict may be focused on a specific body part. Thus more than one patient, terrified of a tonsillectomy, has lost his power of speech. The organ may be directly related to the conflict; a child's hand became paralyzed after he struck his father in anger. Often an organ is suited to expressing the conflict symbolically. Paralysis of the legs can prevent a person who is torn between alternatives from taking any action at all.

A study at Johns Hopkins Hospital revealed that patients with a high degree of medical sophistication exhibited their conversion symptoms in the form of complex diseases. One neurologist's secretary had symptoms mimicking multiple sclerosis. The majority of the patients believed they were organically ill and rejected the recommendation of psychotherapy.

The Attempted Seduction

Conversion reactions are extremely common. One major clinic, treating 5000 general medical cases a year, finds that no less than 18 per cent suffer from conversion symptoms. Most patients with psychogenic pain have conversion reactions.

Conversion reactions, being prevalent and fairly easy to spot, underlay much of Freud's early work. In 1893 he, then practicing as a neurologist, and Joseph Breuer, a general practitioner, published a joint paper entitled "On the Psychical Mechanisms of Hysterical Phenomena," and in 1895 a book *Studies on Hysteria.*

Hysteria is a term less widely used nowadays than in Freud's time. It refers to an illness resulting from emotional conflict and characterized by immaturity, impulsiveness, attention-seeking, and dependency. Most present-day psychotherapists discuss hysteria only in terms of its two principal manifestations. One is the conversion reaction. The other is the dissociative reaction, marked by amnesia, sleepwalking, dreaminess, and sometimes actual physical flight from one's surroundings.

In a study of the conversion reaction, Freud and Breuer reported: "We found to our great surprise at first, that each individual hysterical symptom immediately and permanently disappeared when we had succeeded in bringing clearly to light the memory of the event by which it was provoked." Reasoning back from the cure to the cause of conversion hysteria, they concluded: "In hysteria, the unbearable idea is rendered innocuous by transmuting the quantity of excitation into some bodily form of expression." This discovery was the beginning of the vast research into "the mysterious leap from the mind to the body," which is the subject matter of psychosomatics.

In 1905 Freud reported a classic case of a conversion reaction. It concerned Dora, an eighteen-year-old girl who had been brought to him because of her attacks of coughing and hoarseness. Physical examinations found no cause for her condition.

Dora's symptoms started shortly after an incident by a lake at a resort she went to with her parents and another couple we'll call Max and Sophie Koerner. As Dora well knew, for some years her father had been having an affair with Sophie Koerner. Now, alone by the lake, Max Koerner kissed Dora and sought to seduce her.

"Instead of the genital sensation which would certainly have been felt by a healthy girl in such circumstances," Freud wrote, "Dora was overcome by . . . unpleasurable feeling. . . . The stimulation of her lips by the kiss was no doubt of importance in localizing the feeling at that particular place."

But, Freud knew, a symptom usually has more than one meaning and serves to represent several unconscious processes simultaneously. A single cause will scarcely ever suffice for the production of a symptom.

Therefore, in seeking out why the girl's symptoms arose in her mouth and throat, Freud was impressed by the fact that Dora sucked her thumb until she was five, when her father forced her to give up the habit. Freud further reasoned that Dora probably had had a physiological irritation in her throat, which acted like the grain of sand around which an oyster forms its pearl, and she became fixated on the irritation, making the throat suscept-ible to formation of a symptom. In addition, it developed that she strongly associated the mouth and throat with sexual stimu-lation.

Dora insisted to Freud: "Sophie Koerner loves my father only because he is a man of means."

The way she expressed herself suggested to Freud that she meant the opposite, that her father was a man *without* means. Freud interpreted this in a sexual sense: that her father was impotent.

"That's true," Dora admitted.

"On one hand, you insist that your father's relation with So-phie is a common love affair," Freud pointed out. "On the other hand, you maintain he is impotent, or in other words incapable of carrying on an affair."

"I know very well there's more than one way of obtaining sex-ual gratification," Dora replied.

"You refer to the use of organs other than the genitals?"

"Yes."

"In that case you must be thinking of precisely those parts of the body which in your case are in a state of irritation: the throat and the mouth."

The tickling in Dora's throat, inciting her cough, thus was based on her unconscious picturing of a scene of sexual gratification between two people whose love affair occupied her mind incessantly. At first Dora would not hear of this. Eventually she accepted Freud's explanation, and very shortly afterward her cough vanished.

In a recent seminar at Hahnemann Hospital in Philadelphia, psychiatrist Franklin H. West of Hahnemann Medical College drew upon Dora's case to illuminate the origins and mechanics of the conversion reaction. All conversion reactions, indeed all neurotic responses, begin with childhood impulses and experiences which are repressed into the unconscious. Dora's thumb-sucking till a fairly late age hints at such conflicts, intensified by her father's forcing her to stop.

More immediate to the development of conversion symptoms, a trauma needs to occur in the person's life that stirs repressed conflicts. These attempt to break through to the consciousness against the person's will, imposing great anxiety. Max Koerner's attempted seduction of Dora constituted such a trauma. Repressed sexual impulses were aroused. They found a compromise outlet, in her coughing and hoarseness. This response was an acceptable reversal of the pleasure and receptiveness which her conscious mind found unacceptable.

Dr. West noted that Dora's case is typical of conversion reactions in these ways as well:

• *She has the usual personality of the hysteric.* In Freud's account, Dora comes through as immature, naïve, self-centered, oversensitive, petulant, moody, and given to dramatic emotional displays.

• *She is free of conscious anxiety.* This curious trait—called *la belle indifference*—represents the conversion reaction's success as a defense against anxiety. Dora came to Freud only on her father's insistence and soon broke off treatment abruptly.

• *She uses her symptoms to gain an advantage over others.* By being sick, Dora sought to force her father to leave Sophie Koerner, and also to escape from further attentions from Max Koerner. Such motives play a strong part in the resistance of patients to giving up the symptoms.

• *Her symptoms afford a solution to an unconscious problem.* Dora's memory of the events precipitating the illness was incomplete. At the beginning of her treatment she had no awareness whatever of the meaning of her symptoms.

CHAPTER 11

The Hypochondriacs

They want to be cared for

Acquaintances run when they see him coming.

Physicians call him a "crock" and consider him and his ilk the bane of medical practice, to be referred away to a colleague (preferably a newcomer) as soon as possible.

Quacks prey on him, providing the reassurance and mental comfort he urgently seeks.

Even kindly Ben Franklin was hard on the hypochondriac. "Nothing is more fatal to *Health*," he wrote in *Poor Richard's Almanack*, "than the *over Care* of it."

"Impossible and Ludicrous Company"

The hypochondriac suffers an obsessive preoccupation with his supposed ill health.

He is "impossible and ludicrous company," says psychiatrist Morris D. Riemer, because he gives the impression of relishing his misery. He is wrapped up in his bodily afflictions and will talk endlessly about them.

At the same time, he bemoans his fate and punctuates his self-pitying with expressions of hopelessness. Yet he gives the impression that there is some source of satisfaction for him in being sick. He generally is overdemanding of his doctors, and also unappreciative of their help. Often he seems to take pride in foiling their best efforts. If a physician is persistent in trying to help him, the hypochondriac is likely to become angry. A doctor's psychological explanation will usually only make him more anxious.

The hypochondriac's symptoms rarely fit any pattern known to medicine. They come and go unaccountably, often mysteriously shifting from one part of the body to another. The degree of discomfort he reports is usually excessive for his complaint.

Hypochondriacs generally follow a series of steps, almost a waltz, as they wend their way through the world of medical care. Their unwitting partner is the doctor, and the dance steps go like this: (1) The patient's demands for treatment are met by (2) the physician's determination to examine and reinvestigate, trying one medication after another, to avoid at all cost missing an organic cause. After each trial medication (3) the patient experiences some relief, followed by worsening—the net result being "no change." (4) The patient and the physician become frustrated with each other, and the angry doctor labels the patient a "crackpot" or "untreatable." Then (1) the cycle starts again elsewhere.

Dr. Richard Asher, in writing about such patients, refers to their condition as the "Münchhausen syndrome." Like Baron von Münchhausen, the German cavalry officer who spouted incredible tales, hypochondriacs have a seeming desire to deceive everybody as much as possible. Asher comments on the "enormous waste of time and trouble they are" and "the apparent senselessness of their behavior."

And yet, as annoying as they are to others, hypochondriacs merit sympathy. Psychiatrist David J. Vail of the University of Minnesota School of Medicine feels that the main difficulty doctors have with the hypochondriac is that he does not behave according to accepted patterns in hospital and medical settings. The problem therefore, notes Dr. Vail, is partly that of the physician's expectations.

Moreover, the hypochondriac's pains are totally real to him.

They preempt most of his time. Often they disable him. And he is wholly sincere in his despair that he will never find relief.

Dangerous to Get Well

A Yiddish proverb says, "If things are too good, it's bad."

This might well be the slogan of hypochondria, for it often accounts for the hypochondriac's reluctance to surrender his physical symptoms. Even more than sufferers of other psychosomatic conditions, he unconsciously believes that, as long as he suffers, he is protected from a more dreaded punishment. It would thus, in his mind, be dangerous for him to get well.

The hypochondriac's expectation of punishment is generally the result of unconscious feelings of guilt. Since guilt is painful, it is generally repressed from conscious awareness. It does not, however, cease to exist, but continues to motivate a need for expiation, perhaps in the form of the hypochondriac's symptoms or, as he desperately fears, something worse.

The unconscious follows certain primitive lines of reasoning, and these serve to intensify the hypochondriac's guilt feelings. For example, the infantile mind cannot distinguish between a thought and a deed. To the unconscious, a person is as liable for thinking a thing as doing it. In psychiatrist Charles William Wahl's experience, most hypochondriacs have felt powerful hatred toward their parents and siblings. Merely in wishing them dead, the hypochondriac opens himself up to long-lasting guilt and the expectation of suffering.

Guilt, the unconscious believes, can be relieved only by suffering. A principle of paleologic is the so-called law of talion, a concept that guilt of a crime (be it real or imagined) is assuaged only by an identical or similar punishment. Wishing a parent dead, then, can make a person unconsciously convinced that he too must die. The hypochondriac therefore finds his symptoms welcome. As the Yiddish proverb suggests, if he felt better, he'd be worse off.

A hypochondriac's symptoms can also be a way for him to

assert his identity, a sign of his uncertainty over his inner worth. Lacking self-esteem, he thrusts himself—in the form of his bodily complaints—onto all who will listen. Capturing someone's attention in part is a means of assuring himself that he exists, that he is "some body."

Most psychosomatic disorders achieve for the sufferer an unconscious primary gain, usually relief from anxiety or guilt. Almost always there are also unconscious secondary gains: additional advantages made possible by the illness. These side benefits in turn help perpetuate the disorder.

As an example of secondary gain, physical symptoms may be employed as a cover-up for psychiatric difficulties. To many people it is still debasing and humiliating to have emotional problems but quite acceptable to have a physical illness. Physical illness evokes a wide variety of helping responses. If admitted to a hospital, the patient can gain an honorable retreat from life's defeats and responsibilities.

By contrast, the patient knows, the psychiatric "case" is often an object of dread and aversion to others. Treatment means being "put away"—a far cry from the comfortable bed in a medical hospital where he can be solaced by visitors, surrounded by gifts of candy and flowers, and deluged with get-well cards.

Secondary gains are nowhere more evident than in hypochondria. A hypochondriac, often concerned about being unloved and uncherished, can nurse himself in his illness to compensate for the love he feels he lacks. His illness allows him to be dependent, he can use it to command attention. He can employ it to punish others, as if to say, "Look what you've done to me," and "You're worsening my condition."

George and Wilma and the Headache

Dr. Jackson A. Smith of the Illinois State Psychiatric Institute tells of a headache that is the basis of a marriage.

Wilma is thirty-eight and outweighs her smallish husband by sixty pounds. George worries about Wilma. Not long ago he urged her to visit Dr. Smith to see if there was anything "new" for her old headache.

On the day of their appointment she told George, "I don't feel up to sitting in the waiting room." She stayed in the car while George checked with Dr. Smith's secretary. Then he went to help Wilma in.

"It wasn't immediately clear why a chronic headache would produce an . . . inability to walk alone," notes Dr. Smith. "But in Wilma's case it did." With George's help and with great effort, she made it into the office.

Wilma produced a packet of X rays, lab reports, and consultation notes. "I've had skull X rays to rule out the possibility of a brain tumor," she informed Dr. Smith. While she gave her history, George nodded agreement to each symptom, occasionally emphasizing a pain or ache he felt his wife had insufficiently detailed.

Smith asked George to retire to the waiting room and sought to get more of Wilma's history. She had a headache even as a child, she said. Studying only made her headache worse. She couldn't keep up in class, so she dropped out in her junior year of high school "because I was sick so much."

Her mother, too, has a chronic headache, "more in the back" than Wilma's. She's had every treatment available, even a trip to the Mayo Clinic. "But no one's been able to do much for her trouble," Wilma sighed.

Wilma's first husband was a man who was "most inconsiderate" of her condition. "He was oversexed," Wilma whispered. The marriage soon ended in divorce.

Then George came along. He is sympathetic and sincerely appreciates her condition. He accepts all her complaints and understands how she can seem so well one minute and be so sick the next. He makes no demands on her, sexual or otherwise.

George works hard at a service station he owns. He always goes home for lunch to see how Wilma is feeling and to fix her a bite to eat. In the evenings they watch television together. On long weekends they visit Wilma's mother, who brings them up to date on her condition. Wilma has never made many friends because "folks don't understand sick people."

"To be cured wouldn't offer an awful lot to Wilma," concludes Dr. Smith. She has long since ceased to think of herself as a well person. Her headache is more than a symptom. It's a way of life.

It gives her a reason to avoid the unpleasant. What she can't or doesn't want to do is always the result of her headache rather than her inabilities. Her complaint explains all her shortcomings and is an ever-available topic of conversation.

Without the headache, observes Smith, there is no Wilma. If she were well, she would have to meet the ordinary routines of the day and night without fanfare or special consideration. She would need to forgo the attention and sympathy her headache provides.

Superficially, it appears that George is losing out because of Wilma's condition. "Actually," Smith points out, "he gets everything from life that Wilma does, and besides he doesn't have a headache."

First, all his friends agree he is an admirable character, a "nice little guy." They wonder how he "puts up with her." Next, Wilma's symptoms provide him with the quiet, undisturbed existence that he wants. Being a bachelor was difficult for him because his friends were always trying to get him married. Refusing invitations and saying no to people was unpleasant for him; he hates to hurt anyone's feelings. The marriage solved this problem. He obviously can't go any place because of Wilma's condition.

George had never been comfortable around women unless he was doing something for them. Wilma never deprives him of something to do for her. He has never felt right about sex, and with Wilma he is appreciated for letting her alone. He is intuitive enough never to let his joy over this arrangement shine through.

Finally, Wilma's problems leave him with little opportunity to worry about himself or the future. If by some magic Wilma were cured and became an independent, vigorous, sexually energetic female—"then," cautions Dr. Smith, "it might well be George who had the headache!"

Treating the Untreatable

Barbara walked into a room at the psychiatric clinic of the University of Pittsburgh.

She was a familiar face at various university clinics. For years she had circulated from doctor to doctor, asking for remedies to cure her many and changing ills but unable to obtain relief for long. As her chart grew thick, her doctors' patience wore thin. So as not to see her any more than he had to, a physician would tell her to return after six weeks, three months, or longer. Invariably Barbara would suffer a worsening of symptoms that forced her to come in sooner.

Attempts to refer her away likewise met with resistance. In Barbara's bulging file were notes exchanged between two doctors arguing over who should be considered her primary physician. Neither wanted her.

Now Barbara was one of eight hypochondriacal women placed in experimental group therapy under the guidance of Dr. William D. Ogston, a psychiatrist, and Mary A. Mally, a professor of social work. The women were not considered good candidates for psychotherapy—hypochondriacs generally resist it—but they were offered the weekly group in an effort to afford them some help. Their medical records labeled them "pathetic," "helpless," "troubled," "inadequate." Prognosis for this pioneer effort at therapy was poor.

The women ranged in age from 27 to 56. Their marital pictures were generally dim: Two were single, and five of the remaining six were divorced or separated. None was self-supporting; all got either public assistance or money from relatives.

All had problems related to food. Two were grossly obese. Two others choked when they ate. Four were undernourished. In addition, all had complaints concerning their reproductive organs, such as cramps and vaginal discharge. Half the women had undergone a hysterectomy.

Every one of the women was the least successful member of her family in terms of education, money, social achievement, and marriage. Barbara told the group: "I was hated by my mother, even though I was devoted to her." With one exception, the other women said the same.

Barbara would try to buy warmth and care from her mother by pleasing her with gifts and good deeds. She expected tenfold in return and ended up feeling angry over being used and misunderstood. The other women followed this pattern.

Each also painted a vague picture of her father. Barbara (and three of the others) described hers as a remote, shadowy figure who was a source of apprehension and fear. The others were so emphatic about the intense love and devotion they felt toward their fathers that Dr. Ogston and Professor Mally believed that much of this description was fantasy. It appeared that the women were describing a hoped-for good provider.

In marriage Barbara had expected to be taken care of rather than behave as an adult, responsible wife. Now divorced, she recalled her marriage as turbulent and sexually unsatisfying. Sylvia and Margaret, the two who hadn't married, had had erratic courtships. They finally exhausted the patience of their suitors and remained with their mothers.

In establishing the group, Mally and Ogston hoped to answer: What made these individuals "untreatable"? How effective would group therapy be for them?

Almost immediately the women turned the group to serving their hypochondria. Discussion generally revolved around the subject of symptoms and medications. The women competed for the position of being the "sickest" in hopes of winning the sole interest of the leaders. When a member got into a troubling situation, she and the others expected Mally and Ogston to get her out of it, meanwhile resisting the insights the leaders tried to bring them to.

The group soon became the focus of the women's lives, the only meaningful relationships they had outside their families.

Whenever a member tried to engage in an outside activity, such as getting a job or joining an organization, the others discouraged her. "Perhaps you're not well enough," she'd be told. If she persisted and failed, she would return to the group satisfied that she was ill. The other members welcomed her back with open arms.

It became clear to Ogston and Mally that from such patients there is a lifelong cry to be taken care of. This is mixed with anger that there has never been enough love, protection, affection. Their symptoms arise evidently as a body language expressing their need to be cared for.

In going from doctor to doctor, they are appealing more for pity than for help. Pity is the coin by which they live in their desperate hunt for care. The women in the group rarely saw themselves in terms of having a future. Their day-to-day concern was for present, immediate care.

The group met for about three years, and a seeming paradox emerged. On one hand, the women got little insight into themselves or their hypochondria. Their competitive, demanding, manipulative behavior within the group did not much improve.

On the other hand, there was some relief of their symptoms, and their demands for medication became fewer. One woman had been visiting medical clinics on the average of once a month. After joining the group, she felt no need to go to a clinic for nearly two years. Another had been to clinics no less than 132 times in one year. While attending the group, she went to clinics not much oftener than once every two weeks.

What had happened? Why did treatment that by traditional standards failed have in large part a successful result? Mally and Ogston suggest that while such patients are searching for something, it is not really medical care per se. It is to be *taken care of*. Disregarding this longing, the typical physician pursues the presenting symptoms in the usual manner. He approaches them literally with one biochemical investigation after another, which of course dooms him and the patient to failure in their divergent goals. At some point, both become frustrated and angry, and the patient tries elsewhere.

But from the group these women to a great extent got the care they sought. The women took one another's conditions very seriously. They sympathized with each other, and each had free rein to talk about her health problems. And so, for the first time in years, the women could feel cared for and cared about— and could stop going to doctors.

How to Manage a Hypochondriac

Hypochondriacs are best thought of as chronically handicapped people who require management rather than treatment. Psychiatrist Charles Wahl offers this advice, adaptable for laymen who must deal with the hypochondriac:

• *Listen.* A positive willingness to be listened to, rather than being merely tolerated, is what the hypochondriac wants and needs. He seeks a dependable relationship of trust and confidence. As soon as he is reassured of this, his need for unreasonable amounts of attention ordinarily diminishes.

• *Take his symptoms seriously.* Don't tell him that his pains are imaginary. Rather explain how tension can produce the symptoms that frighten him. Use pictures and diagrams to get anatomic and physiological points across.

• *Focus on feelings.* Encourage him to talk openly about his deep feelings of fear and need. Help him to express other problem areas. Perhaps you can help him see that by concentrating on his health he may be avoiding other areas of difficulty.

• *Accentuate the positive.* Don't suggest alternative fearful possibilities concerning his symptoms. This can terrify him.

Don't urge new tests, either. Hypochondriacs are prone to develop hysterical complications following such procedures as a bronchoscopy or spinal tap. Nor should you advise new medicines. The hypochondriac tends to overdose himself with drugs and become dependent on them.

The Reverse Hypochondriacs

"I guess I'm suffering from the tired housewife syndrome," Lisa said.

She had four small children and a hectic household. This, agreed her doctor, could account for her fatigue and nondescript low-back pain. Bored, harassed homemakers frequently suffer this set of symptoms. The "tired housewife syndrome," as Lisa knew, is nearly always psychogenic.

A less cautious doctor might have simply counseled Lisa to spend more time on herself and sent her off with a prescription for a mild tranquilizer. Fortunately Lisa's physician gave her a physical examination. In her left breast he found a substantial tumor.

Lisa evidently knew about the tumor all the time. But she denied it, put it out of her conscious mind. Even when she went to a tumor clinic on her doctor's recommendation, she talked not about the possible implications of cancer but about the difficulties of raising small children and keeping up with a busy household.

Lisa was manifesting "reverse hypochondria." Whereas the typical hypochondriac uses physical complaints to express an emotional disorder, Lisa was employing psychological symptoms to mask a physical condition.

Technically termed anosognosia, the syndrome is marked by an inability to recognize the existence of a disease. It is potentially far more perilous to the patient than is hypochondria. The typical hypochondriac would do well to be less mindful of his symptoms. The reverse hypochondriac may ignore an organic condition until it is fatal.

Anosognosia is especially common in some catastrophic conditions. For example, sufferers from multiple sclerosis often become euphoric. Their apparent bliss is their means of warding off severe depression over the grave future they face. They counterbalance a painful emotion by going to the opposite extreme.

Denial of illness is often part and parcel of a disease of the brain or central nervous system. The victim's physical functioning may become so altered that he cannot perceive or rationally accept that anything is wrong with him. He is likely to cling to his denial despite direct confrontation. If shown clear evidence that he is ill, he may become inattentive, change the subject, invent explanations.

Dr. Donald Macrae of the University of California School of Medicine in San Francisco tells of a fifty-six-year-old businessman driving home from his office. Suddenly he could not recognize either red or green in the traffic lights. He managed to get home safely by remembering that the red light was on top. Meanwhile he berated himself for being an "overworked neurotic."

Next day his wife heard him stumbling and fumbling. "Nothing's wrong," he told her, believing it even though he couldn't see. While his wife watched in horror, he felt his way from one piece of furniture to another—all the time unaware of the fact that he was blind. Examination by Dr. Macrae showed that he had a defect in the visual center of his brain.

Reverse hypochondria in part results from the public's increasing sophistication about psychiatric ills. People who've learned that mental illness is nothing to be ashamed of may find a psychiatric condition more palatable than a potentially life-threatening physical one. When their doctor asks, "How do you feel?" they are freer to give emotional answers like "Depressed," or "Fed up," instead of ominous physical ones like "Short of breath," or "In pain."

Adolescents characteristically minimize their physical problems. "During the teens the herd instinct is at its peak," notes Dr. Harris C. Faigel. "No adolescent wants to be different from his friends."

Since the teens are generally a healthy time of life, illness makes a youngster feel different. Not wanting to be an exception, he may deny his illness and not follow directions well.

Among adults, denial of an organic illness often stems from

an underlying fear of weakness and helplessness. The patient is likely to admit to physical symptoms but use psychological theory to explain them.

One investigator, psychiatrist Robert Seidenberg of the Up-state Medical Center at Syracuse, New York, has found that many patients "psychologize" their symptoms with the unconscious conviction that a neurotic illness is easier to cure than an organic one. In the face of bodily symptoms, they readily accept and use the concepts of psychosomatic medicine. If their doctor disagrees, they are likely to dismiss him as being psychologically unsophisticated. When confronted with evidence that they have an organic illness, many feel insulted, as if their judgment were thrown open to question.

A forty-two-year-old bachelor we'll call Arthur came to a hospital emergency room complaining of depression and insomnia. "It began about three months ago when I broke up with my girl friend," he told the physician who examined him.

The doctor referred Arthur to an outpatient psychiatric clinic for evaluation. The following week Arthur returned to the emergency room. This time another doctor who saw him noted that he seemed weak and emaciated and had difficulty breathing. He admitted Arthur to the hospital. Cell studies and a biopsy disclosed Arthur had a far-advanced case of cancer.

Arthur was informed that he had a severe physical illness and that, although treatment would be undertaken immediately, his condition was incurable. Over the next few months the diagnosis "cancer" was never explicitly mentioned. But it was implicitly understood, and Arthur was well aware that cancer, not depression, was his primary problem.

Yet, even though he made plans with his family revolving around his terminal illness, he would never openly admit to his impending death. He focused on his depression and talked at length with doctors about his personal problems surrounding his breakup with his girl friend.

He preferred to attribute his insomnia to his depression. In truth it was due to his increasing difficulty in breathing. His depressive mood he ascribed to his shattered romance. Actually, it was a product of his deteriorating physical condition.

About three months after Arthur first came to the hospital, he died. A striking aspect of this case is the fact that Arthur's denial of his illness was contagious. It evidently was caught by the doctor who examined him on his first visit to the emergency room.

Arthur's organic illness even then was readily apparent—it was spotted immediately a few days later. Dr. Bennett L. Rosner of the Indiana University Medical Center observes: "There must have been a fair amount of denial on the part of the physician during the initial contact not to have concluded that this man had more than depression."

The examining physician, Dr. Rosner feels, must have unconsciously entered into Arthur's pattern of denial. In an unspoken conspiracy, he said in effect: "Although you may be gravely physically ill, if we don't talk about it, you can go to a psychiatric clinic for your depression, which of course is something you will get over in time."

PART V

Gut Reactions

The digestive system reacts to stress, often with

stomach pains, diarrhea, and constipation.

Peptic ulcer sufferers commonly hunger for love.

In ulcerative colitis the victim may be bursting

with unexpressed rage. Some people starve themselves,

notably infants who ruminate—i.e., spit up their

food—and teen-agers with anorexia nervosa, who

refuse to eat, though their lives are in danger.

CHAPTER 1 2

Stomaching the Situation

The digestive system reacts to stress

Bill, a quiet newcomer to the encounter group, could contain himself no longer. Turning to Steven, he jumped up and shouted: "I'm fed up. You're a phony from the word go. I don't believe a thing you've said."

Steven paled and gripped his stomach. In a few seconds he recovered and said to the group: "Now I know what's meant by a gut reaction. After Bill said those hostile things to me, I felt a little sick inside. I really felt it in my gut."

As Steven now had reason to know, the gastrointestinal system can be a barometer of psychological stress. Popular speech abounds with examples of the close connection between feelings and the gut: "I can't stomach it." "I'm fed up." "What's eating you?" "She nauseates me." "I can't swallow that story."

A baby's first emotions are strongly associated with his eating cycle. The child's whole universe is centered in his need for food. He experiences his first relief from physical discomfort when he is held and nursed. Eating becomes almost identical with comfort and security. For the child, to be fed is to be loved. Hunger represents rejection and insecurity.

Another complex of emotions soon becomes associated with alimentary processes: possessiveness (of food, love, things), greed, jealousy, envy. These aggressive emotions are often considered antisocial and are likely to be repressed. Thus blocked from expression, they may create a permanent tension and exert a chronic disturbance in the digestive tract.

A child first learns to express his emotions in connection with eating. As an infant, he gurgles contentedly when he's full, complains angrily when he's hungry. Later in childhood he is conscious of giving as well as getting pleasure when he eats well and moves his bowels to his parents' satisfaction.

As you mature, you find other ways of expressing emotion. But, says psychiatrist Don E. Johnson of Hahnemann Medical College, you don't ever quite give up this "eating-digestion-bowel-movement view of life." Observes Dr. Johnson: "We all retain the potential for using our stomachs and intestines . . . in the service of love, hate, dependence, giving, punishing, domination, frustration, and other pleasant and unpleasant feelings."

A person who chronically uses digestive ways of expressing his feelings will start showing symptoms in the misused organs. These symptoms then may develop into full-fledged psychosomatic diseases.

Tom's Stomach

In 1895 a nine-year-old named Tom drank scalding hot clam chowder. The fluid destroyed his esophagus, the tube from the mouth to the stomach. To enable him to eat, surgeons created a hole in his stomach some four inches wide, with an opening in his abdomen. Thereafter, Tom chewed his food, then spit it into a pipe through the opening. Remarkably, he was able to keep his condition a secret from all but his closest friends.

When he was fifty-three, Tom went to the hospital for treatment of severe anemia. There Dr. Stewart Wolf and Dr. Harold G. Wolff recognized the unique opportunity for studying the stomach. They put Tom to work at the hospital and for five years recorded in detail the daily changes in his stomach—its color, acidity, movement. The doctors soon discovered that many of these stomach changes were associated with his emotional life.

Tom's stomach changes vividly point up the almost instantaneous response of the stomach to emotion. It was Tom's job to tidy up the laboratory. One morning an angry doctor came into the lab looking for misplaced instruments. He cursed and pulled open drawers. Tom, fearing that his job was in jeopardy, became silent and pale. It was observed that the mucous membrane of his stomach went from its normal red to nearly white, much of the blood having abruptly drained from it. The stomach remained this way for five minutes, until the doctor located his instruments and left.

In general, Tom's stomach revealed that defeat, fear, and dejection inhibit the stomach's functions. When his nephew died, Tom didn't feel like eating. He felt slightly nauseated and had a "sinking feeling" in his stomach. Doctors observed that his stomach was secreting insufficient amounts of acid.

On another occasion Tom felt threatened by a laboratory technician. For ten months while she worked with him, Tom lost twelve pounds, his appetite decreased, and there was insufficient acid in his stomach. The day after the technician was transferred to another hospital, acid secretions returned to normal.

Conversely, Tom went through a stressful period when he decided to undertake responsibility for the four children of his dead stepdaughter. For some weeks his stomach membrane was engorged and reddened.

His acid secretion, significantly higher than normal, began to eat away at the stomach lining. Such a situation, if it persists, sets the stage for a peptic ulcer. When his pay at the hospital was increased, his anxiety about providing for the children was relieved, and his stomach condition returned to normal.

Hard to Swallow

Digestive disturbances may be symbolic of the patient's problem. A patient who can't "swallow the situation," for example, may develop cardiospasm, a swallowing disorder in which the lower end of the esophagus contracts.

Nausea and vomiting may occur as forms of symbolic rejection. Vomiting is often the response to stressful situations involving guilt about sex. Thirty-year-old Vera became nauseated whenever she attempted to have any social life with men. For twelve years her illness had forced her to abandon almost all social activity, and she had nearly given up all hope of marriage.

Vera was dominated by her ambitious and tyrannical mother. In childhood Vera attempted repeatedly to gain her mother's favor. The mother resented the fact that her husband favored Vera, and began openly to reject her. Vera then became even more emotionally dependent on her mother.

Vera inhibited all sexual activity, which she feared might increase her mother's hostility. Since her mother was the person who originally fed her, guilt and fear felt toward her mother led Vera to reject food. At the age of ten she vomited when a boy brought her food at a party.

When she was twenty-five, a man became interested in her, increasing her guilt and anxiety. Her nausea and vomiting increased to such an extent that she lost twenty-eight pounds in a few months. At a diagnostic clinic Vera was advised to lead a "more active and normal life." She misinterpreted this to mean sexual indulgence.

With her mother's explicit consent and active cooperation, she arranged an affair with her employer's son. During the seven months it lasted, Vera's condition improved, although she found it difficult to eat in the presence of her lover. When he deserted her to get married, her symptoms reappeared, and she returned to live with her mother.

In psychoanalysis Vera with great difficulty acquired some insight into her extreme dependence on her mother and her anxiety-ridden attitudes toward food and sex. She now rarely suffers her previous symptoms.

"I Must Hold On to What I Have"

Chronic psychogenic constipation is another common gastro-intestinal disturbance. Usually it has its antecedents in a strained mother-child relationship in early childhood. When the child reaches the bowel-training stage, he may react to the power struggle with his mother by becoming constipated.

For many children the withholding of feces has the psychologic function of expressing feelings of resistance and negativism toward a world which is perceived as hostile and unaffectionate. Obstinate withholding of feces serves as a symbolic act of defiance and lays the basis for adult constipation problems. What began as partially conscious resistance in childhood later becomes unconscious constipation in adulthood.

The typical sufferer of chronic constipation has a pessimistic, defeatist attitude. He distrusts or lacks confidence in others and feels unloved and rejected. He may have the feeling that he is being persecuted.

The unconscious emotional statement of people with chronic constipation is: "I cannot expect anything from anybody, and therefore I do not need to give anything. I must hold on to what I have." This possessive attitude is the outcome of the feelings of rejection and distrust. The excrement is retained as if it were a valuable possession, an attitude young children often have.

Doris had suffered from chronic constipation since her marriage two years before. She used an enema daily. Doctors reported they could find no organic reason for her difficulty, and diagnosed it as "nervous constipation."

Doris's husband Daniel was a painter who was passionately devoted to his art. Whereas Doris entered marriage expecting great love and tenderness, her husband continued a kind of bachelor life even after he was married. Doris wished for a child, but Daniel feared it would interfere with his work.

In therapy, Doris maintained she was happily married and had no complaints about her husband. The therapist asked to see

Daniel privately. He found him an "entirely self-centered young man" who was completely blind to his wife's emotional needs. The therapist talked to Daniel about his lack of affection toward his wife. "Since the first day of your marriage," the therapist said, "you've never brought her any small sign of attention—flowers or anything else."

The next day Doris reported that for the first time in two years she had had a spontaneous bowel movement before the time for her daily enema. Without making the connection, she also reported that her husband had brought home a bouquet of flowers for her for the first time in their married life.

The laxative effect of these flowers gave a clue to the psychic background of the symptom: Doris had used an infantile way of expressing spite toward her husband as an answer to his loveless behavior. Her constipation expressed the hostile feelings which she did not want to admit to herself and which she had never shown openly.

Bellyaching

Stomach pain is a common reaction to a stressful situation. One boy developed severe abdominal pain every time his mother drove him to boarding school at the start of the school term. But during summer vacation, when he was driven to the school to pick up his bat which had been left behind, he had no stomach pain at all.

Sometimes stomach pain is used as an instrument of punishment and control. Ten-year-old Susie unconsciously used abdominal cramps and diarrhea to rule her parents. When they went out for an evening, they invariably got a frantic call from the babysitter to come home immediately.

Once they found Susie doubled over and screaming with pain. Her pediatrician, Dr. Mary L. Rosenlund of the University of Pennsylvania Medical School, could find no organic reason for the pain. Dr. Rosenlund suggested that Susie's very real stomach pain was one of her most powerful instruments of control, and the prescribed treatment included a concerted effort by Susie's parents to help her accept the controls appropriate to the life of a ten-year-old child.

Stomach symptoms can also be triggered by depression. One young man, Paul, complained of pain in the middle of his stomach which he'd had for more than two months. "The pain can be sharp—so sharp that I feel nauseated—or it can be grinding and dull, and that has the same effect." Since the pain began, Paul had lost about thirty pounds.

Paul had a lot on his mind. He was worried about money. "It's tough living," he told his doctors. "We need money, and if I'm away from work, there just won't be any."

He was upset by the birth of his first child and his own displacement. "Before the baby my wife was always baking and cooking," he complained. "Now it depends on her mood."

Most important, Paul's father had cancer of the bowel. One of his symptoms was severe abdominal cramps. ("He had terrible pains. He told me that he wouldn't want to go through such pains again.") In addition, he lost a considerable amount of weight. Paul's symptoms were thus similar to his father's.

The psychiatrist who treated Paul in the hospital, Dr. Samuel Silverman of Harvard Medical School, concluded that the prime cause of Paul's symptoms was that he is in *mourning* for his dying father. "The pain," writes Dr. Silverman, "represents a somatic identification with his sick father and a physical expression of his reaction to the impending loss of this emotionally important figure for him. Mourning may antedate actual death if the fatal illness is chronic and lingering as it is in this case."

Paul's condition improved in the hospital, a result of a bland diet, supportive therapy, and the fact that the hospital stay was a helpful interruption of his burdensome daily life.

Fear and anger frequently find expression in abdominal cramps and diarrhea. Twenty-two-year-old Richard was discharged from the army because of recurrent attacks of severe abdominal pain and diarrhea. He had been the driver for a captain and had never fought or been in any particular danger.

Richard's mother was a passive, complaining sort of woman

who'd had several abdominal operations and frequent attacks of diarrhea. His father was a dynamic businessman who treated his family like his business, making arbitrary and rapid-fire decisions.

Richard considered that his family life was perfectly fine and left nothing to be desired. "He gave the impression of considerable compliance and complacency," psychiatrists Roy R. Grinker, Sr., and Fred P. Robbins noted.

Richard could not recall any emotional problems he had had at the time of his attacks. To help shake loose the repressed material, the doctors gave him an injection of sodium pentothal. They told him that he was now driving his truck on a particular day when he'd had an attack of cramps and diarrhea. Richard then remembered having heard that enemy troops were in the neighborhood. Suddenly his truck broke down. He could hear shooting behind a hill. Richard was forced to stay with his truck until help arrived.

Under the influence of the drug, Richard verbalized his intense fears: "I'm too young to die. I've been a good boy, I've never harmed anyone. What will Mother do if I'm hurt or killed? Please, God, save me." He perspired and writhed on the bed as he relived this experience.

When the pentothal wore off, Richard remembered that he had been scared and had forgotten about it. In a subsequent pentothal session Richard relived another occasion on which he'd had an abdominal attack. He'd been driving from early morning for his captain, an alcoholic who mistreated his men. At night the captain found shelter in a military police station, leaving Richard to sleep in the truck.

Richard tried to reassure himself that there were no enemy soldiers nearby. He told himself, "I'm perfectly safe." But, he recalled under the influence of pentothal, he was frightened. He couldn't sleep for many hours. When he finally did fall asleep, he was soon awakened by severe cramps and diarrhea.

When urged by the psychiatrists to recall his feelings toward the captain on that occasion, Richard at first defended him, saying, "It was his right to order me as he wished." After a time the pentothal induced Richard to confess his anger and resentment toward the captain. It spilled forth freely and copiously. Richard detailed many incidents of discrimination, unfairness, over-work. The captain, he said, was a "bastard and a no-good son of a bitch" who took advantage of his position of authority.

"And how about your father?" the therapists interrupted.

"He's the same kind of a son of a bitch."

CHAPTER 13

"It's Eating Away at Me"

Peptic ulcer sufferers often hunger for love

"The pain in my stomach is a constant one," Andy was telling his doctor. "The pain is vicious—so vicious I want to tear it out. It gets so bad that I feel like hitting my head against the table. . . . When the pain is at its worst, it's like gnawing, something chewing away inside."

Andy was describing the symptoms of his peptic ulcer. A peptic ulcer is an open sore in the inner wall of the stomach or on the mucous membrane of the duodenum, the part of the small intestine connecting to the stomach. If in the stomach, it's called a gastric ulcer; in the duodenum, a duodenal ulcer. About 1 in 15 adults are prone to ulcer attacks.

A peptic ulcer is almost always the result of stress. In Andy's case, from early in his life his stomach had become sensitive to emotional stress. He'd always been picky about food. "I was never a big eater," he recalls. As a result, "Mother paid special attention to what I ate. My two younger sisters, who had no trouble eating, would get frankfurters, but Mother made sure what I ate was good, like steak."

After Andy's father died, when Andy was six, his mother had to go to work, and her special attention to his eating abruptly stopped. "I had to get my own food until she came back in the evening. There were plenty of lonely, hungry days for me and my sisters then."

Andy first felt his stomach symptoms ten years ago, when he was overseas. "I didn't like being so far away from home," he says. "The food didn't taste right anyway, and I was under a lot of tension with a hard-driving set of fellows around me. When I was in high school and beginning college, I had what you'd call a nervous stomach, butterflies. . . . That would happen especially before exams. . . . When I went to midshipman school, there was terrific pressure and competition, and I'd feel it in my stomach. . . . It seemed the only thing that would help would be rest and being away from my assignment."

Recently Andy's wife had a baby. Andy is resentful and jealous of the infant. "The regular routine of the house has been upset," he complains. "It has to be fed, it cries so much, keeps me awake at night. Well, that doesn't lead to any healing of what's causing my pain."

Andy is also having some trouble professionally. He's a law school graduate trying to get his practice established. "But things have been slow." He's been working nights as a postal clerk. Money problems have forced him to move his family to his mother's house.

In the hospital Andy underwent surgery for a large duodenal ulcer. His condition has improved. Dr. Samuel Silverman of the Harvard Medical School, a psychiatrist who interviewed Andy, concludes that his ulcer was the result of stress situations which extended over a considerable period, and which included competition, separation from home and mother, maintaining two jobs, and the recent arrival of a baby.

"Long-standing intense dependency has been a striking feature of this patient's emotional life," notes Dr. Silverman. "The defenses against this have been principally in the form of over-activity and denial." He adds that these defenses have not succeeded in adequately containing Andy's "basically oral needs." Such needs are part of earliest infancy and are related to the pleasurable experience of sucking. In later life they may determine personality traits.

When their baby was born, Andy's wife's attention was withdrawn from him. His feelings, insufficiently discharged through expressed emotion, were diverted to his stomach.

Who Gets an Ulcer?

A peptic ulcer forms when acid stomach juices eat into the stomach or duodenal wall. The acid first erodes the inner membrane, forming a lesion called an acute ulcer. This ulcer may heal with proper diet, antacid medication, and a decrease in tension.

But if the acid is chronically overproduced, it eventually eats into the deeper muscle layer, forming a chronic ulcer. At last it may perforate the stomach wall entirely, permitting gastric juices to flow directly into the abdomen. Without prompt surgery, perforation may cause death.

The typical ulcer sufferer has a great deal of initiative and drive. He's a go-getter, and is generally successful in his profession. His field is often a demanding one, requiring quick decisions and constant resolving of problems.

But it is not the chronic stress of his job alone that leads to the formation of the ulcer. Rather, within the framework of his occupation, the sufferer is likely to be undergoing a psychological conflict relating to dependence and independence.

Most ulcer sufferers have intense wishes to be dependent. They want to be loved, mothered, cared for. These desires are holdovers from their needs as infants feeding at the breast. Their need to be taken care of is innately bound up with feeding and food, the counterpart of the infant's nourishing at the breast.

"They actually want, as adults, to be dealt with as if they were still being fed at mother's breast," observes Dr. Don E. Johnson of Hahnemann Medical College. "Both psychologically and physiologically [they] respond as if they are hungry all of the time." Their stomachs are constantly secreting as if about to receive food.

These infantile longings are often fought against because they tend to produce feelings of guilt and inferiority. The prospective ulcer patient may overcompensate by exaggerated aggressiveness, ambition, independence. He won't accept any help from anyone and burdens himself with responsibilities.

Alas, his continuous struggle and excessive responsibilities reinforce his wish for a dependent relationship. In the depth of his personality he has an unconscious longing for the sheltered existence of the little child.

This longing is one reason for the beneficial effect of rest cures. The patient is removed from his daily struggle. He can give in openly to his wish to withdraw from his responsibilities and can be passive, demanding, infantile.

Some ulcer patients, on the other hand, don't overcompensate for their dependent desires with an outward show of go-getting activity. Far from being hard-driving executives, many of them are overtly dependent, demanding, and disgruntled. Their dependent tendencies are often frustrated not by internal conflict but by external circumstances, such as marriage or a stint in the army. Military surgeons have learned the futility of trying to treat ulcer cases in the army, except in the rare case in which it is possible to place the soldier in a completely satisfactory job. Most army ulcer patients improve quickly upon discharge from the service.

Once the digestive tract has started to acquire a sore spot because of the dependency conflict, other emotions can contribute to the progress of the disease. Anger, fear, hostility, and resentment are the most common. But any serious emotional shock may stimulate the ulcer process.

Children with Ulcers

Peptic ulcer symptoms of children differ from those of adults. The pain often cannot be precisely located. It is less clearly related to meals and less often relieved by eating. Nausea and vomiting are more common in children. More often than do adult ulcer patients, children with ulcers suffer from loss of appetite, early morning pain, and headaches.

Nine-year-old Peter was admitted to the hospital with symptoms of bloody diarrhea. For two months he had complained of pain which came on from one to three hours after meals. He would sometimes go to bed during the day and cry. Peter has a large duodenal ulcer.

Peter has been seclusive and tense since early childhood. His mother is a cold person who offers little affection or emotional acceptance to her children. When Peter was born, she had been in labor for three days, and there was doubt as to whether he would live. The therapist who interviewed her felt that she would have preferred the death of the child rather than the burden of raising him. Her behavior alternates between rejection and indulgence, but it is always rigidly restrictive and basically hostile and cold.

When Peter was two, he witnessed the violent death of a younger sister in an accident, and at this time he regressed to very babyish behavior. His mother has lost two other children. She says she is quite content that they died, since "I have enough work to do anyway."

She raised Peter in a rigid manner, forcing him to comply with a very precise schedule of feeding and toilet training. The engulfing control which the mother exercised over Peter excluded her husband and prevented any healthy relationship between Peter and his father. His adjustment with other children has been poor, and at school he is a very shy, inhibited boy who makes little contact with either the teachers or the other pupils. He tends to substitute activities with things for activities with people, for he has found relationships with people so painful that he hesitates to reach out to form any new friendships.

In the course of therapy his mother has developed some insight. She has been able to relax some of her control of Peter. His father has become much closer to him. He has begun taking Peter on outings. The improvement in Peter's ulcer has been pronounced.

Children with ulcers tend to be unassertive and to have a great deal of anxiety about expressing aggression or anger. Like Peter, they are children whose need for a secure love relationship with the mother during infancy was not met. They react to emotional stress, especially anger and rejection from other people, with gastrointestinal impairment, including oversecretion of gastric acid. If this state of mind persists, it can lead to an ulcer.

Under such conditions, ulcers can appear even in infancy. Each of three baby boys with ulcers, seen by Dr. Margaret W. Gerard of the Clinical Institute for Psychoanalysis, had an irritable mother who was particularly put out by having to take care of her frequently sick child. One mother handed her baby, who had vomited, to a hospital intern, saying, "Please take him and keep him!" She worried about the baby's dying and called the intern often to ask, "Has he died?"

Each of the mothers was inconsistent. She would threaten her baby, then hug him. She would scold, spank, shout, and shake the baby if he dawdled over eating. None of the babies had been breast fed or held while being bottle fed. All were on strict feeding schedules.

Ulcers in children are sometimes associated with school phobia, the refusal of children to go to school. Eight-year-old Michael first complained of stomach pains shortly after school began. In the morning before school, he would have pain, sometimes with vomiting.

Michael has always disliked school and been reluctant to attend. He is isolated, inhibited, almost friendless. He tends to stay in class alone at recess. Since his ulcer developed, he attends less often than ever.

John is a fourteen-year-old boy with an ulcer. For three years he has resisted going to school. Often he complains of gastrointestinal pains. He has missed as many as forty-five consecutive school days. He spends his days lying in bed, reading, listening to the radio, or sleeping. He is awake most of the night. He has a bad temper and is occasionally destructive.

John's mother is an uncomplaining, resigned woman who

supports her family. His father is passive, ineffectual, and dependent upon his wife. She makes excuses for John's failures and her husband's and is oversympathetic with their "nervousness."

John is much like his father. He is excessively compliant, passive, yet stubborn in his intention not to go to school. He is bland like his mother, with effeminate speech and mannerisms.

Psychiatrist T. P. Millar finds such youngsters were generally strong-willed infants and retain an infantile stubbornness in the struggle to dominate their mothers. They are anxious, fearful of rejection, and hostile. At the same time, they are passive and withdrawn outside the home.

Their mothers are overprotective and set few limits. The fathers hardly exist for the children. While they seem to have received some love from their parents, the youngsters apparently have no experience in tolerating frustration and no coherent view of reality. They retain infantile patterns of behavior, and an abnormal dependence on their mothers.

The sexual stresses of adolescence may find expression in peptic ulcer. Frances, almost twelve, suddenly experienced stomach pain and vomiting of such severity that she was hospitalized. She was found to have a duodenal ulcer. With medical treatment, her symptoms disappeared within a week.

But her incessant preoccupation with questions of sin and guilt convinced her pediatrician that the ulcer was secondary to emotional difficulties. About a month later Frances was readmitted to the hospital with the same symptoms. As before, her symptoms disappeared within a few days. But since her ulcer was not responding to medical management, her physician urged psychiatric evaluation, which the mother finally accepted.

Interviews with Frances's mother at a psychiatric clinic shed further light on the girl's preoccupation with sin. For some time Frances had been asking her mother questions about anatomical differences between the sexes, and other questions concerning the difference between mortal and venial sins. The mother herself told the therapist of her own fear of sexuality and reported that she had always made repeated nightly investigations of

Frances and her fifteen-year-old sister as they slept, "to make sure they haven't touched themselves."

Frances was first seen in the psychiatric clinic a month after her second hospitalization, and at this time she was again experiencing abdominal pain, which had been plaguing her for two or three days. In obvious discomfort, she held her hands tightly pressed against her abdomen. She was pale and tearful and refused to talk with the therapist. However, she did answer direct questions with monosyllables, nods, and shakes of the head, and in this fashion admitted that she was greatly and guiltily preoccupied with questions of sex.

Frances had not yet begun to menstruate and indicated that she knew little about the menstrual cycle. But by this time the cyclic course of her pain and vomiting had become evident: her three bouts had occurred at a twenty-eight-day interval, and each had lasted six days, much like a menstrual period. The psychiatrist offered the opinion that Frances was suffering from a sort of bloodless menstrual disorder. He gave her a brief explanation of menstrual life and some description of the shock of puberty and its bodily changes.

A week later Frances was free of pain and vomiting, but still wouldn't talk to the therapist. She quickly rejected the invitation to talk about menstrual matters. Her last interview coincided with the time for her next "period." She had no abdominal pain or vomiting, but described slight discomfort in her breasts which she had first noticed a day or two before. This time she smiled a little, talked willingly about her interest in sports, and said her mother was always overconcerned with Frances's safety.

Follow-up reports from the mother and from the physician eighteen months later indicated that Frances had experienced no recurrence of pain or vomiting, that her ulcer had responded to conservative medical management, and that her first period had occurred a few months after the clinic experience. She was currently functioning adequately in school, although somewhat socially inhibited.

The psychiatrist, Robert E. Nixon, reported concerning Frances's symptoms: "It seems probable that she suffered principally from her mother's inadvertent efforts to keep her a child. Deeply and pathologically fearful of sexuality, the mother had not only failed to give the child preparation for the menarche, but in addition had made it clear that she would not welcome the advent of adult sexuality in her daughter."

At the same time, the hormonal onslaught of puberty caught Frances in the middle. The result of the conflict between her mother's need to keep her a child and her own bodily need to grow up was her cyclic pain and vomiting.

Hostile Act

Ulcerative colitis victims burst with unexpressed rage

The summer he was eleven, Alex was sexually molested by an older boy in his neighborhood. He was badly frightened, and for a week or more he was exceptionally withdrawn, hardly uttering a word. For months he wouldn't leave the house unless his parents came with him. Alex's father had gone looking for the older boy, threatening to kill him, but he'd disappeared.

A year later the older boy was picked up by the police. Alex emphatically refused to testify in court against his attacker. He was mortified at the thought of having to recount the details of the incident. He was particularly embarrassed because of the women present. But his father, the judge, and the police all exerted strong pressure on Alex to testify. At last he acquiesced.

In court Alex stuttered through his ordeal. A week later he was severely constipated. His parents gave Alex repeated laxatives and enemas.

The constipation then became diarrhea. Alex was having from ten to sixteen watery bowel movements a day. Soon they were mixed with blood and mucus.

Alex rapidly lost more than twenty pounds. His appetite was poor and he was dehydrated and weak. He cried frequently and, recalls his father, "would not let anyone touch him." The family physician diagnosed this condition as ulcerative colitis and recommended various drugs, but Alex's condition grew worse.

He was then hospitalized for two months and gradually improved. Soon he was having only three or four bowel movements a day. He gained weight and seemed almost like his old self again. The physician recommended that Alex remain out of school for the year. Alex mostly "hung around the house," his father recalls. Occasionally a teacher came to tutor him; most days he watched television.

Shortly afterward Alex's father quit his job after a minor back injury. He went on a drinking spree for several weeks. He became overbearing and loud, angrily ordering Alex around, demanding instantaneous compliance. "God damn you, come over here on the double!" he would yell at Alex. When Alex stuttered, his father would shout, "Shut up until you can talk better."

Alex reacted mainly by avoiding his father. Sometimes he would fight back, calling his father "fat boy" or "drunkard." "Why did you marry him?" he asked his mother. "Why do I have to have a dad like that?"

Alex's mother now had to go to work part-time, leaving Alex alone at home with his father. He began to have attacks of bloody diarrhea again, sometimes having twenty bowel movements a day. A month later, when he was admitted to the hospital, he was frightened and cowering.

Now fourteen, he looked more like a boy of nine or ten. He stuttered badly and contorted his face. He was underweight and obviously malnourished. During a psychiatric interview Alex's father, a burly man with a loud, aggressive manner, answered all questions directed to Alex or his mother. The psychiatrist, Dr. Pietro Castelnuovo-Tedesco of the University of California School of Medicine, also noted that Alex's mother remained quiet, with a distant expression on her face. Alex avoided looking at his father. Sometimes, though, he would glance at him furtively out of the corner of his eye.

In the hospital Alex was anxious, depressed, and irritable. He avoided other patients and the hospital staff. He complained about the meals and would eat a full meal only when his mother brought food from home.

Alex had always been overdependent on his mother, and she had encouraged this by overprotecting him. At the same time, her hospital visits were unpredictable, and Alex would frequently wait hours for her. Sometimes she didn't show up at all. Alex's father was also insensitive to his son's situation. As Alex became sicker and often whimpered, the father was concerned only that his behavior was unmanly.

Alex improved very little in the hospital, even with fine medical and psychiatric treatment. Soon he was desperate to go home. He feared he would never get better and be able to be with his mother again. "I don't know why," he told the psychiatrist, "I just feel like giving up." As soon as his mother left each day, Alex became helpless and listless.

At last his doctors decided that Alex should be allowed to go home for the weekend. He returned to the hospital much improved. His mother had spent a great deal of time with him, played his favorite games, and cooked his favorite foods. Alex was soon discharged from the hospital. With frequent psychiatric visits, his ulcerative colitis gradually improved.

Dr. Castelnuovo-Tedesco interprets Alex's illness in the light of his conflicting emotions: Having just entered puberty, Alex was trying to assert himself against an overbearing father who was trying to keep him submissive. At the same time, Alex's father was resentful and jealous of his closeness with his mother. Alex was caught between conflicting desires: wanting to comply with his father's expectations of him, and wanting to rebel against his domination.

The climax of this situation had come in the courtroom. Despite his great reluctance, Alex was coerced into testifying. Even his mother deserted him. In knuckling under and testifying, Alex felt totally defeated. He was overwhelmed with shame and despair.

He also felt hostile and defiant—emotions which he repressed. He complied, but his hostility did not vanish. This complex of emotions often sets the stage for ulcerative colitis. For at one and the same time, the bloody diarrhea can represent loss of control and hostile defiance.

Expression of Rage

Ulcerative colitis is an irritation of the colon—the lower part of the large intestine—due to ulceration. It can be fatal if the ulcer perforates the colon.

The most common symptom is frequent bloody bowel movements. These loose discharges consist mostly of blood, pus, and mucus with some fecal particles. Victims also commonly have abdominal cramps, sometimes with fever, vomiting, loss of appetite, and dramatic weight loss.

The disease usually has many relapses and remissions before it becomes chronic. These remissions may be distinctly correlated with the patient's emotional life. One college student's parents fought incessantly. Often the young man himself was the target of his father's anger. When he developed ulcerative colitis, a psychiatrist advised that he go to an out-of-town college. There his symptoms disappeared.

After graduation he returned to live with his parents. Very soon he once more showed symptoms of severe ulcerative colitis. Within a year he required surgery.

The colon reacts sharply to emotion. During periods of tranquillity it is pale and quiet, its secretions of enzymes low. During periods of anger and resentment, however, it becomes engorged with blood and very active. Secretions increase. Spots of abnormal tissue may occur.

Ulcerative colitis is thought to develop when a predisposed person fails to express chronic resentment and anger. On an unconscious level, the mucous membrane of his colon *does* respond to these repressed emotions. The ensuing engorgement and hyperactivity produces bleeding. Enzymes secreted by the intestine further erode the membrane, leaving it open to bacterial invasion.

Ulcerative colitis is often accompanied by severe depression and feelings of hopelessness and despair. The typical victim is immature and dependent, particularly on his mother. He often is perfectionistic and rigid and tends to be wary of other people. Generally one parent is domineering and threatening; the other, though quiet and seemingly submissive and martyrlike, controls through aloofness and inconsistency.

Symptoms of ulcerative colitis frequently appear when a person is faced with a situation which he feels he cannot deal with. In one study fully 86 per cent of ulcerative colitis patients had a well-defined and serious life crisis in the six months before they became ill. These included job changes, moving to a new home, death in the family, and other upsetting situations.

One woman was partly responsible for her son's being severely burned. She shortly afterward developed severe ulcerative colitis. In the hospital for surgery, she became psychotic. The night before her operation she was found wandering in the street outside the hospital, trailing her intravenous infusion. She died just after surgery.

Colitis patients are often worried about finances and preoccupied with money matters. The disease may occur in response to financial obligations which are beyond a person's means.

In periods of change an individual must respond to a challenging situation with responsibility, effort, and concentration. But persons who develop ulcerative colitis are inclined to give up easily in the face of obstacles. They are easily frustrated and soon start to feel hopeless and helpless. They are thus involved in an overwhelming struggle to assert themselves and accomplish a difficult task.

Some potential colitis victims may have a fixation at the infantile level, according to one widely accepted interpretation. Whenever they are faced with a need to give or to accomplish a task, they may respond in an infantile way by producing bowel movements. Thus, instead of meeting the obligations of motherhood, job changes, financial necessity, or similar developments, some people unconsciously employ colitis as a substitute for real accomplishment.

Too Much Mother

"You can't go out tonight," Cynthia's parents tell her, "because so many people are getting raped and knifed."

"Don't walk with your hands in your pockets," Jeff is cautioned, "because you'll hurt yourself when you fall."

Barbara's mother worries constantly about germs. "She cracks up at the slightest injury to any of us," Barbara comments. "She wants us in a straitjacket so we won't get hurt."

Harvey's parents rarely go out, because "we're afraid the children might burn the house down while we're gone."

Paul's family doesn't take trips together because "it's too much of a chore to be constantly preoccupied with looking for rest room signs."

Adam's mother won't allow him to go hunting and fishing with his father.

Each of these children suffers from ulcerative colitis. In a study of eight families of children with ulcerative colitis, Dr. Don D. Jackson and Dr. Irvin Yalom of the Stanford University School of Medicine found all the families to be severely restricted and restrictive.

They lead extremely narrow lives, seeing few people and engaging in few activities outside the home. Humor, novelty, and creativity are actively discouraged. The parents restrict their children's activities as well as their own. They convey the impression that branching out on one's own is fraught with danger.

The fathers in these families are all unhappy with their jobs and are strikingly lacking in ambition. They have low self-esteem and seem resigned to the role of mere breadwinner. Cynthia's father wants her to get a good education so she can get "a better husband than her mother got." The mothers are the dominant figures in these families.

These families are exceptionally quiet. There seems to be an unspoken rule that interactions between family members will be limited. They hold each other in check by placating or subduing each other. Arguments, anger, emotional expression of any kind are usually avoided. Jackson and Yalom observe: "There appears to be a conscious awareness of pain, disharmony, and unhappiness in the family and yet an agreement that this will not be mentioned."

Susan's family, for example, was uncommunicative and indirect in interviews with the therapists. Her relatives seemed constantly embarrassed and were often silent. When they spoke, it was in quiet, expressionless voices. They seemed to give all information in a loose, tentative fashion, so it could be easily altered by another family member who might object. In this way they could maintain a façade of solidarity.

Jackson and Yalom reported: "The hesitation in the family became . . . a major subject of the interview sessions. Each time we mentioned their reluctance to answer they suggested that they simply could think of nothing to say. Finally we advanced the question of whether they had really had nothing to say or whether they felt that they were not permitted to say things within the family."

At this, Susan's sister Anita blurted out a memory. "When I was younger I would want to talk. I would come into the room, but everyone would tell me to be quiet because they were watching television." The mother and father adamantly denied that this was true. Within a few minutes Anita herself denied she had ever mentioned any such thing.

Concealment of emotion was the family's lifeblood. In one of the interviews it was learned that there had been some kind of "unpleasant episode" the previous Saturday morning. With persistent inquiry the therapist was able to find out that Susan's brother Ken—who was always polite, laconic, and virtually expressionless—had expected to be picked up by two other boys in his class at 7 A.M.

He arose early and waited for them. At 10 A.M. he was still waiting. His father suggested that he telephone one of the boys to find out what had happened to him. Ken learned that he had been stood up.

In the presence of the therapist, the father complimented his son on his not being upset by the incident, or at least not being "really" upset. The therapist suggested to the boy, "Perhaps you waited three hours before telephoning because you didn't want to find out that you'd been stood up." Ken showed some feeling, appearing to be at the point of tears.

The father became annoyed. "There's no use making a big deal out of it," he said. The family rallied, changed the topic, and the door was closed on the episode.

Most commonly, ulcerative colitis afflicts children more than eight years of age. It is sometimes associated with arthritis, growth retardation, skin disease, and anemia. While some children suffer continuous symptoms, the majority have a pattern of intermittent easing, then worsening. Relapses are usually more frequent and severe during the first few years of the illness. At any point the symptoms may either disappear or become chronic.

In general, children with ulcerative colitis are constricted, defensive, and guilty. They tend to be rigid and oversensitive. Often they have problems involving their sexual identification. They usually have conflicts in dealing with their aggressive impulses and keep their hostility concealed. It is common for them to be chronically depressed.

Almost invariably these children have overprotective mothers on whom they are overdependent. Indeed, in many cases the onset of illness can be traced to a real or fantasied disruption in their relationships with their mothers.

These children are usually torn between the healthy need to express hostility and independence in regard to the mother, and the abnormal need to have a close dependent relationship with her. All children with ulcerative colitis in one study view their mothers as dominating and inconsistent, hostile and overprotective. The typical such child feels his mother basically rejects him and is insensitive to his needs. She prohibits direct expressions of his sexual and aggressive impulses and requires conformity with strict standards. He sees his father as passive, ineffective, and unimportant.

The conflict between the child's need for dependence and his need to express his hostility and strike out for independence is likely to be particularly stressful at certain stages of his development. The first is the period of toilet training, when the child wants both to please his mother and to resist her. The second is the start of school, when the child may be unwilling to part from his mother. The third is puberty and early adolescence, when the child may be unable to feel independent of his mother and form new relationships. Ulcerative colitis in children frequently develops at these critical times.

In some cases the problem may arise mainly out of the mother's inability to allow a child to grow up. For example, Elizabeth had just reached puberty. Just after her first menstrual period, her relationship with her mother rapidly deteriorated. The mother began a thorough check on all areas of Elizabeth's life. She even insisted on accompanying her to the bathroom. Elizabeth resented this invasion of her privacy, but she was unable to express her anger. If she had, it might have relieved the situation.

As it was, Elizabeth had an acute onset of ulcerative colitis and required hospitalization. Psychiatric consultation revealed that the main problem was with Elizabeth's mother. Within a month the mother was able to accept the psychiatrist's suggestions that she allow Elizabeth more independence. Elizabeth's colitis subsided very soon afterward.

CHAPTER 15

The People Who Starve Themselves

Some infants spit up everything; some teen-agers won't eat anything

Mysteriously, despite regular and plentiful feedings, seven-month-old Jason was starving to death. His arms and legs were twigs, his body underdeveloped. He whimpered constantly and was listless.

In the hospital he took little notice of people who approached his crib. But whenever a nurse picked him up, he immediately stopped crying and clung desperately to her. He cried vigorously when she put him down.

When a nurse brought Jason a bottle of formula, he went for it hungrily. He would suck voraciously and cry when the milk was gone. Soon he would revert to his steady whine and blank stare.

Psychiatrist Donald T. Fullerton of the University of Wisconsin School of Medicine was called in for consultation. A few minutes after Jason's meal, Dr. Fullerton observed, the baby's tongue protruded a little, curved into a spoon-shaped groove. Jason's abdominal and chest muscles jerked a few times. The previously swallowed formula ran slowly into his mouth. The infant continued to chew and eventually reswallowed part of the vomitus.

Jason was suffering from infantile rumination. As cows and other ruminants rechew their cud, the infant was bringing up and rechewing the contents of his stomach. Since much of the regurgitated food was dribbling down his chin, he was losing two ounces a day and was becoming dangerously dehydrated. Jason was slowly starving himself. Only intravenous feeding could keep him alive.

The mothers of babies who ruminate are almost invariably immature and dependent. They are incapable of providing warm, comfortable, and intimate physical care for their babies. Often they are severely depressed and spend little time caring for the infant.

One woman neglected a baby, boarded as a foster child in her home, because of the demands of her own children. She isolated him in a back room, propped his bottles, and didn't allow the other children to visit him. The baby learned few motor skills. He habitually rocked his head from side to side and soon began to ruminate.

Since infants so coldly treated receive very little comfort from the outside world, researchers speculate that they seek some gratification from within. Feeding is likely to be their greatest source of satisfaction. They therefore attempt to extract a bit more pleasure from life by refeeding themselves.

Also, a preverbal child can communicate only through his body. The mother's attitude toward the infant is often succinctly conveyed in the way she handles and addresses him when she feeds him. The baby responds in kind. He signals his distress by his pathological gastrointestinal functioning after feeding.

In Jason Langer's case, his mother had had a miserable childhood caring for a psychotic mother. She remembers feeling trapped and resentful. As an adolescent, she became promiscuous and nearly alcoholic. Shortly after graduating from high school, she met and quickly married a career Navy man in an attempt to escape her problems.

Jason was an adopted child. The Langers had come to adopt him in an unusual way. They were friendly with another couple, the Oslers. Mrs. Osler became pregnant by a man not her husband. The Oslers persuaded the Langers to adopt the baby in order to "save our marriage."

Sally and Jim Langer were ambivalent about the arrangement from the start. They felt obliged to take Jason but unprepared to care for him. "All of a sudden we had a baby on our hands," Jim recalls.

Sally was confused and anxious. "He cried a lot more than necessary," she remembers. She responded by spanking him.

When he spit up, she would jerk him away so that he wouldn't soil her or the furniture. She became even angrier at him when she discovered that he seldom spat up when a babysitter fed him. She rarely held him. "It spoils a child to cuddle him," she'd say. She left him alone most of the time.

At the hospital she was observed while she fed him. She sat rigidly and held him in an uncomfortable position. Jason had trouble keeping his head up. He had to arch his back and keep his head sharply turned in order to get at the bottle.

When he finished the bottle, she placed him on her shoulder and pounded him sharply on the back. "It makes me happy when I get a good burp," she said. Indeed, she struck him so hard that some vomitus was forced into his mouth. Dr. Fullerton commented that when speaking of the infant, Sally sounded as if she were "talking about a defective machine."

The recommended treatment for infantile rumination is to hospitalize the child, thereby temporarily separating him from his mother. At the same time, a member of the hospital staff provides the kind of warm, encouraging environment a baby needs in order to thrive.

Jason was assigned a special nurse who spent eight hours a day with him. She was a mature, warm woman who enjoyed fondling Jason and playing with him. Jason at first clung desperately to her. During the first day with her his rumination came to a near halt. But when she left he cried violently and ruminated again.

During the next several days he ruminated less and less and clung less to the nurse. He was now gaining weight, smiling, and making contented baby noises.

After three weeks Jason left the hospital. In the meantime, with a psychiatrist's help, Sally had gained insight into her own problems and the baby's emotional needs. His rumination stopped completely. He continued to gain weight normally, smile readily, and respond easily to people.

Aversion to Food

"It sometimes happens that a physician has patients—they are more apt to be women—whose appearance is truly shocking," report Dr. J. Dejerine and Dr. E. Gauckler.

"Their eyes seem brilliant. Their cheeks are hollow, and their cheekbones seem to protrude through the skin. Their withered breasts hang from the walls of their chests. Every rib stands out.

"Their shoulder blades appear to be loosened from their frame. Every vertebra shows through the skin. The abdominal wall sinks in below the floating rib and forms a hollow like a basin. The thighs and the calves of their legs are reduced to a skeleton.

"One would say it was the picture of an immured nun, such as the old masters have portrayed. These women appear to be fifty or sixty years old. . . .

"Are they tuberculous or cancerous patients, or muscular atrophies in the last stages, these women who in misery and hunger have reduced to this frightful gauntness? Nothing of the kind. Their lungs are healthy, there is no sign of any organic affection. Although they look so old, they are young women, girls and sometimes children."

Dr. Dejerine and Dr. Gauckler are describing a syndrome called anorexia nervosa—loss of appetite of psychic origin. It is often a misnomer, since many sufferers (called anorectics) are painfully hungry, especially in the beginning. Yet they cannot or will not eat. About 10 per cent of anorectics starve themselves to death.

The syndrome was first described and named by Sir William Gull in 1874. He noticed that, although it does occur in males, the typical anorectic is a teen-aged girl. Sir William could find no physical disorder that might account for such starvation. He concluded that it resulted from "a perversion of the ego . . . a morbid mental state."

The anorectic is often overactive—"sustained by some unknown miracle of energy„" Dejerine and Gauckler have observed. Once the syndrome has developed, some symptoms are likely to last for from three to five years. Relapses may occur for years, with the person from time to time losing considerable amounts of weight and requiring hospital admission.

Most anorectics have developed a morbid aversion to food. It may have started with certain foods and then been generalized to all food. Some anorectics are afraid to eat because they feel the food will make them sick or in some other way harm them.

At the same time, the anorectic is likely to have a tremendous preoccupation with food. One group of hospitalized children frequently had vivid daydreams of food and eating. They often thought about cooking, eating, and feeding others. Dr. John Blitzer and his colleagues at the Children's Hospital Medical Center in Boston report: "One would see a severely emaciated child pushing a loaded food cart down the hospital corridor, serving the other patients, and urging them to finish their meals. . . . Many of the children ate secretly. Some hid food. Others would 'steal' food rather than eat the food that had been served to them."

Their food fantasies often had to do with aggression. One girl, when she ate, made believe she was stuffing food into someone else. "I pretend they don't want to take it and I force them," she said. Another girl couldn't eat when given a plate. "Can't they understand what I want to do is to take it . . . away from somebody?"

Linked with the anorexia snydrome is apparently a grossly distorted body image. Reports Dr. Blitzer: "The most striking aspect of the starved children of our study was their denial of emaciation. Although most of the patients resemble the starved inmates of a Nazi concentration camp, not one expressed the slightest concern about being so thin. On the contrary, many insisted they were too fat."

Power Play

For many anorectic children, not eating represents a power play. Food provides weaponry in the struggle between the child and his parents. The reaction of a starving youngster's family is naturally to urge him to eat. Parents often become desperate and try to force their anorectic child to take food. The child in turn resorts to ruses to give the impression of having eaten, perhaps by flushing food down the toilet. Many anorectic children demand special foods prepared in a particular way before they will eat.

In early childhood food is a battleground for autonomy. In the first year of life most children begin to assert their independence by grabbing the spoon out of their mother's hand or by rejecting certain foods. At the same time, food represents dependence and the mother's love for the child.

In adolescence, at an impasse between childhood and adulthood, the youngster may crave both independence and dependence. In psychological terms, not eating represents giving up dependence on the mother and can also express hostility toward the mother. At the same time, the solicitude of the mother toward the anorectic is greatly increased. She becomes deeply involved in his eating and very much concerned with his health.

The anorectic thus has it both ways. He acts independent of his mother, yet he has her hovering over him. Many anorectics regress to childlike thinking and acting. One girl told her mother: "I just want to lie down and disintegrate. I want a nurse who will do even more for me than you do."

She became incapacitated and had to be dressed and pushed around the hospital in a wheelchair. If the nurse tried to force her to walk, the girl would sink down to the floor and stay there until she was picked up. As her anorexia nervosa improved, she also became more mature in her behavior.

An anorectic may plunge deeper into his regression as a result of his parents' inability to cope with it. Parents typically resent the child, then react to their anxiety, hostility, and guilt with overprotectiveness. They try to meet all the child's demands, often fostering a deeper egression.

Often hospitalized anorectic children try to set up the same sort of relationships with the hospital staff that they had at home. Dr. Leonard I. Lesser and his associates at the University of Miami School of Medicine studied fifteen anorectic girls and report that their patients "displayed considerable skill in playing the members of the hospital staff one against another," much as they might do with family members.

A girl might choose a particular nurse as a confidante and flatter her to secure special favors. Or the girl might lie to her pediatrician that her psychiatrist had promised her a particular privilege. The pediatrician might reluctantly agree, while resenting the psychiatrist and doubting his wisdom. "Whenever communication between staff members was inadequate," reports the study team, "the patients were unerringly adroit in exploiting this opportunity to defeat the therapeutic program."

"I Could Get a Baby That Way"

In many adolescent anorectics, food represents budding sexuality. Young women sometimes become anorectic soon after their first menstruation. While they are anorectic, it is rare for girls to menstruate.

Many youngsters begin a reducing diet because they think they are too fat. Actually the fat may be nothing more than the rounding out of sexual development. At a normal weight, an adolescent girl cannot deny her developing breasts and rounding hips. By starving herself, however, she can try to return to a stage of relative asexuality. Such seems to be the unconscious motivation in many cases of anorexia nervosa in young girls. One girl told doctors she was afraid of gaining weight lest she become "too sexy."

Many anorectic youngsters, both boys and girls, stop eating because of fantasies of oral impregnation: they imagine they can become pregnant through the mouth. Some have the impression that obesity and pregnancy are the same thing. Said one: "I'm scared to eat, because that would make me fat and I would get a baby that way." Others objected to eating because they associated feeling full with pregnancy.

Dr. John Blitzer and his colleagues have found that oral impregnation is often linked with incest fantasies. One girl was upset because she thought her father wanted to make her fat. She couldn't understand it, since he liked her mother best and "wouldn't want to marry me."

A boy compared conception, pregnancy, and delivery with eating and digestion. "Something goes into your body, it undergoes a process there, and then comes out," he said. Another boy connected being fat with being feminine. He started dieting when he felt "flabby and girlish."

A teen-aged girl started developing and becoming heavier. Her classmates teased her about having a baby in her stomach. She developed anorexia nervosa after a young woman she was close to became pregnant. Her father lost his temper over her inability to eat, and her symptoms worsened.

Many anorectic children pick up strange ideas about eating from their parents. Often the parents are excessively concerned about weight, dieting unnecessarily. Diane's father indulged in food fads. He connected food, pregnancy, and growths inside the body. He told Diane that his own mother's illness after pregnancy was cured by diet. "Every ounce of food has to come out in a bowel movement," he'd say, "or it will kill you."

Diane had her first period at thirteen. Boys began to whistle at her. Half a year later she missed two periods. Fearing that something was wrong organically, she had her mother take her to several doctors, all of whom reassured her that occasonal missed periods at her age are normal.

But knowing that periods stop during pregnancy, Diane became so frightened that she had to be hospitalized and sedated. In the hospital she got an unusually heavy period. Her appetite disappeared. Thereafter, she was anorectic and again stopped menstruating.

The crippling anxiety Diane felt, reports the Blitzer team, was probably related to body sensations which she connected with sexuality, menstruation, and pregnancy fantasies. "The fantasies revived older infantile incestuous wishes and ideas of impregnation concerning the father." Diane's father reinforced her fears about food and sex. When her mother wasn't around, he secretly told Diane the facts of life.

"I Can't Stomach Him"

Sometimes anorexia nervosa seems to grow out of an extremely ambivalent and guilt-provoking relationship with a parent.

Arlene, a bright twelve-year-old, had such a relationship with her father. She was admitted to the hospital after losing sixteen pounds. She had regarded herself as obese—"the bottom of a pyramid," like an acrobat who bears the weight of others on his shoulders—and so began to diet.

This provoked a major struggle with the family concerning eating. To both parents, a plump child meant a happy family and the successful fulfillment of parental responsibility. Alarmed, they made Arlene the center of a culinary circus. A pediatrician suggested that they be less solicitous. But they were unable to refrain for long.

In psychiatric interviews Arlene was superficially friendly but tried to defend herself against personal questions. On the Rorschach, her most frequent response was that of a clown's mask, symbolizing her sense of acting a role and keeping her feelings concealed. Although she claimed she had "nothing to hide," she denied that she suffered from any emotional or physical illness.

In the ward Arlene was friendly and assisted the nurses in their duties. The attitude of the staff, initially favorable to Arlene, became ambivalent as she succeeded in producing misunderstandings between staff members by misquoting them.

In describing her feelings about her father, Arlene said: "I cannot stomach him because I feel he is always pushing something down my throat." She was uncomfortable in his presence and regarded him as disgusting. At the same time, she was seductive toward him, as he was to her.

He told the psychiatrist, "Of course I love her. Every time I see her, I want to pinch her behind." As he said this, his face flushed with embarrassment, and he added, "Do you think maybe she is too old for me to do that any more?"

Arlene's discomfort with the assumption of an adult psychosexual role may be a consequence of the failure to develop an adequate relationship with her father. The erotic components between father and daughter were uncomfortably close to the surface for both of them. Arlene repeatedly seduced her father into some gesture about which both felt guilty. She would then regress to a very dependent relationship with her mother.

Anorexia evidently served the purposes of punishing her father while keeping her mother protective. An end to solicitousness—and ultimately an end to her anorexia—came after Arlene continued to lose weight. Her doctors decided to institute tube feedings. She responded with tears and bitter complaints. Just before the tube feedings were to start, she began to eat everything offered to her and to ask for extras.

Savage Attack on Food

Frequently anorectics go on binges of uncontrolled eating. The condition, known as bulimia, often springs from a depressed or violent mood. A bulimic eats voraciously and indiscriminately, sometimes to the point of unconsciousness. Vast quantities of food may be gobbled up—loaves of bread, meats by the pound, whole cheeses. The overeating is generally a form of aggression. One girl entirely consumed her sister's very large wedding cake on the night before the wedding.

In one extreme case a woman's emaciation is due to a bizarre syndrome of bulimia and vomiting. Beatrice is five feet two inches tall and weighs less than seventy-five pounds. Her preoccupation with her body weight began at the age of fifteen when she was embarrassed at being thirty pounds overweight and was angry at herself for overeating. During the next few years, urged by her mother, she would go on a strict diet and drop to a normal 112 pounds, only to gain all the weight back when she was away from home at camp.

At the age of eighteen she realized she could eat all she wanted yet stay thin by inducing vomiting after voracious overeating. She soon was vomiting spontaneously. She derived conscious pleasure at seeing her mother go into a rage, then plead with her not to vomit.

Beatrice began to steal money to finance her four or five lunches, which she ate and threw up. Menstruation ceased at nineteen. She took enemas surreptitiously, consumed more than a cup of laxative nightly, and exercised vigorously, all in a conscious attempt to lose weight.

Beatrice's mother was an excitable, self-centered, domineering woman. When Beatrice was four, her mother had given birth to a longed-for son, and mother and son immediately entered into an intimate relationship; it continues to the present with much mutual lip kissing and caressing. Beatrice grew up feeling abandoned by her mother and hating her brother. When consciously angry at him, she experienced a desire to put something in her mouth.

Between the ages of seven and twelve she had bouts of abdominal pain and vomiting. She grew up through adolescence feeling neglected, insecure, and disapproved of. She wondered if she was adopted. Socially she was flamboyant, seeking attention from others in any way possible.

Beatrice's sexual ideal was to be held in the arms of a man, kissing without genital contact. At seventeen, a year before vomiting began, she performed fellatio with a boyfriend on numerous occasions, feeling nauseated afterward. When faced with intercourse in her late teens, she said: "I froze up when I thought of what my mother would think."

Between nineteen and twenty she lost sixty pounds and was hospitalized. She brought her vomiting under control, but her bulimia continued, often with food she stole. She was discharged after nine months, overweight at 138 pounds.

Back home, she quickly began again to overeat large amounts and vomit afterward. At twenty-four she married, but from the start the marriage was filled with discord. She began consuming more than a fifth of alcohol each evening in an attempt to control her frenzied overeating and vomiting which otherwise would go on all night.

Her husband divorced her and she lived with her two children, withdrawing socially, and becoming more preoccupied with her increasingly bizarre eating pattern. Her life for the next ten years consisted mainly in procuring and preparing large amounts of food, much of it spoiled, followed by nine-hour "bathroom sessions."

In these sessions she consumed about five pounds of food at a time. Then she vomited and simultaneously defecated, eating and vomiting five or six times with increasing frenzy until she was exhausted and fell asleep. On awakening she went out for food and the cycle began again. She packed her refrigerator with food until it overflowed. The kitchen and the bathroom were filled with foul odors from bowls of food left around in various stages of decomposition.

Beatrice's daughter, Sara, was thus brought up in a household dominated by her mother's unusual eating habits. Sara recalls that her mother would weigh her daily and say understandingly: "I know you don't really want to gain weight and can't help yourself . . . you will feel better when you can feel every bone . . . you'll be happy when the scale gets lower."

Almost inevitably Sara developed anorexia nervosa. "Not eating," says Sara, "made me feel closer to my mother. I couldn't do it any other way."

PART VI

Closets in Your Skeleton

Your emotions may be expressed through muscular

disorders, bone deformities, headache, backache,

fatigue. Rheumatoid arthritis victims tend

to be seeming martyrs who seek to rule their

families with an iron hand.

CHAPTER 16

High Tension

Bone deformities, headache, backache, fatigue—your muscles express your emotions

There is a type of personality often revealed by a tight jaw. Mark is such a person. Getting him to talk is like pulling teeth. He holds things in: emotions, ideas, words. He tends to be stingy; he gives little away, either of himself or his possessions.

Mark's physical appearance matches his personality, understandable since the tensions forming both personality and physique are the same. Mark's parents laughed at him when he expressed his feelings or desires. They treated harshly any strong statement he made in his own behalf. Before Mark entered grammar school, he learned that to talk was to risk ridicule and punishment.

In inhibiting his urges to speak, he unconsciously clamped his jaws. From a lifetime of this habit, his jaw muscles are overdeveloped, bulging his face where his jaws meet. His jawline has been pulled into a triangle, giving him a canine look. He is tight-lipped in all senses of the word.

Your Personality Made Visible

Your body is your personality made visible, for your emotions lead you to adopt special body attitudes. Every expression of your body has a meaning and a history: the quality of your hand-shake, your posture, the look in your eyes, the tone of your voice, your way of moving. So notes psychiatrist Alexander Lowen, an authority on the effect of emotions on the anatomy.

Form follows function in body development. Obviously, if you're on a track team, your legs will become thickly muscled from running. Muscles also can be developed from isometric exercises, in which you tense your muscles while you yourself are stationary. By contrast, if you're bedridden and don't exercise, your legs will become scrawny and weak.

Less well realized are Lowen's findings that emotional factors can promote similar development or atrophying. Harry, a commodities broker, has calf muscles so bulging that people often ask him, "Were you a track star?" Harry in fact never was athletic and now rarely moves from his telephone. Psychologically, however, he's running all the time. Though his legs aren't racing literally, they're always getting ready to run. The constant stretching and pushing, though done unconsciously and in a sitting position, are like isometric exercises and have given Harry the legs of a long-distance runner.

Conversely, Emil is the inheritor of a large family business, though personally he is weak and insecure. Feeling menaced since childhood, he has stepped through life gingerly, sensing little support. Now at fifty, despite his large head and solid body, his legs are flimsy and poorly developed.

A muscle ordinarily lengthens and contracts, somewhat like a rubber band. Many muscles work in pairs, so that one muscle bends your arm, while an opposing one straightens it. Ideally, muscles are relaxed and highly elastic. Under emotional stress, however, a muscle may remain abnormally contracted.

Such muscular tension, however slight, can be measured by an electromyogram, or EMG, a machine that records electrical impulses generated along muscle fiber. EMG readings profile what psychologist Robert B. Malmo of McGill University calls the "uptight response," the typical reaction pattern of chronically tense people. When startled by a sudden sound, both normal and anxious people show a comparable rise in muscle tension for the first two-tenths of a second. A normal person's muscle tension drops quickly. But in anxious people, whose degree of muscle contraction is high to begin with, the tension continues to rise and remains high for a prolonged period.

When tense muscles chronically pull on bone, they can cause the bone to become deformed. Psychiatrist Arnold W. Wilson of the University of Southern California School of Medicine tells of Josef, a young man who was unable to open his mouth more than an inch—about half the normal opening. Josef's memories date back to his early childhood in Poland. His mother was a domineering, punishing figure, his father kindly but ineffective. When Josef was five, the war forced his parents to flee Poland. They arranged for him to go to a foster home in a neutral country. They told him, however, that he was going for a summer vacation with relatives.

When he landed at the foreign port, he experienced abject terror and desolation, then years of torment in the foster home. "You must obey me without question," his foster mother would tell him. "Above all, you must not cry."

Ultimately Josef joined his parents in the United States. At thirteen he underwent a sharp personality change, becoming excessively timid and developing a severe stammer. He had increasing difficulty opening his mouth, until he could part his jaws no more than an inch.

At twenty-three Josef consulted Dr. Wilson. After three years of psychoanalysis, his stammer and excessive shyness disappeared. Unaccountably, he remained unable to open his mouth.

Dr. Wilson suggested physiological studies. All efforts to stretch the muscles of Josef's mouth under anesthesia failed. An internist observed: "It's as if there were an invisible chain connecting his upper and lower teeth, and when the chain is taut that's as far as he can open." At last a dental surgeon deduced from an X ray that a projecting point of Josef's jawbone had overgrown, causing it to stick in the arch under his cheekbone. Removal of the excess bone enabled Josef to open his mouth in a completely normal manner.

There is considerable evidence that muscle tension can stimulate the growth of the bones on which the muscle is anchored. Dr. Wilson speculates that prohibitions placed on Josef's expressing his hostility toward his parents and foster mother caused him unconsciously to tense his jaw muscles. The chronic tension led to an overdevelopment of parts of the jawbone, obstructing the range of motion of his jaw.

Muscular tension can thus cause profound changes in stature and bearing. Dr. Graham Fagg, an English pediatrician, has studied how posture can reveal fixed emotional attitudes. One example is what he calls the "fear-hate" posture, which signals pent-up aggression. The person has permanently lifted and drawn in his shoulders and pulled his head downward by tightening the muscles at the back of his neck. This is the posture of the underdog, of the child under attack by an adult.

Another posture is often assumed by a person who sees himself as a member of the Establishment facing down a challenge to his authority. His neck is stiffened up and his chin drawn in—"the typical posture of the judge or the elderly spinster schoolmistress." Fagg observes that recent leaders of Britain's Labour Party have the typical underdog posture, while Conservative leaders tend toward the posture of reined-in authority.

Aching Head

Headaches may be caused by tension of the muscles binding the neck and the head. Additional pain may result from the constriction of arteries supplying the scalp and brain, the product of the tightening of muscles surrounding the blood vessels.

While the vast majority of headaches are caused by emotional stress, headache can be a symptom of a serious bodily condition. Among the organic disorders signaled by headache are kidney disease, liver and gallbladder disturbances, hypertension, and brain tumor. The fact that constipation and indigestion often are accompanied by a headache has given rise to the folk notion that a good laxative is the best cure for an aching head. That may work for constipation, but not for tension.

The tension headache often has symbolic significance. In 1911 a psychoanalyst named Sadger reported on a woman who had three types of headaches: pressure felt from outside, piercing headache, and pressure felt from within. The pressure from outside Sadger traced to an experience in infancy. As a little girl, the woman had been taken into bed by her father and felt the tremendous weight and pressure of his body. Her piercing headache was associated with masturbating with a girl friend when she was three or four years old. Her pressure headaches from within were based on early painful yet pleasurable experiences moving her bowels.

Psychoanalyst Otto Fenichel had a patient whose headache reminded him of intestinal worms he'd had as a child. "What do the worms remind you of?" Fenichel asked.

"Feces," replied the patient.

"And what does the feces remind you of?"

The patient replied: "My thoughts."

Dr. Franz Alexander once had as a patient a middle-aged spinster, a virgin. She felt her headache as an internal pressure threatening to burst her skull. In therapy she concluded the sensation was a symbolic expression of her repressed desire for pregnancy.

Dizziness, like headache, may be of emotional origin. Dr. Gordon Hoople of Syracuse, New York, an ear, nose, and throat specialist, tells of a fifty-year-old woman who had been constantly dizzy for three or four weeks. A physical examination revealed no defects. Reluctantly the woman told Dr. Hoople her story:

She was the youngest child in a family of ten and had enjoyed a wonderfully happy family life. A week before the onset of her dizziness, she learned for the first time that she was born out of wedlock. Her oldest "sister," eighteen years older than she, was actually her mother, and her "mother" was in truth her grandmother. The woman was literally sent into a spin.

Raging Migraine

Migraine is more than just a bad headache. An attack often begins with spots before the eyes, numbness, and speech difficulties. When the headache hits, it always occurs on only one side and is frequently accompanied by vomiting, nausea, chills, and fatigue. After the attack the sufferer usually enjoys a temporary sensation of well-being.

The pain of migraine results from the abnormal expansion of arteries to the cranium, the portion of the skull encasing the brain. Migraine afflicts about one in ten people. Generally it first strikes the victim in adolescence or young adulthood. Common migraine, popularly called a "sick headache," may last from a few hours to several days. A second type, "classic" migraine, is often accompanied by visual distortions, with throbbing pain lasting from four to six hours. The visions reported by some mystics are thought to be visual auras caused by classic migraine. A third type, "cluster" migraine, generally occurs without warning in a series of short attacks, usually from twenty to ninety minutes long, then may disappear for months or even years.

Common migraine seems especially likely to arise in response to specific events. Sometimes merely a loud noise or a bad smell may trigger an attack. Dr. Oliver Sacks, a neurologist at the Albert Einstein College of Medicine, recommends that migraine patients keep two diaries, one recording migraine attacks and the other daily events. Taken together, the diaries may reveal a pattern and disclose what kinds of circumstances precipitate attacks.

Neurologist Arnold P. Friedman of the Columbia University College of Physicians and Surgeons finds that most of the migraine patients he treats come from families which are undemonstrative and which suppress feelings of aggression and hostility. They enforce rigid norms and place high value on attainment —doing well in school, making a lot of money. A young person brought up in such a family is often unable to express his anger toward his parents. This, says Dr. Friedman, leads to emotional conflict, and this in turn triggers migraine.

A migraine sufferer is typically perfectionistic, ambitious, rigid, and orderly. He is excessively competitive and unable to delegate responsibility. Such people often have an attitude of chronic resentment and are frustrated in not being able to live up to their unrealistic ideas. Faced with an insuperable task, they may come down with an attack of migraine. Panic is a frequent precipitant of attacks.

The most common prelude to migraine is repressed rage. Psychoanalysts treating migraine patients have observed that an attack may disappear when a patient gives vent to his hostility. Migraine attacks, says Dr. Friedman, are "inextricably bound with psychiatric symptoms of life situations or a relatively short-term emotional crisis." Even if a particular attack can be controlled, the attacks are likely to recur if the underlying factors are not resolved.

Ralph, for example, was the youngest child in his family. His parents always treated him as a baby and overprotected him. He was brought up by strict moral codes.

As he approached adolescence, he began to realize that these codes were hypocritical. Then at fourteen he was sexually seduced by his twenty-seven-year-old sister. He now felt unworthy of his parents' love. At the same time he was resentful of their moralizing. This conflict plagued Ralph until, at seventeen, he enlisted in the Navy. It was in the process of deciding to enlist that he had his first migraine attacks.

In the Navy Ralph felt secure because of the strict regulations he had to conform to. But for about a year after discharge he felt lost. He drank heavily and was sexually promiscuous—behavior which his parents had always condemned. Abruptly Ralph reformed and decided to become an "honest and sincere" person. He married Edith, who was an invalid and completely dependent on him. They soon had children.

Recently, after some twenty years of marriage, Edith underwent surgery. Her condition has greatly improved. She has become much more aggressive and has gradually assumed the leading role in the family. Their teen-aged children, in the meantime, have become ever more independent.

Ralph has again begun to suffer from migraine. He has been almost incapacitated by his frequent attacks and is in danger of losing his job. He denies that he has any emotional conflicts, but he does recognize that his migraines coincide with the change in his wife's personality and the growing up of his children. His doctor has referred him to a psychiatrist, the only hope he holds for relieving Ralph's condition.

Stresses on the Spine

Joe, an inarticulate, stocky man in his thirties, was married to Millie, a whiny, clinging asthmatic. Complaining of low-back pain, Joe consulted Dr. Howard D. Zucker, now a professor of psychiatry at the Mount Sinai School of Medicine. Dr. Zucker found no evidence of physical damage. He injected novocain into Joe's back. Immediately Joe felt much relieved.

"I knew something of the ways in which people unconsciously use their bodies to express mental metaphors," Zucker recalls. He wondered if Joe might have recently met someone more appealing than the sick, complaining Millie. Zucker mused aloud: "You know, sometimes people lean over backwards trying to avoid temptation."

Joe jerked as if he had been hit, and exclaimed, "Oh, Doc, you've given me back my pain."

In the low-back syndrome, the sufferer's back is stiff and he has difficulty bending and moving. His muscles are abnormally contracted and tender. Often there are shooting pains into his buttocks and legs.

Low-back pain is much like headache. It is very common, and possible causes include some extremely serious bodily conditions. Cancer, tuberculosis, and kidney disorders are among the severe organic problems producing backache.

A high percentage of physiologic low-back pain is associated with the intervertebral disks—the cushions of elastic tissue separating the vertebrae. A disk sometimes ruptures ("slips") or degenerates, often from repeated minor injuries. One frequent cause of back injury is lifting a heavy object with the spine bent instead of straight. A slipped disk may press on nerves attached to the spinal cord or on the cord itself. If the disk degenerates, the vertebrae may pinch a nerve.

Underlying much back pain is the fact that man evolved as an erect, two-legged animal, acquiring a number of physical difficulties that had not troubled his four-legged ancestors. The spine has had the greatest difficulty adjusting to an erect position. Bearing the weight of the head, it must be rigid. Yet, to allow body movement, it must maintain a certain amount of flexibility.

This is accomplished through long muscles which run from the head to the end of the spinal column. A continual tension is necessary to maintain both rigidity and flexibility. A failure of the back muscles to balance correctly may throw unusual stress upon the spine, producing discomfort. Such failure is largely due to abnormal muscle tensions. With the pain, further muscular contraction occurs, intensifying the symptoms.

Most back pain, like most headaches, is either emotional in origin or represents a minor local condition intensified by psychological factors. Emotional conflicts can contract muscles and constrict blood vessels in the back. These tensions and constrictions can mimic the back pain caused by a slipped or degenerated disk.

"Psychologic disturbances play a much more important . . . role in backache than has been generally recognized," says Dr. Louis A. Gottschalk of the University of Cincinnati College of Medicine. One study of patients at an Air Force convalescent hospital revealed that fully 96 per cent of the backache cases were caused by emotional problems alone or by emotional factors complicating a minor organic disorder. Another study, of workers in heavy industry, found that 4 out of 5 of the backaches were caused wholly or largely by emotional factors.

Backache is often a conversion reaction (see Chapter 10), representing repressed desires to attack. The stiffness and pain are thought to stem from an unconscious blocking of movements expressing impulses toward destruction. The muscular contraction giving rise to the pain may keep the conflict from reaching conscious thought, where it would cause anxiety. Guilt-ridden sexual drives play a considerable part in causing muscular tension in the pelvis.

Muscular contractions are common during attacks of anxiety. Some patients in psychotherapy develop backaches when they are on the verge of a breakthrough. Widespread muscular contraction is the patient's last-ditch, anxiety-laden defense against a painful insight.

Myrna, a forty-year-old childless divorcee, had suffered episodes of what was thought to be a slipped disk that had followed a youthful experiment with water-skiing. Her attacks became more severe. Doctors advised surgery.

Myrna was aware that her condition was related to a conflict between her passion for Gary, an unmarriageable man, and her anxiety over the possibility that she would never have a family. She moved to a lonely house in the woods where Gary stayed with her from time to time. For four years she could find no solution. Then one evening after Gary had left she found herself literally "floored" for a whole night, unable to get up.

After this episode psychiatrist Gotthard Booth was able to help her in the resolution of her conflict. Her attacks of "slipped disk" disappeared, and her passion for Gary waned. At the age of forty-nine she found a happy family life with a widower, his children, and grandchildren.

Upright Individuals

Dr. James L. Halliday, a British pioneer in psychosomatic medicine, feels that people with backache are often very upright individuals. They tend to be markedly devoted to duty, and in general show the typical characteristics of an "obsessive" type of personality: cold, perfectionistic, and inflexible.

Since they are rigid, sensitive, and touchy before illness, Dr.

Halliday suggests, it is no surprise that they suffer parallel symptoms in the muscles.

Obsessive types of personality often develop their characteristics as a reaction to a stern authoritarian figure in childhood, usually represented by the father. They develop an overpowering moral conscience, along with a great deal of repressed resentment, hostility, and guilt. All of these make them rigid in their emotions, leading to the same quality in their musculature.

Backache is often a reaction to depression. Psychiatrist Howard Zucker calls one type of low-back pain a "depressive equivalent": It is unconsciously substituted for what otherwise would be an out-and-out case of depression. Sufferers often discuss their backaches in terms that also typify depression. For example, they may be self-condemning ("I have a *bad* back") or despairing ("If I don't get help, I'll kill myself").

Bernie, a thirty-four-year-old art goods salesman, developed intractable low-back and leg pain at Thanksgiving two years ago. Earlier that year his older brother Fred had failed to attend the *bris*, the Jewish ritual circumcision, of Bernie's son, which Bernie deeply resented. Then, as Thanksgiving approached, Bernie and his family were all laid low with influenza. His mother, instead of helping them out in their illness, "went to my older brother, and I was mad."

Retorted his father: "No matter what you say, your older brother is always right."

"Right then," Bernie recalls, "it was like a wall set down in front of me." And in this situation, a typical cause of severe depression, he developed depressive-equivalent low-back pain.

Another major source of backache is the post-traumatic neurosis, a common reaction to sudden physical injury, as from an automobile accident. The sharp impingement of a force threatening to life or limb is likely to cause otherwise normal people to lose the ability to maintain their psychological equilibrium. A major personality upheaval may result immediately after the accident. Often it occurs several weeks later, after the person has become consciously aware of the peril he has been through.

"It is quite apparent that any human being receiving a sudden threatening injury will react emotionally to it and will have to make some psychological adjustment," observes psychiatrist Robert L. Leopold of the University of Pennsylvania School of Medicine. Most sufferers of post-traumatic neurosis become anxious and irritable. Many also develop physical symptoms, of which backache is among the most frequent.

The post-traumatic neurosis is widely pooh-poohed, suggesting to many a "phony" illness or a "padded" law suit. Actually, says Dr. Leopold, "this is no truer . . . than the statement that a person with [any other type of] neurosis is 'weak'."

A claim for compensation may tend to prolong the genuine pain the sufferer feels from his backache. If physical fitness is important to his job, he is likely to be anxious over his poor prospects for employment. His wish to become well may unconsciously be outweighed by the security promised from compensation. He also may have dependency needs he is unaware of, and these may be satisfied by his remaining disabled.

His backache may well worsen as his claims are viewed suspiciously by doctors and rejected by the powers that be. He is likely to take their rejection personally and resent it. "His 'back is up,' " comments Dr. Salek Minc, an authority on the psychological aspects of backache. "It is tense and painful. He will not get better."

Backache in a compensation case usually improves only after the claim is settled. Though some unsympathetic souls may smirk at the "miraculous recovery," physicians such as the University of Cincinnati's Louis Gottschalk nonetheless observe that an early cash settlement greatly facilitates rehabilitation. The pressure to remain ill is off the patient, and he can direct his energies to recovering.

"Massage is a standard treatment for inflamed muscles, and equally valuable for inflamed emotions," observes the physician-novelist Frank G. Slaughter. The subjectiveness of back pain means that sometimes psychotherapy succeeds where all else fails.

In one unconventional course of therapy thirty-seven-year-old

Lydia was administered behavior-modification techniques. Physical rehabilitation specialists at the University of Washington School of Medicine concluded that Lydia's continuous backache was a habit that she would discontinue if she received the right combination of encouragement and discouragement.

When Lydia was admitted to the university hospital, she was given a narcotic prescription whenever she felt pain. This had the effect of encouraging her to feel pain, since she enjoyed the narcotic high that resulted from it. She was consuming four or five tablets a day.

Doctors put her medication on a strict timetable, removing that incentive to experience pain. During the next forty days less and less narcotic was put in her prescription, and finally none at all. Lydia never realized the difference.

Everyone on the staff was instructed to use attention as a reinforcer. When Lydia complained about her pain, the doctors, nurses, and other ward personnel were as unresponsive as they could be. But when she got up and moved around, they were lavish in their praise.

By judiciously giving attention and praise when Lydia showed progress, and being unresponsive when she lagged, the staff saw a remarkable change in her. Virtually bedridden at the outset, by the end of two months she could walk nearly a mile without resting, at twice the normal walking speed—all free of pain.

No Oomph

Backache is not the only condition masking depression. Impotence, insomnia, numbness, gastrointestinal disorders, heart palpitations—all are often depressive equivalents. About a fifth of all hypochondriacs are thought to be suffering from underlying depressions. Of severely depressed patients, about 25 per cent come to the doctor with organic complaints.

The depressed person tends to have symptoms that are generalized and a bit vague. Internist Michael J. Halberstam of the George Washington University Medical School tells of seven depressed patients each of whom made an appointment because of "flu" or a "cold that won't go away." "Their symptoms had nothing to do with viral disease or the respiratory system," Dr. Halberstam recalls. "Instead, they were tired, couldn't concentrate, and had difficulty getting up in the morning."

Two other patients presented themselves to Halberstam with "eye infections." Both had been to ophthalmologists, but their examinations had reported their eyes normal. The eyes of one "felt heavy," and the other "had trouble reading." His actual problem was not visual but in concentrating on what he was reading.

A depressed person often feels pressure and a diffuse, burning pain inside the chest. A physician may ask him: "Where do you feel it?" He is likely to reply, "Right here," and press one hand against his chest—the characteristic "depressive gesture."

Fatigue is another common symptom of the depressed. The sufferer of fatigue may be unable to perform his daily duties. The slightest task may be a heavy burden. Such exhaustion can be perfectly normal after intense or extended stress. A temporary inability to respond to stimuli seems to be one of the body's ways of restoring equilibrium after unusual effort.

But most cases of prolonged fatigue, in which the person feels excessively tired after only mild exertion, arise from emotional causes. A study of 300 patients suffering from fatigue showed that only 20 per cent had an organic disease, such as anemia, vitamin deficiency, or liver disease. "Even in these cases," notes Dr. Nathaniel Shafer of New York Medical College, "it is not certain that the organic illness was the cause of the fatigue since many patients with these diseases do not suffer from fatigue."

Psychiatrist Morris D. Riemer describes inertia, a characteristic of fatigue, as a prevailing immobility of the whole person. There is stifling of initiative, ambition, productivity, and creativity. The sufferer usually attributes his inability to work to his need for rest. He may also say that he fears he'll bungle a job, pointing to the facts that he has difficulty remembering and that he finds it hard to plan his work.

The person suffering chronic fatigue often cannot make decisions involving the slightest responsibility. When given an assignment, he becomes utterly confused and helpless. Throughout the day he remains drowsy. He takes to his bed as a haven.

His reaction to his inertia is generally acceptance rather than objection or amazement. He dwells on his tiredness and his need to lie down. He is unable to be with other people for any length of time without becoming restless; other people find it difficult to be with him since he is depressing and uncommunicative. He finds comfort and safety in blanking out, having no feelings or thoughts. In this trance state he has a sense of invulnerability to any demands put upon him.

A physical impairment, not in itself disabling, can be blown up into a full-fledged disability with the onset of inertia. Dr. Riemer, experienced in psychiatric evaluation of compensation cases, has found that inertia can "lock in" a disability, making a sufferer feel it is impossible for him to work. "The avalanche of symptomatology is incongruous to the degree of physical damage," Riemer observes.

One of Riemer's patients, a fifty-two-year-old maintenance man, slipped while operating a floor waxer. He was propelled against some furnishings and suffered some minor cuts and bruises. He has tried to go back to work several times since, but blacks out each time.

Fatigue has now set in. For no apparent reason and without any exertion on his part, the tiredness overcomes him to the point of his hardly being able to move. He has difficulty reading newspapers and can't concentrate on television. When people talk to him, he gets distracted and can't follow their train of thought. For the most part he feels like doing nothing at all and sits idly, with a blank mind, gazing into space.

While such extreme tiredness seems to express a muscular weakness, the immediate physiological cause may be a deficiency in blood sugar. It is believed that fear and anger are not the only emotions that can stimulate the flow of adrenalin and, in consequence, an increase in the blood's sugar content. Enthusiasm, zest, and purposeful striving are also thought to have a tuning-up effect on the adrenal system.

As you've probably observed in your own experience, work you dislike can be more fatiguing than a more strenuous activity you carry out with interest or pleasure. One reason for this may be that, while you outwardly push yourself through a job, you inwardly withdraw. You therefore lack the needed adrenal stimulation, and indeed go into a "vegetative retreat": Emotionally and physiologically you behave as if you were resting, a state marked by a diminishment in blood-sugar content.

(Doses of sugar, however, have only a short-term effect, if any, in combating fatigue. The condition then may be aggravated as the sugar provokes a counterreaction in the form of an excessive secretion of insulin. A better bet is to avoid sugar altogether, which may also cut down insulin flow and leave a higher sugar content in the blood.)

Fatigue often results from a conflict between passive, dependent wishes and active, aggressive ambition. The fatigued person may suffer a lack of hope of achieving some cherished goal, perhaps a frustrating struggle against insuperable odds. Or he may lack a genuine incentive. Routine activities often are carried out primarily under external pressure or on account of internal compulsion, but not on the basis of absorbing interest.

In many cases the prolonged frustrations create hostile aggressiveness, which leads to anxiety. This may further contribute to an unconscious retreat from activity.

Franz Alexander and his associate Dr. Sidney A. Portis examined nine people suffering from fatigue and showing abnormally low blood sugar. All the individuals had no oomph, no pep or interest in life. They completely lacked initiative at home, on their jobs, everywhere. In most cases the fatigue developed after the person had to abandon a cherished goal, giving up hope and resigning himself to continue with some distasteful routine which he revolted against internally. He went on an emotional sit-down strike.

A businessman seen by Alexander and Portis developed fatigue when the main incentive of his work—the guidance and approval of his superiors—ceased, ironically because he was promoted to a job in which he had more independence and responsibility. A physician developed fatigue attacks after he went into private practice against his own inclination. An artist developed his attacks immediately after he accepted a position in a business office, which required him to give up the art career that was his aim in life. A housewife developed fatigue attacks after her husband refused to have children or to adopt one. Because she had to give up her ardent hope for a child, life became aimless and intolerable for her.

Many fatigued people can be helped by a change in their external circumstances, permitting them to pursue their real inclinations. If internal conflicts do not allow such a simple solution, psychotherapy is generally the only answer.

CHAPTER 17

Iron Hand

Rheumatoid arthritics may sacrifice themselves to rule

"Mama was a powerhouse."

Ginny grimaced. Her mother had complained constantly that she was sacrificing her life for her children. She demanded absolute subservience from them. Her notion of a well-behaved child was one who sat quietly on a chair, touched nothing, and caused no trouble.

Ginny's father, a bus driver, was rarely at home. "I hardly knew him," Ginny recalled. When she was eighteen, he died. She went to work to help support her family.

"I was a whirlwind," Ginny remembered. She would walk several miles from home to work and back. Then, in the evenings, she'd roller-skate for hours. She also did all the building and fixing around the house.

Ginny and a young man named Harold decided to get married. The engagement dragged on. One evening, when Ginny was thirty-four, Harold told her: "I'm not sure I want to marry you."

Shortly thereafter Ginny developed painful swelling in her fingers, toes, and ankles. The doctors gave her the name for her condition: rheumatoid arthritis.

Twin Under Stress

There are several kinds of arthritis (Greek: "inflammation of joint"). The arthritis that occurs in many people after the age of fifty is *osteo*arthritis, a result of aging, trauma to the joints, and normal wear and tear. It is commoner than rheumatoid arthritis and as a rule less damaging. The arthritis referred to in this chapter is entirely rheumatoid.

In rheumatoid arthritis there is inflammation of the joints, usually those of the extremities. Damage is often irreversible. Tissue may fill the fluid sacs between the bones, solidifying the joint and leaving the sufferer stiff and crippled.

The rheumatoid arthritic is three times as likely to be a woman as a man. While the disease can begin at any age, it largely starts off in young adults—the average age at onset is about thirty-five. It is one of the five leading causes of disability among workers.

Rheumatoid arthritis is thought to begin with an inherited susceptibility. An indicator of a person's vulnerability to the disease is possibly a blood protein termed the "rheumatoid factor." It is found in at least half of all rheumatoid arthritics and frequently in their close relatives. Found also in some other diseases, it is rare in the population at large. When the rheumatoid factor is present, it may be a sign that changes have taken place within the person's body, increasing his likelihood of getting rheumatoid arthritis, among other diseases.

Emotional stress evidently tips the balance so that the vulnerable person develops actual symptoms. "Only those individuals with significant emotional conflict go on to the development of disease," theorize Dr. George F. Solomon and Dr. Rudolf H. Moos of the Stanford University School of Medicine. "The rate of progression . . . may be related to the degree of psychic turmoil."

The interplay between emotional and hereditary factors is shown in a study of sets of identical twins of whom one has rheumatoid arthritis. Dr. Sanford Meyerowitz of the University of Rochester School of Medicine and Dentistry reasoned that identical twins have equal hereditary susceptibility to the disease. Therefore psychological differences between them could be significant. Dr. Meyerowitz found each twin in a pair very much like the other in personality and life style, but with this striking and consistent difference: The twin who developed rheumatoid arthritis was involved, shortly before his illness, in a demanding and restricting situation.

He suffered what Dr. Meyerowitz called an entrapment. He had either lost someone close to him or was unable to separate from this person. In all. cases he had undergone severe emotional stress.

Psychological Straitjacket

Another predisposing factor can be the person's craving for physical activity. Rheumatoid arthritics often recall early pleasure in movement. They tend to take on a glow when they speak of hard work, dancing, ball games, and other forms of physical activity. Women tell of being tomboys and recall with delight their girlhood feats on the playing field.

This craving for movement may stem from earliest childhood. Infants seem to have inborn preferences concerning ways of discharging tension. Some babies prefer an employment of their muscles; they may kick and thrash about, or tense opposing muscles and go rigid. Generally these infants grow into active, always-on-the-go children.

Such a child has an overpowering need to use his muscles, as innate to him as crying or sucking is in infants. Some parents, however, find the child *too* active. They may punish him, physically or by withholding affection, for running and jumping as much as he'd like.

In the child's mind, the physical discharge which he urgently needs becomes associated with fear and guilt. He seeks to release tension and anger through physical activity. At the same time, he is inhibited by the disapproval of his parents.

He is put, in Dr. Franz Alexander's phrase, into a psychological straitjacket. The child usually tries to discharge his feelings through muscular activity in acceptable channels. He loves sports and exercise, for these activities bring him relief.

Much as the exercise is enjoyed, in cases of rheumatoid arthritis this effort at relieving tension is only partly successful. The child, and the adult he becomes, is left in a state of muscular contraction. Rheumatoid arthritics commonly recall sleeping in rigid, overflexed positions. Muscular stiffness and pain are frequent precursors of the first arthritic attack.

Moreover, the rheumatoid arthritic as an adult does essentially what he did as an infant: To a greater degree than normal, he reacts to emotional stimuli by unconscious muscular contraction. This physical response has been inhibited since childhood, and so he unconsciously also activates the opposing muscles. This psychological straitjacket, suggests Franz Alexander, may injure his joints and intensify his predisposition to rheumatoid arthritis.

Dr. Irene M. Josselyn, a psychiatrist in Phoenix, Arizona, speculates that the increased tension in a joint may make the joint particularly susceptible to bacterial invasion. Once an infection is introduced, tension increases still further. Arthritic changes may then take place as part of the body's defense against the infection and pain.

Parents and Anger

Not only running and jumping are restricted in the typical arthritic's childhood. Restraining his movement is often part of a family pattern that is generally restrictive. Just as his physical activity is confined, so also is he likely to be kept from acting in accord with his own likes and dislikes. He may especially be forbidden to express his anger over being so restricted. Little girls frequently have the additional burden of being overprotected.

Punishment in such families is common, often involving the curtailment of physical freedom. Discipline tends to be strict, frequently enforced by a father who otherwise may be a distant figure: uncommunicative or often away from home. Many arthritics remember that as children they knew what the boundaries were and they never dared cross them. One patient says of her father: "He never took us over his knee. But he didn't need to."

Aside from a general tendency toward strict discipline, the fathers of rheumatoid arthritics fall into no clear description. Some are recalled as being affectionate, wonderful, kind, good-natured. By contrast, others are remembered as being completely irresponsible, unreliable, unambitious, unreasonable, high-tempered, overdominating.

For example, one father is described by his arthritic daughter as being a habitual drunk and wife-beater. Once he set fire to his wife's bed when she wouldn't sleep with him. He tried to "get fresh with me, his own daughter."

Another daughter of his says that she always lived in fear of him and that he used a leather strap to punish her. "I have absolute contempt for him and can never forgive him," she declares. "If he died tomorrow, I wouldn't shed a tear."

Mothers, on the other hand, are recalled with great consistency as strong, controlling women. "Hard-working," "efficient," "self-sacrificing" are adjectives often used by arthritics to describe their mothers.

The mother of an infant with rheumatoid arthritis was described by a social worker as resembling the frozen-faced farm wife in Grant Wood's painting *American Gothic*. Unemotional and perfectionistic, she held the baby stiffly, with a firmness that inhibited the child's movement. When asked why she never caressed the baby, she replied: "Should one? Wouldn't it spoil her?"

Control may be naked domineering, and many arthritics describe their mothers as cold, intolerant, and impatient. But the armored fist may also be in a velvet glove, and arthritics commonly speak of their mothers in very positive terms: "She had a lovely disposition and was very sweet." "She was a nice, sunny personality and easy to talk to." "Nothing ever bothered her." Further discussion generally reveals that as a child the arthritic was dominated and restricted, however subtly.

Rheumatoid arthritics typically have great difficulty in letting out anger. In a study of 16 women with rheumatoid arthritis, Dr. Solomon and Dr. Moos found only 2 who would admit to ever having any angry feelings. In a situation where most people would be "mad as hell," these women would "feel hurt" or "get upset." Almost never would they reveal their anger to their husbands and children.

The feebleness of their anger is shown by one woman who mentioned a "serious disagreement" with her husband. One night he said, "You're henpecking me." This caused her to rush to her car, drive some distance, park for a while, and think—the total extent of their "serious disagreement." She regarded it as an outburst.

Inability to express anger may make some situations more stressful to the arthritic than to most people. It is generally less stressful for a person to discharge his anger at once, releasing it rather than letting it seethe as resentment. The arthritic's bottled-up hostility thus provides a chronic stress that can promote the formation of this painful disease.

Need to Serve

In addition to controlling their emotional expression, rheumatoid arthritics may seek to dominate in their personal relationships. Franz Alexander notes that patients with rheumatoid arthritis try to control their environment with an "iron hand"—a symbolic and dramatic depiction of the physical deformities often seen in advanced stages of the disease.

The typical female rheumatoid arthritic falls into a well-defined personality pattern. She is generally demanding and exacting toward her children. At the same time she will worry about them and do a great deal for them. At first glance, her self-sacrifice may seem in contradiction to aggressive domination. But, possibly as it was for her mother, it is an unconscious tactic that works: While sacrificing herself for her family, she is also controlling them.

Moreover, her attention to duty is physically rigorous and helps her discharge her pent-up hostility. The self-punishing aspect of her labors for others also serves to relieve her guilt over feeling angry. The way she sees herself is: "dependable"; devoted"; "active"; "a good hard worker."

She tends to be perfectionistic and compulsive. She often is nervous, although this may not be apparent to others since she is likely to be introverted. Beneath her reserve, she is depressed, moody, and easily upset. She generally has a strong need for security and tends to be conservative and conforming.

Jessica, a thirty-two-year-old mother of three, personifies the rheumatoid arthritic's masochistic need to serve. As a small child, she did heavy housework and helped her father do farm chores. Instead of going to college, as did her eight brothers and sisters, she went to live with an older sister in order to help care for the sister's children. The same slavish servitude carried into her own marriage.

After developing rheumatoid arthritis, she spoke as if she needed to justify her wish to be rid of a painful disease: "I am very anxious to get over my arthritis so I can finish having my family." She even sought to offer a charitable reason for entering psychotherapy. "I have no emotional problems," she told her psychiatrist, "but I am happy to do anything for science."

The 16 women in the investigation conducted by Dr. Solomon and Dr. Moos tend to describe their marriages at opposite extremes: as either extremely good or extremely bad. On the favorable side, the women say of their husbands: "He's so good to me it's pathetic." "He's marvelous, very easygoing, calm, and relaxed." "He's patient, kind, helpful." "He's just a good, good person." Many arthritic women have selected compliant and passive men as their mates. Far more husbands have physical defects than can be easily explained by coincidence.

On the other hand, when the marriages are bad, they are very, very bad. "He's mean. He used to toture me," says one woman of her husband. "He gets provoked very easily and is impossible to understand," declares another.

And yet, in keeping with their general martyrdom, the women have tended to endure their marriages. Evelyn, for example, has been married to an irresponsible alcoholic. Even though he has habitually stayed out and spent all their money, she thinks, "Well, maybe I'm at fault," and gives him another chance. She's had few arguments with him.

Debra has received grotesque beatings from her husband. He would choke her and hold the bed covers over her head. Debra has never complained. "I'm probably to blame for the whole situation," she'll say.

Ernestine has lived for twenty years with a man she has nothing in common with. The solution she's long hoped for: "He'll fall in love with somebody else and leave me."

Mona has been married to her husband for twenty-seven years. She's always been sure that he doesn't love her. "But," she says, "I've always felt sorry for him and want to help him out."

Last Straws

A disruption in the potential arthritic's pattern of behavior may lead to the disease.

Symptoms generally develop in conjunction with a stress situation. One woman had her first attack after having to move from town to town, much against her wishes. Another had had a traumatic experience with surgery. A third has been through a year in which her father had a stroke, her brother-in-law died, her mother-in-law came to live with her, and her house caught fire.

Often the stress involves the loss of a significant emotional tie. Psychiatrist Alfred C. Ludwig of the Harvard Medical School cites these circumstances preceding the onset of symptoms in a group of his patients:

• Angela: Death of mother followed by threat of father to remarry

• Marie: Separation from husband by his entry into military service
• Phyllis: Emotional rejection by husband
• Melvyn: Separation from family during military service
• Anton: Entrance to college
• Fritz: Death of grandmother, separation from fiancée, and loss of security from change in employment

The disease may also be precipitated by events which increase hostility. A woman's husband took to beating her. Another woman gave birth, and the child reactivated old sibling rivalry. Sometimes there is a period of idleness, which deprives the person of the physical activity he greatly needs to discharge his hostility.

An increase in the burden of guilt may be a last straw. Guilt may spill over when the person's opportunity for sacrifice becomes thwarted. He may be forced into a situation where he must accept help beyond his ability to compensate with service.

Rheumatoid arthritics commonly deny the effects of the disease and will do everything in their power to remain independent. Their answer to "How are you?" is likely to be "I feel fine" or "I don't need anything from anyone." While in the throes of an attack, they may drive themselves into overactivity, far beyond their capabilities. Often they are unable to accept help, even from their doctors. Among physicians, rheumatoid arthritics are notorious for their resistance to treatment.

Because arthritics typically hate to get help and need to give it, a disabling rheumatoid arthritis condition can spiral. The more impaired an arthritic is, the more help he needs, the less he can discharge hostility and guilt, the worse may become his symptoms. Arthritis frequently recurs when the sufferer is deprived of opportunities to perform masochistic service, perhaps because someone is doing the patient a "favor."

Conversely, the symptoms often subside when self-sacrifice is again demanded by family conditions. One woman with severe arthritis had to be carried about by her husband. He died suddenly. She made an immediate recovery, took charge of everything, even traveled across the country for the funeral.

The disease may afflict women whose unconscious rebellion and resentment against men has been increased by vicissitudes of life—for example, when she is abandoned by a man with whom she felt safe, or when a previously compliant man becomes more assertive.

Sylvia developed painful, stiff muscles immediately after she discovered that her husband was having a love affair. After persistent pain and stiffness for several months, she developed arthritis.

Sylvia's mother was a conscientious but cold woman. Her father had deserted the family when Sylvia was two years old. She felt that her mother's role, and that of woman in general, was unbearable. "I'd rather die than tell my husband I love him, even if I did," she'd say. "Then I could never be on top."

For several months after marriage she refused to have sexual intercourse, and thereafter agreed to sexual relations only infrequently. Though she was a frail-appearing little woman and her husband had been a prize fighter, she ran the home and made all the important decisions.

Her husband's infidelity was her first hint that he was rebelling and she could not control him. When her domination of him was clearly ending, her hostility increased, found no outlet, and her arthritis developed. Subsequently he was unfaithful to her a second time. When she found out, she suffered an abrupt worsening of her illness.

The typical rheumatoid arthritic, then, is a woman who has a physiologic predisposition to the disease. She is brought up in a restrictive household. Her rebellion against her restrictions leads to anxiety. She represses her rebellious tendencies, expressing them only in sports and other acceptable physical activities.

In marriage following her mother's footsteps, she seeks to control the home, employing a self-sacrificing need to serve. Ultimately her successful pattern of dominating her family is interrupted. This intensifies her muscular tension, her characteristic way of responding to stress. Resulting injury to the joints leads to arthritis.

PART VII

Sex Problems

A woman's menstruation, intercourse, and childbirth

may be obstructed by feelings of guilt and fear.

A man's resentment toward women may cause him

impotence and sterility.

CHAPTER 18

Flight from Womanhood

*Guilt and fear can obstruct menstruation, sexual
intercourse, and childbirth*

Although Nancy's menstrual period lasts only one day, her
symptoms are so severe that she often has to be hospitalized. She
has "awful pains" in her head and a "black mist" before her eyes.
She feels giddy, and her lower back and thighs ache. Sometimes
she feels nauseated and vomits. Often her legs give way and she
collapses, then suffers from amnesia.

Nancy's distress springs from a fear of sex, observes her psychiatrist, Dr. Desmond O'Neill of the Chelsea Hospital for
Women in London. An anxiety-ridden attitude toward sex and
bodily functions was instilled in her throughout her childhood by
her "harsh, brutal, and narrow-minded mother."

Red Badge of Womanhood

A negative attitude toward menstruation is reflected—and
also promoted—by popular terminology: "being unwell," "sick,"
"having the curse."

Often, too, a girl has been inadequately prepared for her first
period. So instead of feeling proud and grown up at this sign of
womanhood, she is likely to feel frightened, repelled, and guilty.
If a young girl has her first period in a setting of insecurity and

family strife, she may thereafter be plagued by abnormally painful periods, called dysmenorrhea.

Women with dysmenorrhea tend to fall into two personality types. The first type of woman is like Denise. She is timid and shy, with a small childlike face and fragile physique. As a child, Denise was overprotected and spoiled by her parents, possibly because she was sickly. "I hate to menstruate," says Denise, "because it's so dirty."

The other type of woman is like Fran, who resents the female role. She is hard and aggressive, with a masculine voice and manner. As a child, Fran was a tomboy, fond of rough games and excelling in sports. Most of her friends were boys. The relationship to a man she prefers is as "just another guy" or as "a sister," rather than a lover. She resents menstruation because "it's messy" and because it is an unfair handicap in competition.

Sometimes painful menstruation stems from a wish to retreat from adult sexuality. Eleanor had no menstrual trouble until she went to college, where she had a few sexual experiences. She suddenly began to have extremely painful periods. After marriage her dysmenorrhea became complicated by severe premenstrual tension. Dr. Therese Benedek of the Chicago Institute for Psychoanalysis suggests that Eleanor's menstrual problems began when erotic stimulation made sexuality emotionally threatening.

Dysmenorrhea may also be a reaction against motherhood. May, a mother of two young children, never had any menstrual difficulties or problems with pregnancy. When her youngest child was a year and a half, she began to have strong hostile feelings toward her children. Her periods became severely painful.

Apparently, her doctor concludes, May equated menstruation with abortion and suffered anxiety and guilt because she didn't want more children. She also felt anxious and guilty over her hostility toward her children. Anxiety and guilt can cause abnormal muscular contractions and also disturb hormone balance, the two major physiological factors in dysmenorrhea.

Excessive menstrual bleeding is another symptom associated with emotional problems. Dr. Desmond O'Neill treated 12 women who bled abnormally. None had an organic disorder. Each woman had begun profuse menstrual bleeding at a time of unusual difficulty and distress. Heavy bleeding occurred whenever the woman was in a situation arousing emotional tension.

The women suffered anxiety, depression, headache, and fatigue. One woman would begin bleeding during any vivid emotional experience. After psychotherapy, 7 of the women returned to normal menstrual function. Two improved, but relapsed under new stress.

In a similar study Dr. Helen Flanders Dunbar reports that most of 45 women with excessive menstrual bleeding were cured with "psychotherapy of a superficial sort." Forty-four of the women began bleeding heavily after undergoing a particular sharply stressful situation.

Skipped Period

For emotional reasons a woman's period may stop altogether. This condition, known as amenorrhea, may last from a month to many years. Often it is the result of shock or stress. In London during World War II many women failed to have their periods after heavy bombings. They began menstruating again when they became less tense. Women who have been the victims of rape or attempted rape may develop amenorrhea, apparently a result of sex-related fright.

Failure to menstruate seems to be relieved in particular by hypnosis. One woman had been suffering from amenorrhea for two and a half years. A hypnotist regulated her periods to occur on the first day of each month at 7 A.M. and to last for three days.

Amenorrhea can be *induced* by hypnosis. Hypnotist G. R. Heyer frequently helped dancers and musicians delay or skip their periods so they wouldn't interfere with a performance.

The condition may be associated with guilt and fear about sex. A woman may stop menstruating during an extramarital affair, a cruel irony since she will immediately suspect she is pregnant. A young girl faced with the prospect of intercourse may fail to have her period as an unconscious way of returning to the less threatening days of childhood.

Some young women stop menstruating if they strive to take on the responsibilities of adult life prematurely. They may leave home and take a job before they are emotionally ready. "If in this fashion she approaches adulthood too rapidly," says Dr. Robert E. Nixon, "she may well maintain equilibrium by delaying . . . sexual maturity [through the development of] amenorrhea."

Loss of menstruation may occur when a woman is depressed, particularly about her sex life. Kathy, unmarried at twenty-five, says, "I'm making a mess of my life." She's been the mistress of three married men and doesn't know how to break the pattern. Six months ago she stopped menstruating. Assuming she was pregnant, she left her lover. She in fact is not pregnant, but she hasn't had a period since.

Guilt about incest precipitated amenorrhea in Ann, a nineteen-year-old girl who says she is "not a normal woman." She feels she has too much facial hair, and she hasn't menstruated in two years. She is excessively neat and has an agitated manner. With boys, she is tongue-tied. But she has sexual longings and dreams of marriage.

With great embarrassment, Ann told her doctor that at six she indulged in mutual exploration with her seven-year-old brother. She didn't tell anyone, and she began to worry about death and damnation. At twelve, she says, she yielded to his urgings to have intercourse. Then she was afraid she was pregnant.

Her doctor's sympathetic understanding lessened Ann's guilt about her secret. Two days later she menstruated. But since she did not really resolve her conflicts, her menstrual problem returned several months later.

Pelvic Pains

Guilt and fear about sexual matters can result in a woman's suffering from a wide variety of symptoms in the genital area.

Andrea is a forty-year-old woman who has been married for two years. She came to gynecologist Ernest W. Page of the University of California Medical Center complaining of incapacitating pelvic pain. Doctors had removed her appendix and part of her right ovary, to no avail. Since her marriage, the pain had become worse, and Andrea told Dr. Page she was sure she had "pus and corruption" in her uterus.

Eight years before, she confessed, she had had an illegal abortion which had resulted in a uterine infection. She'd never told her husband about it. Page saw that she became very agitated when she discussed it, and he conjectured that the "severe guilt complex" with respect to the abortion was the basis of her pain. She refused to see a psychiatrist and told Page, "I resent your suggestion that I need one."

Dr. Page referred Andrea to an internist who specializes in psychosomatic illnesses. The internist was convinced that Andrea was suffering from an emotional illness. She had already had any number of tests performed to try to determine an organic cause for her pain. Now she insisted upon having her uterus reexamined for a uterine infection. Since Dr. Page was on vacation, the internist referred her to another gynecologist for a pelvic examination under anesthesia.

As she was losing consciousness, the gynecologist tried an experiment in hypnosis. "I am going to perform some procedures," he told her. "The pain in your pelvis will disappear. But you might have some trouble with headaches for a while."

Shortly afterward, the internist sent the gynecologist this letter: "Damn your hide! Her pelvic pain is better, but her headaches are intolerable, and I can't relieve them. The next time you try hypnotherapy, suggest a pain in your own area, not mine!"

In a while, though, Andrea's pelvic pain returned, possibly because she still could not admit the abortion to her husband. She rejected the suggestion that she seek psychotherapy and has found a surgeon who will remove her uterus. But this operation, like the others, will probably not bring lasting relief from her pain.

Women who suffer from chronic psychogenic pelvic pain usually have had several operations in an attempt to relieve it. In a study of 36 women with pelvic pain, it was found that most had insecure childhoods. They are immature as adults and suffer from various types of neuroses.

Some women suffer from the "irritable bladder syndrome," which is nearly always sex-related. It is characterized by urgency and frequency of urination. "Frequency is sometimes so severe," says Dr. Leon Chertok of La Rochefoucauld Institute in Paris, "that patients are unable to leave their home, because they are obliged to urinate every five minutes."

The illness may take the form of acute attacks or there may be constant discomfort. Women with this ailment may feel continuous pelvic and genital pains—dull, sharp, shooting, throbbing, or burning. Says Dr. Chertok: "One finds patients who are unable to sit, so painful is this whole area."

Often the women can't clearly define or localize the pain. Their descriptions frequently point up the symbolic nature of the ailment. "It's as if I were receiving a knife thrust in the vagina," says one woman. "It's as if something were being forced into the urethra," says another. "Like a little band on my clitoris," says a third.

When organic causes for the syndrome have been ruled out, researchers find that it often coincides with conflictual or traumatic situations in a woman's sexual life, such as divorce, abortion, menopause, surgery on the genital system.

The symptoms frequently are associated with long-standing sexual difficulties. In one study fully 90 per cent of women with irritable bladders did not have orgasms. Many of them refused to have sexual intercourse. The onset of the illness often coincides with a woman's first sexual experience.

In cases of extreme aversion to sex, a woman may involuntarily contract her vaginal muscles, a reflex much like blinking an eye when an object comes toward it. This contraction, called vaginismus, may painfully grip the penis during intercourse.

Indeed, vaginismus may make it impossible for the penis to penetrate the vagina at all. In a study of 100 cases of vaginismus, Dr. Carice Ellison of the Psychosexual Clinic of Maudsley Hospital in London found that some couples had not had sexual intercourse in as much as ten years of marriage. Most of the women felt that their vaginas were "too small" for intercourse, although in no case was this the fact. Surprisingly, their husbands seemed to agree. Apparently husband and wife shared feelings of fear and guilt about sex, which accounted for the amount of time these couples let elapse before seeking help. Possibly these women unconsciously chose as husbands timid men who would not be sexually aggressive. In many cases the woman's mother had been dominant, her father submissive like her husband.

Often women with vaginismus are ignorant and fearful that intercourse will be painful. Guilt about sex makes them expect punishment. Some of the women in the Ellison study thought of sex as violent aggression. They compared their husband's penises to daggers or big snakes. One woman said: "It's like a large leather mouse."

Imaginary Pregnancy

In 1554 Mary, Queen of England, married Philip, King of Spain. Mary was nearly forty, a hard and embittered woman. Philip was handsome, pleasure-loving, and twelve years younger. He didn't particularly like his wife or her country.

Mary was desperate to provide an heir to her throne, for her half sister Elizabeth was waiting in the wings. Before long she recognized the symptoms of pregnancy in herself and made a public announcement. But expectancy became embarrassment and embarrassment became despair as the months of waiting dragged into years. A child was never born, and Philip went home to Spain.

Mary was suffering from pseudocyesis, commonly known as false pregnancy. Like Mary, many of the women who suffer from this condition are extremely anxious to become pregnant. Naomi is a twenty-seven-year-old woman whose husband wants children very much. She's been afraid she would disappoint him by not being able to conceive.

For the past four or five months Naomi has been pleased to note that her breasts have gotten larger and her abdomen has been steadily swelling. She's gained twenty-five pounds. She gets morning sickness every day, and her hands and feet are swollen. Her menstruation has all but ceased.

Recently, Naomi tells her doctor, she's begun to feel the fetus moving. She's been busy making baby clothes. But Naomi isn't pregnant—her condition is entirely psychogenic.

Pseudocyesis also occurs in women who feel the opposite about pregnancy: they fear and loathe the thought of it. Sometimes, too, women may be suffering from a physical condition, such as a uterine tumor, which may terminate menstruation. They may thus think they are pregnant, and begin to show physiological signs.

In some cases of false pregnancy the women are so convinced they are pregnant that they cling to the delusion long after their "pregnancy" has been diagnosed as pseudocyesis. Sometimes they even progress to having false labor pains. Some women will give up the fixation only after being given hormones which at last induce menstruation.

Most women with false pregnancy are between twenty and forty-four years old. Occasionally, however, a child may develop the condition. Doris was a six-year-old girl with curly pale-blond hair and large blue eyes. She looked like a cherub.

For a few weeks she had been suffering from strange symptoms. Her abdomen was enlarged. She had nausea and vomiting in the morning, and pain in her stomach. Her ankles were swollen.

In the hospital, doctors ruled out any organic disturbance. "My tummy is big because I'm going to have a baby," Doris told the hospital staff. "I want a baby to take care of and God put a baby inside me by magic."

She wanted a baby, Doris told one doctor, so she could have a playmate. She put oranges under her nightshirt and showed him that now she had breasts. "My mother is too busy and tired to have another baby, so I decided to have one."

To check on every possibility, her doctors decided to perform an exploratory operation in Doris's abdomen. Before the operation Doris was given an enema. Her distended abdomen immediately became much smaller. It had been filled with gas and fecal matter.

The doctors proceeded with the exploratory surgery. They found nothing wrong and removed her appendix. Although they informed Doris about her operation, she became convinced that the doctors had actually taken her baby out of her.

When it was time for Doris to leave the hospital, her mother refused to take her home. She'd visited Doris only once in the month-long hospital stay and showed no interest in the child.

Doris was placed in a child-care center. Still convinced that she had been and was pregnant, Doris often told her counselors that she had a baby inside her, that she could feel its head and feel it move. She refused desserts, because "when you're going to have a baby you can't eat sweets."

Doris's mother was a promiscuous, sadistic, and neglectful woman. She'd had four illegitimate children and a great number of lovers. Some of them had beaten her and her children. To punish Doris, her mother would often lock her in a small room for two or three days without food. Another punishment was forcing her to eat cereal mixed with mustard and pepper.

Doris had no toys and often had to do the housework. She wasn't sent to school. "I don't think my mother loved me at all except when I was a baby," she said.

For more than a year Doris was in the care of a warm and encouraging woman, psychiatrist Joae Graham Selzer of Harvard Medical School. It became clear to Dr. Selzer that Doris, abused and deprived, wanted very much to be grown up, "believing that only adult women had anything of value: rings, high-heeled shoes, husbands, and babies." Doris had intense wishes to be fed and loved and filled up. She was also painfully lonely. The conviction that she was going to have a baby helped relieve these feelings.

With Dr. Selzer's help, Doris gradually gave up the belief that she had been pregnant. Instead of playing mother to dolls, she began to experience happy moments in playing as a child. Finally Doris was adopted by an older couple who had waited many years for a child. She feels wanted and loved, and her symptoms have not returned.

Conflict Over Motherhood

Farm animals respond to social stress with disturbances of the reproductive cycle. If you move hens from one barn to another, their egg production will fall off for a time.

In the female of our species, too, stress—particularly stress resulting from conflicts over pregnancy and birth—can interfere with the reproductive process.

Women who are ambivalent about becoming mothers are likely to develop complications during pregnancy. "It is now generally accepted," says Marilyn T. Erickson of the North Carolina Memorial Hospital, "that psychological disturbances can adversely affect the course of pregnancy, labor, and delivery."

Women who suffer from such complications as toxemia of pregnancy, excessive nausea and vomiting, and abnormal weight gain tend to be more anxious in general than women with normal pregnancies. They are likely to be more concerned with their bodily functions, more withdrawn. They often have negative attitudes toward sex, menstruation, and marriage. Typically, they are more dependent, resentful, and childish than women who carry to term without complications.

In nearly all cases the women have a marked ambivalence about the expected baby. They have a conflict between wanting and not wanting the unborn child.

Anxiety about the birth of a child may be responsible for many cases of prolonged and difficult labor and delivery. In one study women who had expressed fears for themselves and their babies had a much higher rate of complicated labors than women who were not particularly fearful. In a study of women enduring prolonged labor (more than twenty-four hours), researchers found a strong correlation between anxiety and the duration of labor. Women who suffer from prolonged labor were also likely to be introspective and sensitive. Their relationships with their mothers were generally poor.

Unconscious fear of pregnancy frequently keeps a woman childless. Rena married at twenty and wanted to start a family right away. Three years later she hadn't conceived, and she went to a doctor in great distress.

The first test the doctor performed to find the cause of her sterility was to see if her Fallopian tubes were open. It is through these tubes that the egg passes into the uterus, where it meets the sperm. If the tubes are blocked, the egg cannot possibly make contact with the sperm.

For many years it was thought that only an injury or an infection could cause the Fallopian tubes to close. "It is now known," says Flanders Dunbar, that "an emotional crisis or shock may close these tubes just as it may make one clench one's fist." A woman's emotional problems may make her Fallopian tubes involuntarily contract at the time of ovulation—when the egg is produced—making conception impossible.

Rena's doctor found that her Fallopian tubes were closed during ovulation. But some days later, when ovulation was over, she was tested again. This time her tubes were open. "The obvious conclusion," says Dr. Dunbar, "was that the muscles contracted involuntarily at the time of ovulation."

The reason for Rena's inability to conceive probably lay in her fears about pregnancy. As a young girl she had heard several conversations among women about the dangers and pains of pregnancy. She heard gory and probably exaggerated stories and developed a great deal of anxiety about becoming pregnant. After marriage Rena thought she had escaped her fears. "There's nothing I want so much as a baby," she would tell people. But her involuntary nervous system expressed her buried fear by keeping her from becoming pregnant.

Other women may unconsciously avoid pregnancy by becoming ill for the few days when conception is possible. Although consciously they ardently desire children, they may develop severe headaches or nausea during ovulation and thus avoid intercourse. Or they may become extremely tired during those days, or may plan a trip away from home. The net result is that intercourse takes place only when the woman can't become pregnant.

Still other women, for no physical reason that doctors can determine, simply fail to ovulate. Their ovaries stop producing eggs, and it is thus impossible for them to become pregnant. Claire entered psychoanalysis when a doctor diagnosed her inability to ovulate as a "psychological block." She worked out some problems in relation to her father. Almost immediately she became pregnant.

The typical infertile woman was ailing and timid as a child. She was lacking in self-confidence and had difficulty getting along with other children. As an adult, she seems self-centered and cold. Actually she may be simply unable to show affection.

Other women unable to have children may be aggressive and domineering, professionally as well as personally. They often are excessively orderly and well-organized and may unconsciously feel that a child would disrupt the carefully maintained organization of their lives.

Psychogenic sterility can apparently be relieved in any number of unlikely ways. Women frequently become pregnant just after taking the test to see if their tubes are open. This happens even though the test shows the tubes were closed. Sometimes a woman has been sterile for many years. She finally decides to do something about it and makes an appointment with a doctor. Before the consultation even takes place, she becomes pregnant.

A childless couple may conceive after they have adopted a child, sometimes after they've merely decided to file for adoption. A woman's sterility may be the result of a lack of confidence in herself as a mother. If she adopts a child—or even resolves to try to adopt one—she may gain self-confidence and become able to have a child of her own.

Dr. Bernard Sandler of the Infertility Clinic at the Victoria Memorial Jewish Hospital in Manchester, England, has arrived at this conclusion: "A woman may conceive, not because of any particular treatment, but because she [is] emotionally ready to deal with conflicts about conception."

"Why Do I Kill So Many Babies?"

Unconscious resistance to motherhood can play a significant part in the occurrence of miscarriages. Many women who have a history of miscarriages have difficulty in accepting the role of mother. Although such women may express strong desires to have children, unconsciously they have conflicts which result in miscarriages.

Some investigators suggest that miscarriage may come about when emotional factors precipitate endocrine changes, such as an increase in adrenalin secretion. This can cause premature contractions of the uterus.

Endocrine changes may also bring about a weakness in the musculature of the cervix, the opening between the uterus and the vagina. This might lead to premature expulsion of the fetus. Although the condition is found among women who have normal pregnancies, it is frequent in women who habitually miscarry.

In one study nine women who had had at least three miscarriages were operated on to correct this defect in the cervix. Premature widening of the cervix was prevented, and the women were able to carry their babies to term. Indeed, in a sense they were forced to do so, for surgery made the cervical muscles resistant to opening.

Of these 9 women, 3 became emotionally disturbed enough to seek psychotherapy as their pregnancies progressed. After delivery, fully 5 of the other 6 women developed psychoses. "By . . . forcing the patient into motherhood," the researchers conclude, "the underlying unconscious emotional conflicts [were] precipitated and exacerbated." Since these women could not resolve their conflicts physiologically by miscarrying, they were forced into psychological forms of expression.

At thirty, Viola had had nine miscarriages. She and her husband were profoundly affected by the trauma of each lost baby. At last Viola decided that she would never bear a live child unless she could "figure out why I kill so many babies."

As she began exploring her feelings about having a baby, Viola remembered that her father had frequently given her enemas when she was a child. She'd been warned to hold them in as long as she could, until she felt "stretched." Thereafter, when something inside her made her feel stretched, "I had to get it out." Her miscarriages had all occurred at the point in pregnancy when she began to feel stretched and had to get out what was inside her.

With tears and anger, Viola now recalled the basis of another conflict she had about childbirth. She remembered her father telling her mother that he would not live with a woman who had a baby. She'd thus come to despise her mother and all other women who had babies. As an adult, she had the unconscious fear that her husband would despise her if she had a child.

Women with a history of miscarriage frequently have unstable and unhappy marriages. The wife often has an infantile attachment to her husband together with hostility toward her mother. In an unsatisfactory marriage a woman may feel that the birth of a child may put an end to fighting with her husband and prevent divorce. But on another level she may know that a baby can never save a marriage, and may thus miscarry.

Sometimes organic problems combine with an emotional upset to trigger a miscarriage. One overwrought woman in her forties was suffering from an abnormality of the uterus. At a family dinner one Wednesday night she had a violent quarrel with her father-in-law and had a miscarriage that night.

It is possible for quick and apt psychotherapy to help avert a miscarriage in progress. One young woman wanted ardently to have a baby. But in her fourth month of pregnancy she suddenly started to have profuse hemorrhages. Her gynecologist considered surgically terminating the pregnancy.

The husband, however, decided to call in a psychiatrist. From her dreams, he determined that the woman was suffering from a conflict with her father. She was his only daughter, and he was unusually attached to her. He had objected to her marriage. When she married despite his objections, he sank into a deep depression and cursed her, wishing her never to have any children.

The woman realized how this problem with her father might be interfering with her pregnancy. Her bleeding stopped. Several months later she had a baby boy.

CHAPTER 19

Pursuit of Manhood

Resentment toward women can lead to
impotence and sterility

In some primitive cultures the husband takes to his bed when his wife is having a baby. When the child is born, he takes care of it and submits to any fasting, purification rites, or taboos attendant to the birth of a child. The custom is called couvade, from the French meaning hatch or incubate.

Modern men also suffer from a couvade syndrome, having psychogenic symptoms during their wives' pregnancies. Surveys show that as many as half of all expectant fathers have physiological disorders ordinarily associated with women approaching childbirth.

One man suffered from a large array of problems during each of his wife's six pregnancies, although he was healthy in between. When his wife became pregnant, he lost his appetite and had indigestion. Headaches and insomnia troubled him, and he often had morning sickness. Like a pregnant woman, he had to urinate frequently.

During his wife's labors he would have abdominal cramps and chest pain. He could barely concentrate and found himself doing odd things. During one labor he assisted in the hatching of chicken eggs.

Although women rarely have excessive dental problems during pregnancy, their husbands frequently do. One twenty-four-year-old man developed a toothache about halfway through his wife's first pregnancy, when she developed a complication and had to go to the hospital. His dentist could find nothing to account for it. The usual painkillers afforded him little relief. The wife, on the other hand, had several medical problems during her pregnancy, but none of them was toothache.

When his wife was discharged from the hospital two weeks later, her husband's toothache disappeared. It came back during her labor. Then, like most couvade symptoms, it disappeared for good when the baby was born.

Researchers speculate that the couvade toothache derives from the old folk saying, "For every child a tooth." With poor nutrition, a woman's bones may lack enough calcium during pregnancy, but her teeth are unaffected. Nevertheless, many people, even medical students and nurses, believe that pregnancy commonly damages a woman's teeth. Apparently, many husbands believe it as well, and their teeth may begin to ache.

Lost Erection

A tall husky man showed up at the medical clinic. With great embarrassment he confessed: "I'm losing my nature." He was down to having intercourse only twice a night, he explained. On the weekends one of his three girl friends was beginning to complain.

This bedroom athlete suffers from anxiety about impotence, the inability to have sexual intercourse. The anxiety may account for his heroic performance, for our culture makes sexual prowess essential to the self-esteem of most men. Psychiatrist A. H. Chapman of the Greater Kansas City Mental Health Foundation has remarked: "Though a man be a dignified judge, a captain of industry, a national golf champion, or a distinguished physicist, he feels worthless and debased if he cannot perform an act which he shares in common with dogs, rabbits, cattle, and rats."

In the Middle Ages it was believed that impotence was the result of sorcery: A witch tied knots in a cord or strip of leather and hid it. Until the man found the cord and untied the knots, his impotence would persist. Modern man is not much more enlightened—witness the large number of "potency formulas" available in any drugstore.

At one time or another every man is impotent. An erection develops when minute reservoirs under the skin of the penis fill with blood. The mechanism controlling the reservoir valves is so delicate that a slight stress will cause them to open, rendering the penis limp. Anxiety, fatigue, a strange bedroom, coughing children in the next room, any of a hundred other disturbances can make a man sexually inactive for a night or several weeks. If he begins to brood and worry—or if his partner is taunting or complaining—the condition can become chronic.

Impotence is almost entirely psychogenic and is the most common psychosomatic complaint of men. In only about 5 per cent of cases is impotence largely physical. Many diabetic men suffer from the condition. Prostate surgery in older men sometimes produces impotence. Alcohol and drugs can markedly interfere with potency. Remarked Shakespeare of drink: "It provokes the desire, but it takes away the performance."

In the most common type of impotence, the penis either will not become erect or will lose erection shortly after entering the vagina. If a young man's first attempt at sex with a woman is traumatic, chronic impotence may result.

Allan had always felt guilty and fearful about masturbating. As a child, his father was punitive, and his mother conveyed to him the "badness" of sexual activity. When Allan was eighteen, friends took him—half drunk—to a prostitute. He was unable to perform, and the woman teased him about it. Now, in addition to guilt about masturbation, Allan was deeply worried about his masculinity.

In the years ahead, Allan often had rich sexual fantasies about women, particularly when he masturbated. He tried on numerous occasions to have sexual intercourse. Now, at thirty-one, he was still unsuccessful and was finally moved to seek psychotherapy.

A man can be impotent with one woman but not with another.

He may be impotent with his wife, but not with other women. On the other hand, he may be impotent with any woman except his wife. On occasion, a man is impotent just those times of the month when his wife is most likely to conceive.

Some studies have shown that the impotent man was often suppressed by his parents. He was never encouraged to be a man, or at least not as much of a man as his father. He is likely to be relatively ignorant about sex and he usually has severe guilt feelings about sexual activity.

Deep down, he often hates women and is ambivalent about men. His impotence may be a way of withholding sexual pleasure from his wife. Eddie is a forty-three-year-old scientist who's been unhappily married for years. Although he and his wife, Pam, do not express anger openly, they have other ways of showing their dissatisfaction with each other.

When Pam is angry at Eddie, she gets a headache and goes to bed for two or three days, leaving him to take care of the house and the children. When he's angry with her, he becomes silent for days.

Sexual relations between them have not been frequent for years, but did occur with some regularity. Then Eddie found another way of expressing anger at his wife. He became unable to have an erection. Pam doesn't complain, but she sometimes walks through the house restlessly at night. Since Eddie's impotence involves a conflict with Pam in particular, it is probable that he would be potent with other women.

Impotence may also be a way of trying to repress sadistic impulses and fantasies. Some men, says Dr. Therese Benedek of the Chicago Institute for Psychoanalysis, unconsciously fantasize that "the penis is a powerful destructive organ which could do irrevocable harm to the loved woman." This may spring from the man's unconscious anxiety over castration, which Freudian psychoanalysts believe is the basic motivation of sexual inhibitions. The unconscious fear of losing the penis may interfere with developing erections, or may cause loss of erection shortly after intercourse begins.

Some men in their thirties or forties become impotent after

many years of normal potency. Often the impotence coincides with a symbolic loss of potency in work: not getting a raise, losing a job, being passed over for promotion.

Andre is a thirty-five-year-old executive who's been married eight years and has two children. His parents considered his success their goal, and made tremendous sacrifices to send him through college and graduate school.

Competitive and ambitious, Andre was successful while still young. Last year, however, several important opportunities fell through. Andre began doubting his competence and judgment. His wife was understanding and encouraging, but anxieties nagged at him, and he became depressed.

At the same time, Andre noticed a gradual slackening of sexual performance. He became progressively less capable of having intercourse with his wife. After his first few failures apprehension and humiliation made it almost certain that he would fail again. Before long he was unable to have an erection.

Another sort of impotence is premature ejaculation. This condition is characterized by the man's ejaculating too soon—just as his penis touches the vagina, or at the first few movements, or sometimes even before his clothes are off. This may happen on occasion to a man who has abstained for quite a while.

If the man ejaculates prematurely several times in succession —and if the woman criticizes or derides him—the condition may become chronic. The man fears that he is failing to function adequately as a man and that he is disappointing the woman. He may feel anxious, depressed, and guilty, states of mind which increase the risk of future failure.

Since there is no chance of the woman having an orgasm through coitus, she is likely to be even more frustrated than the man. Indeed, it is often the wife who first brings the condition to a doctor's attention.

Sometimes premature ejaculation, like impotence, expresses hatred, rejection, and contempt for the woman. It may also be a method of revenge, either for something the woman has done to him or for something another woman (often his mother) has done to him.

When Arthur would begin caressing his wife, he would soon either lose interest entirely or ejaculate prematurely. As a child, Arthur recalls, he was often left in the care of a governess. He conjectures that his birth was probably unplanned, since he seemed to interrupt a project his energetic mother was working on. She continued to work on it for years afterward.

Arthur remembers bitterly how he resented his mother's frequent desertion of him. When he protested by fierce crying, he was punished for his "temper tantrums." He felt terribly thwarted by his mother. He felt a wish to thwart her in return.

This desire to thwart a woman was carried over to his sexual relationship with his wife. He was trying to frustrate and punish her. She intuitively perceived the hostile nature of the act and reacted hysterically. She would cry and strike him with her fists. Arthur would then become remorseful and depressed.

Holding It In

Children often have the notion that the sexual act their parents perform has to do with urination, so closely are genital and urinary functions connected both in the anatomy and in the unconscious. Conflicts about sex often show up in urinary disorders.

Psychiatrist Charles William Wahl and his associates at the University of California studied eight patients who couldn't urinate. "Sexual conflicts of a repressed character were discovered in all of these patients," reports Wahl. "The genitals were considered tabooed areas of exploration . . . and pleasure. The performance of the act of urination had become . . . invested with forbidden, voluptuous, erotic feelings."

Men may unconsciously equate the length and force of their urine stream with sexual competence. This is one reason why some men are unable to urinate in public places, especially when others may be looking.

Masturbation can unconsciously be equated with urination and lead to urinary retention. As a teen-ager, Stan had masturbated a great deal; "excessively" is the word he used. At twenty-eight he married, but found himself completely impotent. He conjectured that continued masturbation might be the cause of his impotence, and he stopped masturbating.

Still impotent, he found that now he could urinate only in certain circumstances. He had to be in a darkened room with his eyes closed and with absolute silence. These were also the circumstances under which he used to masturbate.

At forty, Stan was admitted to the hospital because of his chronic urinary retention. Doctors found no organic reason for his trouble. They concluded that for Stan urinating had become a substitute for masturbation.

Often, men with urinary retention are repressing hostility and murderous rage. At the same time, they may unconsciously believe that, like those repressed emotions, urine is poisonous and defiling. The primitive logic of the unconscious then may translate the emotional act of holding in emotions into the physical act of holding in urine.

Doubts and guilts about sexuality may combine with repressed aggression to produce urinary retention. Roger, now a scientist in his forties, was an only child. His father was often away, and when home was disapproving. Roger felt he was never good enough to win his father's encouragement or interest. His mother was distant and unloving.

As a child Roger was extremely concerned about the size of his penis. He remembered equating free and forceful urinating with sexual prowess. He was also troubled with guilt about masturbating. As an adult he was unable to urinate in a public place and feared he might be a homosexual because he became sexually excited seeing another man urinate.

Roger described his eighteen-year marriage as "hell on earth." Before finally getting a divorce, he often wished his wife dead. He had also had strong death wishes toward his mother. She died of a stroke, and he regarded his wishes as magically and frighteningly fulfilled. He was very anxious for several months after her death, fearing he'd be killed in retaliation.

After his divorce Roger felt burdened and guilty about his new sexual freedom. It aroused an underlying guilt about promiscuity and raised doubts in him about his sexual adequacy.

Now a chance factor brought Roger's problems to the fore. On a scientific expedition to India, Roger witnessed the death of a colleague from urinary disease. One of the symptoms was an inability to urinate for two or three days before death.

Roger developed the conviction that he would die in just six months. When five months were up, he began to have trouble urinating. He was certain that this symptom foretold his death. Then for four days he was unable to urinate at all. Roger went to the hospital in a state of panic. Tests clearly established his symptoms as psychogenic.

At the hospital, psychiatrists helped Roger see how his death wishes toward his wife and mother led him to expect to die, for the primitive logic of the unconscious follows the principle of tit for tat. His own great fear of death was reactivated by the way in which his colleague died, and it helped account for Roger's choice of symptoms. The symptom was also an expression of Roger's guilt and feelings of inadequacy about sex. It had the advantage, too, of taking him out of the sexual arena. Roger accepted these interpretations and made a quick recovery.

It is possible for emotional trauma to affect not only the retention of urine but the actual *production* of urine. Twenty-nine-year-old Fred had been married for six months. It was a stormy marriage, marked by frequent quarreling.

After one particularly violent fight Fred found it impossible to urinate because he had no urine. He didn't feel like urinating either. But he perspired a great deal and his bowel movement was more fluid than usual. Fred's doctor found his bladder empty, but no signs of illness. During the next few days his bladder returned to normal.

Fred began to notice that after any upset he would have no urine for from ten to twelve hours. Admitted to the hospital, Fred continued to be unable to urinate. After thirty hours he was hypnotized and given a posthypnotic suggestion: four hours afterward he would urinate. At exactly that time Fred passed a normal amount of urine.

For the sake of experiment Fred was again hypnotized and told not to urinate. He was given a normal amount of fluids and placed under the constant observation of a nurse. His bowel movements were not abnormally fluid, and he had no urge to urinate. Thirty-two hours later there was still no urine in Fred's bladder. Mysteriously, the fluid evidently stayed in his tissues. The doctors retracted the hypnotic suggestion, and soon Fred urinated.

Bad Seed

Edgar is a quiet man who has been married seven years and has no children. His sperm is normal, but Edgar has very little interest in sex. "I'm too tired from teaching to have intercourse more than twice a month," he says. With sex so infrequent, it is highly unlikely that his wife will ever become pregnant.

Sam is a twenty-five-year-old man, pleasant and bland. Nothing bothers him, nothing excites him—including sex. He is interested in having intercourse with his wife only when he is fully rested on Sunday afternoons. His wife is sexually responsive and wants to have children. Sam is not particularly anxious to. "We might adopt two children," he says.

The male's non-interest in sex is one of the reasons for a couple's childlessness. The typical such male comes from a household dominated by an aggressive mother. She controlled him by threatening to withdraw her love if he wasn't a "good" boy. Among the bad things of life, she conveyed to him, was sex. Observes Dr. Robert N. Rutherford of the University of Washington, an expert in the treatment of infertility: "Somewhere in his sexual conditioning he learned that sexual activity with women was naughty and that erotic behavior with himself or with a female might lose him his most precious possession—his mother's love."

As a young adult, he is likely to be unaggressive sexually. The girls he dates may consider this a sign of strength on his part and respect for them. After marriage, however, the woman will expect him to become more interested in sex.

Alas, the man will be tentative and will often expect his wife to initiate the sexual activity. She may become resentful and uncooperative, trying to goad her husband into making the first move. The result is a stalemate, with very little sexual activity and no children.

In some cases ignorance about sex is the cause of childlessness. Homer and Ellen had been married six years and wanted children. Ellen said they had intercourse every one or two months. During a physical checkup, however, her doctor was surprised to find that Ellen had an intact hymen which admitted only a fingertip.

She finally told her doctor the truth: Homer attempted intercourse only once or twice a year and had never penetrated. Ellen and Homer had both had strict religious childhoods and had no idea about how reproduction was accomplished.

Sterility in males is sometimes the result of a psychogenic problem with sperm. "There is little doubt," says Dr. Z. Palti of Hadassah University Hospital in Jerusalem, "that sterility in the male due to disturbed spermatogenesis [production of sperm] may result from emotional stress."

Under conditions of emotional stress some men chronically produce less sperm or none at all. To collect sperm for analysis, men have to masturbate. In some men this act produces anxiety and guilt, and their semen produced by masturbation may show no live sperm. On the other hand, the semen ejaculated in sexual intercourse will have a normal live sperm count.

Ambivalence toward fatherhood and other emotional problems cause some men to be sterile only when their wives can conceive. Chris is a mild-mannered public accountant who has been married for seven childless years. His childhood was stormy. When he was nine, his mother divorced his alcoholic father. His stepfather was critical and jealous of the boy, so Chris decided to live with his father.

The father died of cancer when Chris was in high school.

When Chris married, he was very shy and had never had sexual intercourse. Now doctors have found that Chris's sperm is perfectly normal during or just after his wife's period—a time when it is rare for a woman to conceive. Two weeks later, when she is ovulating and likely to conceive, Chris produces semen with no live sperm.

In some men such ambivalence about fatherhood can combine with hostility toward the wife—and can result in a rare condition called retrograde ejaculation, also known as dry coitus. Instead of being ejaculated out of the penis, the semen is propelled backward into the urinary bladder. This wrong-way run can be caused by organic disorders such as diabetes mellitus and neurological diseases. It sometimes follows the removal of the prostate.

In some cases, however, no organic cause is found. Dr. Palti theorizes that during orgasm emotional stress triggers the muscle which closes off the urethra, the tube through the penis. Thus obstructed, the semen travels backward into the bladder.

Michael is a thirty-two-year-old man who's been married for seven years and purports to want children badly. He's been very much disturbed at his inability to impregnate his wife. All Michael's thoughts have become focused on his infertility.

Doctors have found that Michael has the normal feelings of orgasm during intercourse, except that his sperm passes backward into his bladder. Michael, it has turned out, is extremely hostile toward his wife. His infertility is an unconscious way of punishing her by depriving her of children.

PART VIII

Breath, Skin, and the Supernatural

Respiratory infections, tuberculosis, and asthma

have emotional components, as do many skin conditions,

such as itches, eczema, and hair loss. Psychosomatic

principles may account for seemingly supernatural

phenomena like religious zealots bleeding from

Christ's wounds, and voodoo deaths.

CHAPTER 20

Out of Breath

Colds, TB, and asthma have emotional components

"I have so much difficulty breathing," eighteen-year-old Katharina told Sigmund Freud. "Sometimes it catches me so that I believe I am choking. It suddenly comes upon me. There is first a pressure on my eyes. My head becomes so heavy, and it hums so that I can hardly bear it, and then I become so dizzy that I believe I am falling, and then my chest begins to press together so that I cannot get my breath."

Freud came to the conclusion that Katharina's breathing problem was associated with anxiety. She had her first attack after finding her uncle in an act of adultery. The uncle had earlier made attempts to seduce her.

Freud determined that Katharina's breathing difficulty was related to traumatic sexual feelings related to this uncle. Indeed, she realized that the frightening face she hallucinated during her choking attacks was the distorted, enraged face of her uncle. She recalled that when he found out that she had told her aunt about the incident with the other woman, he threatened to "do something to me . . . his face became tense with rage."

Choking Fits

Shortness of breath is often a symptom of respiratory or heart disease. In many cases, though, it is purely a reaction to stress. A truck loader named Charles complains of chronic shortness of breath. "I can't seem to take a deep breath and get enough air in," he says. "I can feel my heart pounding like a son of a bitch."

Charles says he gets tired after only ten or fifteen minutes of work and then has to sit down. He often stays home from work two or three days a week. He's concerned about his heart. "It seems to be getting worse," he says. "Often at work I'll take my pulse, it'll move one, then three, then skip, then one, then skip. That's when I start losing my breath." Extensive laboratory tests find no physical abnormality. Occasional skipping of the heartbeat is perfectly normal.

Charles's doctors conclude that he is anxious and depressed. He is excessively preoccupied with his body and inordinately affected by minor upsets. He is particularly concerned about being less and less able to meet his everyday responsibilities.

Of particular importance is the fact that Charles's young son died just a year ago of congenital heart disease. "If the baby cried he would turn blue," Charles recalls. "When he died he went right before our eyes." In recent weeks Charles's breathing difficulty has worsened. His doctors believe that this is due to his unconscious reaction to the anniversary of his son's death combined with his usual fears about his health.

Many people react to stress by hyperventilating, breathing too deeply or too fast or both. You may notice this in yourself when you're in the grip of a strong emotion. Some people hyperventilate briefly in their sleep, reacting to feelings arising from dreams.

Usually hyperventilation passes after a few minutes as you recover your equilibrium. But if you continue to hyperventilate, other changes in your body can soon occur. The level of carbon dioxide in the blood is reduced, causing numbness, tingling, and rapid heartbeat. Before long you may feel weak and faint. You may experience abdominal cramps.

The hyperventilator may also feel short of breath and suffocating. One woman describes hyperventilating as "gasping for breath like you're drowning . . . swimming as far as you can and then you can't go any farther." Says another hyperventilator: "You have to breathe fast in order to keep from smothering." Remarked a student who hyperventilated for an experiment: "I was taking in deeper breaths and at the same time felt as though I were hardly breathing."

If a person continues to hyperventilate, he may begin twitching all over and have convulsions. Although quickly reversible with medical aid, the experience is likely to be terrifying. People who have been through a severe attack of hyperventilation often feel they're having heart attacks or losing their minds. Others are certain they're on the verge of death.

The Cold War

Some people seem extraordinarily susceptible to colds. They are frequently laid low with stuffed heads, bleary eyes, aching muscles. Since everyone is exposed more or less constantly to cold germs, why do some people contract colds so much more than others?

Recent studies suggest that psychological factors play an important part in determining who will get cold symptoms and who won't. The symptoms may arise due to emotional bugs as well as microscopic ones. For example, the mucous lining of the nose swells in response to emotional stress as well as to viral attack. After you've cried, you usually find that you have to blow your nose. For a short while afterward you may have the typical symptoms of a cold. Psychiatrists sometimes find that chronic cold symptoms are a substitute for suppressed crying. After the person discharges his grief and sorrow, his supposed cold disappears.

Sometimes the symptoms can bring about changes which a person desires, causing him unconsciously to cling to the cold. One young man had a squeaky effeminate voice which was a standing joke to his friends. When he had a cold his voice sounded husky and fierce. He had colds frequently and for weeks at a time.

Another man with an abnormal predisposition to colds was subject to fits of uproarious sneezing. In his daily life this man was passive and inadequate. When faced with a situation that made him feel resentful, he remained outwardly unassertive, but he developed a cold and began to sneeze. In therapy it became clear that his sneezing represented a release of hostility, a safe expression of resentment. When he learned to use his aggressive impulses more constructively, he stopped having colds so often.

Investigators have worked with cold-prone people at the first sign of a cold. In the course of an interview devoted to interpreting the emotional needs for the cold, the person's symptoms often abate or even disappear. A cold coming on may thus be averted by psychotherapy.

For many people, having a cold can serve an important emotional function. It allows a person to have a legitimate excuse to rest and regress for a few days, possibly protecting him from serious emotional problems.

Dr. Martin A. Jacobs and his colleagues at the Boston University School of Medicine studied male college students who suffered from bad sore throats and severe upper respiratory infections. Most of them, the investigators found, had recently been through distressing life changes which they could not cope with. Unable to meet the challenge, they were disappointed in themselves and felt like failures. The respiratory infection soon followed.

Rob, for example, had started college only two months previously. He was under great pressure to do well, since his brother had been expelled the year before. Rob had expected college to be easy, but now he was dangerously close to flunking out.

In addition, he felt guilty for going out with girls at college, since his girl friend back home had made him promise to be true to her. Thanksgiving recess was coming up, and Rob felt that when he went home he'd have to tell his mother about his low grades, his girl about his dating. He was discouraged and fed up with himself. Rather than go home, he thought of joining the Army. In this setting he developed a bad sore throat.

Alex, another student in the study, had just moved away from his invalid mother into an apartment of his own. His father was separated from his mother. Alex hoped to make him responsible for her and get himself off the hook. At the same time, he knew that his father was involved in gangland operations and was marked for murder. He was unable to influence this extreme situation and soon developed a severe upper respiratory infection.

Emotional factors may also influence a person's susceptibility to tuberculosis germs. At the beginning of the century, most TB patients lived in dirty, airless, damp and overcrowded rooms. They were usually undernourished. Living in such conditions, it was thought, made people vulnerable to TB germs.

In recent years, however, researchers have noted that TB patients are often well-nourished and have lived in comfort all their lives. Investigators conclude that a person's state of mind can increase his susceptibility to TB and influence the outcome of his treatment.

Susan, for example, developed TB after a long period of emotional turmoil. Ten years before, she'd had a child by a man who was an alcoholic. She was unable to decide whether or not to marry him. Still indecisive, she had another child with him. They finally married, but soon divorced.   '

She married a temperamental artist. Dissatisfied with herself, she took it out on one of her sons who was much like her. She had a negative attitude toward men and great feelings of weakness. After a year of this marriage she developed tuberculosis.

In the sanatorium Susan's condition grew worse instead of better. A psychiatrist found that she had strong suicidal drives. Susan described a dream about drowning and remarked that it was the kind of death she would prefer. The psychiatrist noted the similarity between death by drowning and collapse of the lungs in TB.

With continued psychotherapy and medication, Susan's condition began to improve. An improved mental outlook brought with it a corresponding improvement in her lungs. "Until there was some attention paid to her emotional problems," says the psychiatrist, "not even the most expert physical care could halt the deterioration of her lungs."

The Paper Rose

The young man was allergic to roses. Suddenly someone handed him a rose. He began to sneeze and his eyes teared. His nose began to run. A noteworthy fact: The rose was made out of paper.

A group of hay-fever sufferers were sitting in their allergist's waiting room. They noticed that the pollen count on the doctor's chart showed a great deal of pollen in the air. Several of the patients immediately developed severe hay-fever symptoms. Actually the pollen count was not nearly as high as the chart showed. The allergist had arbitrarily raised the figure to test his patients' reactions.

These anecdotes illustrate the strong link between allergy and psychological factors. An allergy is a condition of unusual sensitivity which some people may develop to substances harmless to others. Called allergens, these substances include foods, pollens, house dust, cosmetics, animal hair, medicines, and many others.

When an allergen is taken into the body, antibodies are produced. They treat the allergen as if it were a threatening microbe or dangerous foreign body. After repeated contacts with the allergen, the allergic person may show symptoms in such particularly sensitive tissues as the nose, the eyes, the bronchial tubes, and the skin.

Allergic reactions seem to be partly hereditary. People with allergies commonly have a family history of allergy. But a potentially allergic person may never show any symptoms of allergy. Some people are found through skin tests to be sensitive to many substances, yet they have been totally free of allergic symptoms.

Emotion can cause symptoms to appear in people who have a potential for allergic reactions. A person who has a hereditary predisposition to allergy may have his symptoms triggered by stressful situations. Hay-fever victims often have more severe symptoms during periods of emotional turmoil. Conversely, they may display few symptoms during periods of tranquility, even though the pollen count may be high.

Asthma, among the potentially most serious allergies, is characterized by obstruction of the small bronchial tubes. In an asthma attack, the lungs become distended and breathing becomes increasingly labored. The sufferer makes wheezing noises as he tries to force air through the plugged tubes. His neck muscles strain, his veins become engorged, his chest swells.

The attack may last for a few hours or for days and even weeks. Although the victim is in intense distress, the asthma attack itself is rarely fatal. But asthma does contribute to an estimated 5000 deaths in the United States each year, chiefly among people suffering heart and lung damage.

About three out of four people who have asthma are allergic to one or more substances. The asthma is often precipitated by emotional states. Dr. Hyman Miller and Dr. Dorothy W. Baruch have observed and treated allergic patients in Los Angeles for more than twenty years, and have confirmed that asthma attacks "may be set off and continued by emotional causes."

Parents of asthmatic children are often fully aware of the emotional component of the disease. One mother reported that her son could bring on an attack at will. "The first few days of school went fine," she said. "Then he heard he could stay away from school by having asthma. He would work up an attack and come home." Instead of allowing him to come home during an attack, the mother arranged for her son to lie down in the health room. "He never got an attack at school again," she reports.

Researchers note the power of suggestion in bringing on an attack of asthma. One investigator put asthma sufferers in a situation in which they had previously been exposed to allergens and developed attacks. Now they again had asthma attacks, even without the presence of the allergen.

Even more dramatic are the results of research conducted by Dr. Thomas Luparello and his colleagues at the Downstate Medical Center in Brooklyn. They told each of forty asthma sufferers that he would be inhaling increasing concentrations of the allergen which usually brought on an asthma attack.

After inhaling, fully nineteen patients showed significant disturbances in breathing. Twelve went on to have full-blown asthma attacks, with wheezing and shortness of breath. Actually, they hadn't been inhaling allergens at all. The substance was a harmless salt solution.

So great was the strength of suggestion that one woman, told she was inhaling pollen, developed hay fever as well as asthma. Afterward, true to the sufferers' suggestibility, all the asthma attacks were successfully treated with a placebo.

The First Cry

Researchers remark that an asthma attack resembles the infant's first cry—"the shrieking, helplessly sprawling newborn child with blood-red swollen face," in the words of investigator Eduardo Weiss.

The similarity may be more than coincidental. Evidence suggests that the asthma attack is a substitute for crying, that it is a suppressed cry. Most asthma patients, says Franz Alexander, spontaneously report that it is difficult for them to cry. "Moreover," he says, "attacks of asthma have been repeatedly observed to terminate when the patient could give vent to his feeling by crying."

A number of male asthmatics were frozen into supermasculine roles—cold, tough, unemotional. Their asthma improved when they were able to weep over feelings of loneliness. Some asthmatics learn to avert attacks by weeping.

The newborn child's cry is thought to express an urge to return to the safe haven of its mother's body. Correspondingly, most asthma patients have dependent attachments to their mothers and an intense need to maintain a strong bond with them.

Often an asthmatic child's overdependence on his mother is fostered by the mother's overprotectiveness. The child may come to feel that he is valued only when he is sick. Dr. Melitta Sperling of the Downstate Medical Center in Brooklyn has termed this the "psychosomatic type" of relationship between mother and child. "The child is rejected by his mother only when he is healthy and evidences strivings of independence. . . . [He] is in fact rewarded for being sick and helpless by the special care and attention given to him at such time."

Dr. Sperling feels that the child's asthma attacks are in compliance with the mother's unconscious desire to control the child. By his illness, the child shows how dependent he is on his mother, thereby gratifying her wishes. But the child at the same time is bound to feel frustration and resentment toward the manipulative mother.

Dr. John C. Coolidge of the Massachusetts General Hospital describes one case in which a mother derives a "conscious and direct sense of pleasure . . . from her child's asthma." The mother, May, was herself asthmatic and felt that her son Teddy was very much like her in being asthmatic too.

"It made me feel better and closer to him when he was sick," May says. "I drop everything and just tend to [him]. . . . When Teddy gets asthma I breathe with him almost the way my mother does with me. I can understand him better, feel so close to him." This close bond between May and Teddy excludes her other child and her husband.

The first attack of asthma is sometimes precipitated by a breaking of the dependent bond between mother and child. Alfred, for example, slept in the same bed with his mother. Then, when he was 11, he touched her breasts one night. The mother sent Alfred away to camp, which was his first separation from her. Immediately he got his first attack of hay fever. Years later Alfred married against his mother's wishes and developed asthma.

In some cases children have severe asthma which fails to respond to the most intensive therapy. For such intractably asthmatic children, allergist Murray M. Peshkin of New York recommends the "parentectomy," the removal of the child from his parents.

In 1940 Dr. Peshkin helped establish a residential treatment center in Denver designed to rehabilitate the child with intractable asthma. Children between the ages of five and fifteen are accepted from all over the world and remain there for from eighteen months to two years. In the meantime, the parents often undergo psychotherapy in an effort to improve the quality of the home life the child will return to.

"At the Institute in Denver," Dr. Peshkin says, "the parents know that the independence of the child is encouraged. The parents must adapt to a child who has been subjected not to the neurotic needs of parents to maintain their children at childhood levels, but to demands where every opportunity is given for maturation to proceed uninhibited by parental fears." Particular care is given to helping the parents establish a good relationship with each other, which Dr. Peshkin considers a "necessary condition for the successful treatment of intractable asthma."

The success of the parentectomy, a largely emotional balm, has been remarkable. Fully 90 per cent of the children recovered substantially or completely while at the treatment center. Of these, 97 per cent maintained this improvement during the year after returning to their homes.

Many parents of asthmatics steadfastly insist that the child's condition is due entirely to an allergy, with few or no psychological causes. This insistence often represents the parent's effort to stave off feelings of guilt and blame. But the evidence in many cases suggests that the allergic component of asthma is secondary to the emotional.

Children who develop asthma at home often recover immediately in the hospital. The parents may explain: "He's allergic to the dust at home." But even if the dust from the house is vacuumed up and discharged into the hospital room, the child remains free of symptoms. The instant his parents come to visit, however, he may get an attack. One of Dr. Peshkin's recurrent problems is to remind parents that the child is in the Denver Institute not only because of mountain air but because it's away from home.

CHAPTER 21

Thin Skin

From itching and hair loss to the seemingly supernatural

The skin is a prime target for the allergic response. Hives, eczema, and rashes are common skin allergies. Yet these and other skin disorders also occur in people who show no sign of allergy in skin tests.

As you've probably noticed, your skin is extremely responsive to your state of mind. The next time you're feeling a strong emotion, notice what's happening to your skin. If you're feeling embarrassed or conspicuous, are you blushing? If you're afraid, does your skin feel cold? Are you in a sweat about something? Or hot under the collar with rage? When you're impatient, are you literally itching to do something?

Dermatologists and psychiatrists find that emotions play a large role in disturbances of the skin. Itching, for example, is often associated with inhibited sexual excitement. This is particularly true of itching of the anus or genitals, erogenous zones which give sexual pleasure when they're scratched. At the same time, the pain and rawness which result from scratching is built-in punishment for the sexual feelings.

One recently widowed woman was being treated for urinary incontinence with a urethral apparatus. Erotically stimulated by this treatment, she became anxious and guilty about her sexual feelings. She developed an itch on her genitals. By scratching, she gratified sexual feelings. And her sleepless nights punished her for her forbidden pleasure.

Dr. Herman Musaph of the University of Amsterdam in the Netherlands concludes that "itching may result from the thwarting of an emotion." He treated one woman who had an intense itch on her head, throat, and arms. It soon became clear that she experienced this itch whenever she was on the verge of feeling anxious. "Itching here," says Dr. Musaph, "was a substitute for anxiety."

He has also found that repressed rage can produce itching. One man had to wait for Dr. Musaph much longer than he expected. Just as Musaph entered the waiting room, the man experienced a frenzy of itching.

Emotional states seem to play an important part in skin diseases such as acne rosacea and eczema. Eileen is a twenty-two-year-old girl who all her life has suffered on and off from eczema. She would get red, raw itching areas on her face, arms, and legs, and would scratch at the sores furiously. Often she would wake up in the morning to find the sores weeping and bleeding. She thus spent much of her life looking disfigured.

Eileen had one affair after another. With immediate gratification of sexual impulses would come guilt. When it became clear that the men were not really interested in her, she would feel depressed and hostile toward them. Whenever a romance ended, Eileen would suffer a severe eczema attack.

She saw a number of dermatologists, but they all told her they couldn't help her because her condition was due to emotional factors. Eileen at last sought psychotherapy.

In the course of three years of therapy Eileen came to see that she felt hostile toward her father for abandoning her and her mother in her childhood. She looked to men to satisfy her longing for a father, using sex to make them fulfill her needs. When they inevitably abandoned her, she turned her guilty, hostile feelings against herself by disfiguring herself. Finally Eileen was able to form a good relationship with a man she later married. Her skin lesions cleared and have not recurred.

Dr. Rene Spitz, in a study of infants who developed eczema,

concluded that they generally have an abnormally great need to be touched and held; their skin surfaces cry out for stimulation and gratification. At the same time, their mothers often don't like to touch and care for them, depriving them of the very contact they crave.

Bald as a Billiard Ball

Sudden hair loss (alopecia) is another skin-related condition that seems strongly associated with emotional factors. The victim may lose hair in patches, or he may become as bald as a billiard ball, losing even his eyebrows. Dr. Irwin I. Lubowe, a New York dermatologist, and Dr. Irvin H. Cohen, a Maryland psychiatrist, agree that frequently "there is a history of sudden nervous shock preceding the occurrence" of partial or total hair loss. The common incidents, in their experience, are the sudden loss of a loved one, a car accident, financial loss, or broken engagement.

Treatment of the condition is usually unsatisfactory, especially after it's been present for five to ten years. About 30 per cent of the people who lose all their hair continue hairless.

In his private practice Dr. Cohen was treating thirty-two-year-old Sarah for severe anxiety attacks. After some months and a great deal of improvement he suggested that her therapy might be terminated. Soon afterward she lost a patch of hair from her scalp the size of a silver dollar.

Thereafter, whenever Sarah thought about stopping therapy, she found that she would lose an excessive amount of hair. In the course of therapy it became clear that the significance of hair to Sarah grew out of her relationship to her mother. She recalled that as a child her mother would relentlessly comb Sarah's curls until they were perfect. Often Sarah would fuss over the pain of her mother's combing out the tangles. She remembered times when she was afraid she would be late for school because her mother would literally hold her by the hair to continue the combing.

Her hair became the focus of feelings of sexual attractiveness. Sarah knew that men found her sexually desirable, and she was afraid of the possibility of losing control of her sexual impulses. Becoming bald made her feel ugly and afforded some protection from sexual advances. When Sarah had worked through her difficulties with her mother, she was able to leave therapy without losing any more hair.

Dr. Robert D. Mehlman and his associates at the Children's Hospital Medical Center in Boston investigated the relationship between traumatic events and hair loss in children. One two-and-a-half-year-old boy suddenly lost all his hair, including his eyebrows and eyelashes, two weeks after he'd been abruptly weaned from his bottle. His hair partially grew back when his mother gave him back his bottle.

Several children seemed to lose hair as a response to feelings of abandonment. A girl, two and a half, lost clumps of hair after her mother left her father and took the children to live with their grandmother. An eight-year-old girl had experienced hair loss since she was two, whenever her parents' tumultuous marriage seemed about to break up. Another child started losing hair after her mother took a job.

Hair loss was associated in several cases with the birth of brothers and sisters. A ten-year-old boy lost a great deal of hair after the birth of a sibling. His mother had abruptly transferred all her attention from the boy to the baby.

The Wounds of Christ

One curious skin condition strongly associated with emotional factors is painful spontaneous bruising, termed autoerythrocyte sensitization. The condition usually affects women and is characterized by a sudden pain in an area of the body. A lump appears, then discoloration as blood rises to the surface. There is bleeding under the skin. The bruises can be very large and nearly incapacitating.

Dr. Frank Gardner and Dr. Louis Diamond of Harvard have

found that most people with spontaneous bruising at one time suffered a physical trauma, such as being hit by a car. They speculate that these patients developed a skin sensitivity to their own red blood cells. In one experiment they injected a small amount of a patient's blood into his skin. Within a few hours the area was painful, swollen, and bruised.

People who develop this condition usually exhibit psychological symptoms of emotional origin, such as severe headaches, fainting spells, numbness, partial paralysis. Dr. David P. Agle and his associates at Case Western Reserve University Medical School in Cleveland observe that the character structure of patients with the condition "exhibits strong hysterical and masochistic features."

They've found, too, that episodes of spontaneous bruising are frequently related to emotionally stressful situations. One woman saw a gunshot wound above the right knee of a man who resembled her brother. Soon she developed a painful bruise in the very same spot.

Another woman experienced spontaneous bruising on the back of her right hand after she had strongly resisted an impulse to strike an annoying person. As she walked away she felt an initial burning sensation and saw that the back of her right hand was turning black. A second episode occurred when she was about to shout in anger at her son for carelessly causing an accident. But when she saw him covered with bandages she felt tense all over and noted a burning sensation on the back of her left leg. She saw a red lump and then a slowly developing huge black-and-blue mark. She was so incapacitated that she had to be hospitalized for several weeks.

A person with spontaneous bruising sometimes bleeds through his skin. Usually the skin doesn't break, but the blood seems to ooze up through the hair follicles.

A combination of spontaneous bruising and psychogenic bleeding may account for the phenomenon of religious stigmata, the wounds of Christ on the cross. Through the centuries more than three hundred people, mostly women, have been recorded as afflicted with Christ's injuries. A stigmatic may spontaneously bleed from her hands, feet, and sides, or from the shoulder where Christ bore the cross. Some have scalp bleeding as if from a crown of thorns.

Most stigmatics have disturbed personalities and have long shown hysterical symptoms. Theresa Neumann, a Bavarian peasant girl, was hospitalized with severe hysteria after an accident. For several years she was unable to walk, speak, or hear. But when Saint Theresa of Lisieux was canonized in 1925, the girl's symptoms disappeared.

Theresa Neumann first experienced stigmata—on her hands and feet—on Good Friday, 1926. Half a year later she began bleeding from her scalp and side and to weep bloody tears. She would frequently go into trances and speak in a strange tongue before her stigmata began to bleed.

The appearance of stigmata sometimes follows an intense religious experience. In Sicily in 1918 a thirty-year-old friar named Padre Pio suddenly cried out in pain and fell unconscious to the floor during prayers at the monastery. He was bleeding from his hands, feet, and side. A doctor who examined him reported that "the lesions in Padre Pio's hands are covered with a fine membrane of a pink color. There are no fissures, no swelling, no inflammation of the tissues."

Padre Pio later recalled that as he prayed before the crucifix, five beams of light seemed to shoot from the wounds of Christ to the same areas of his own body. He'd felt unbearable pain and joy before he fell into a faint and began to bleed.

Today, more than fifty years later, Padre Pio still bleeds from these wounds.

Voodoo

Another seemingly supernatural phenomenon is the voodoo death.

For hundreds of years the Western world has received reports of mysterious death among primitive people. A young African unknowingly eats a taboo wild hen. When he discovers his transgression, he shudders with fear and is dead before the day is out.

In New Zealand a Maori woman eats some fruit. When told it has been taken from a forbidden grove, she exclaims: "The sanctity of the chief has been profaned. His spirit will kill me." Within twenty-four hours she is dead. An anthropologist observing African tribes reports: "I have seen more than one hardened old [warrior] dying steadily and by inches because he believed himself to be bewitched."

Among the aborigines of Australia, anyone who breaks a tribal taboo or offends an enemy may be cursed by having a bone pointed at him. Reports Dr. Herbert Basedow from direct observation: "The man who discovers that he is being boned by an enemy is a pitiable sight. He stands aghast . . . his cheeks blanch . . . his eyes become glassy and . . . his face becomes horribly distorted. . . . He attempts to shriek, but usually the sound chokes in his throat."

The man may froth at the mouth. His body begins to tremble and his muscles twitch. He writhes and moans. After a while he crawls home, where he sickens and refuses food. Inevitably he dies. But if the medicine man reverses the curse, a near-dead person can be restored to perfect health within hours.

From experiments with animals, Dr. Curt P. Richter of Johns Hopkins Medical School suggests that voodoo deaths in man result from overstimulation of the parasympathetic nervous system, which causes the heart rate and breathing to slow and body temperature to drop. Within fifteen minutes after Richter trimmed the whiskers and facial hair of a rat, depriving the animal of possibly its most important means of contact with the outside world, the animal—otherwise unharmed—would be dead.

Death among these rats seems to follow from a strong feeling of hopelessness and isolation. In primitive societies voodoo death seems to stem from similar emotions. W. L. Warner, who worked among aborigines in Australia, observes that a recipient of a curse is suddenly thrust into a position of utter isolation. Everyone he knows—all his family and friends—casts him into the realm of the taboo and withdraws from him. They act toward him only as if they expected him to die. The victim, himself a believer in black magic, becomes what his tribe wills him to be and concurs in committing a kind of suicide.

Dr. Walter B. Cannon of Harvard Medical School suggests that voodoo death may be explained as "due to shocking emotional stress—to obvious or repressed terror." For, says Dr. Cannon, the phenomenon is characteristic among human beings "so primitive, so superstitious . . . bewildered strangers in a hostile world." Their fertile imaginations "fill their environment with all manner of evil spirits capable of affecting their lives disastrously."

It is thus even more surprising that an apparent voodoo death can take place in twentieth-century America. Dr. James L. Mathis of the University of Oklahoma Medical Center reports what he calls a "sophisticated version of voodoo death"—a suggestible son evidently hexed by his domineering mother.

Robert bought a nightclub with financial help from his mother. She kept the accounts of this very successful business. After more than a decade Robert received a very good offer for the club. His mother was distraught at the prospect of the sale. She warned: "Do this and something dire will happen to you."

Two days later Robert had a mild spell of wheezing. The day after the sale was completed, he came down with a bad attack of asthma, a condition he'd never had before. He had to be hospitalized. "Something will strike you," his mother warned again.

Thereafter, Robert needed to be hospitalized three or four times a week for asthmatic attacks and convulsions. He wondered if his mother was not right, after all. He felt that his asthma condition was hopeless.

"After all," he reasoned, "she's been infallible in her predictions." He'd been married twice. "It won't last," his mother had predicted each time. Both marriages ended in divorce.

With the help of a psychiatrist, Robert was able to see some connection between his asthma and his mother. He felt he was "allergic" to her. Still, he was afraid of her.

Now in reasonably good health, Robert considered investing

his money in another venture, one excluding his mother. He called her to tell her of his plans.

"Regardless of what the doctors tell you," she warned him, "remember my prediction of dire results."

In less than an hour Robert had succumbed to a fatal attack of asthma.

PART IX

Heart Disease and Cancer

Heartfelt emotions can lead to circulatory diseases,

including hypertension and heart attacks. Some forms

of cancer evidently occur frequently in certain

personalities—studies link despair and suggestibility

to the development of malignant growths.

CHAPTER 2 2

Heartfelt Emotions

. . . can lead to circulatory diseases, including
hypertension and heart attacks

In the early seventeenth century William Harvey, the physician and anatomist who discovered that blood circulates through the body, noticed the effects of emotion upon heart action.

"Every affection of the mind that is attended with either pain or pleasure, hope or fear, is the cause of an agitation whose influence extends to the heart," he wrote in his *De Motu Cordis* (*On the movement of the Heart*). Harvey marveled that "in modesty the cheeks are suffused with blushes; . . . in lust how quickly is the member distended with blood and erected!"

Popular expressions also recognize the close link between states of mind and the heart. Someone who suffers a grave disappointment is said to be brokenhearted. In great happiness the heart leaps for joy. In fright the heart is said to stop. After a terrifying crisis you might hear someone say, "My heart was in my mouth." Your heart goes out to someone in sympathy. You give your heart in love.

A series of stressful situations can profoundly alter the heartbeat. Eleven-year-old Don had never had any heart problems. Then one morning he woke up with a rare and often fatal heart abnormality, paroxysmal ventricular tachycardia. His heart was beating excessively fast and irregularly. It was enlarged and his chest was congested. From lack of sufficient oxygen he was starting to turn blue.

In the preceding few months Don's life had changed drastically. He'd had his own room in the same house and had essentially the same friends and activities for eight years. But recently his family had begun to build a house. The construction took longer and was more expensive than they had anticipated. While the house was under construction, Don's family rented a small house.

Don had to share a room with his two younger brothers. A neat and ordered person, Don found his new living arrangement filthy and chaotic. His father had to work overtime to help meet the unexpected expenses of the new house. The family missed their summer vacation. Meals and bedtimes became irregular.

When the family finally moved to their partially completed house, Don was faced with the additional pressure of going to a new school. It was soon afterward that his heart problem developed.

For several months after the initial attack, Don continued to have bouts of pounding and erratic heartbeat. When his parents attempted to control his misbehavior, he would throw himself on the floor screaming and thrashing. Fearing he would have a fatal heart attack, his parents began catering to Don's every whim so as to avert his temper tantrums. Don would escalate his demands, and his parents would angrily and guiltily accede. Since medicine seemed unable adequately to control his heart condition, Don was referred to a psychiatric clinic.

To help illuminate the way in which Don's emotions were affecting his heart, psychiatrists had his parents keep a heart-rate diary. Four times a day they took Don's pulse and made a note on his general mood and recent events.

Soon a pattern began to emerge. When Don was impatient, frustrated, annoyed, or competitive, his pulse rate was markedly higher. Don's statements in such situations evidenced a wish to speed things up, possibly accounting for his unconsciously speeded-up heart rate. Once while waiting an hour for a bus at the depot, Don's heart beat excessively fast. "I wanted to get out of there," he recalls. "I kept waiting for the bus to come."

Normal pulse readings were associated with feelings of contentment and achievement. Lower pulse readings also followed the resolution of unsettling experiences. On one occasion, for example, Don was frustrated and disappointed over not being able to take part in some school sports for medical reasons. After he released his pent-up frustration with a good cry, his pulse rate was the lowest since the diary had begun.

The same was true after Don received a deserved punishment from his parents. This helped convince his parents that they could enforce discipline without fear that Don would have a fatal heart attack. Before long his temper tantrums disappeared. With psychotherapy and continued medication, Don has remained in good health.

High Pressure

During states of emotional tension the circulation of people with both normal and diseased hearts is slow to recover after exercise. Often, merely discussing a charged subject can cause changes in the circulatory system. In one study researchers found that when people talked about highly personal matters, there were changes in their heart rates and electrocardiograms greater than after physical exercise.

Stress is increasingly recognized as a precipitating factor in heart disease (the general term covering a number of illnesses of the circulatory system). Fully 76 per cent of patients admitted to one large city hospital with heart disease had emotional factors as a precipitating cause.

The same was true of a high proportion of cardiac patients in a Cincinnati clinic. Investigators found that during the relatively stable periods in their lives, the heart conditions of these patients improved. The rate of progression of the disease slowed, and the intensity of their symptoms was reduced. On the other hand, sudden worsening of heart problems was almost always related to severe stress in these patients' lives.

Some studies suggest that the personality of the typical heart patient makes it difficult for him to avoid stress. Indeed, he seems to have built it into the fabric of his life. He is typically a person with great control and persistence, constantly striving for success and accomplishment. He usually works toward long-term goals, postponing early gratification. He is aggressive and competitive. Often he has a sense of urgency about time, since he is plagued by deadlines.

As in most research of this sort, there is contrary evidence that must be considered. For example, heart attacks were relatively rare before the early 1900s. A pure personality theory would presume that people before then did not have the drive, ambition, and other characteristics often ascribed to present-day victims of heart attacks. Internist Lawrence E. Lamb warns: "One must be most cautious in ascribing to personality or psychic factors the dominant role in such events."

At the same time, contemporary researchers compared a group of hard-driving men who constantly had to meet deadlines with a second group of the same age who were easygoing, noncompetitive men. Both groups were similar in their drinking, smoking, eating and exercise habits—the only significant difference was in personality. In the hard-driving group the incidence of heart disease was seven times greater.

Researchers have found a particularly close association between emotions and hypertension, high blood pressure. In hypertension the blood pushes with greater force against the artery walls. The heart tends to enlarge, often with impairment of its functioning. Hypertension is a major contributor to stroke and often damages the kidneys and adrenal glands. Untreated, it is usually fatal within twenty years.

In a small percentage of cases chronic high blood pressure can be traced to a specific physiological disease: Cushing's syndrome, toxemia of pregnancy, lead poisoning, ovarian tumor, pyelonephritis, and other kidney disorders. For most cases of hypertension the cause is not organic but psychological.

In people with normal blood pressure strong emotions can cause a temporary rise in blood pressure. Hooked to an apparatus that was registering his blood pressure, a pilot was about to take off when a mechanical difficulty forced him to wait. For four hours technicians poked around, trying to find out what was wrong. As the pilot's frustration and anger mounted, so did his blood pressure. Finally he took off. Once in the air, his blood pressure dropped. It rose briefly again during the preparations for landing. On another occasion a pilot hooked to a blood-pressure apparatus overheard a disparaging remark which he took personally. Immediately his pressure jumped almost 50 per cent.

People who are going through stress may experience high blood pressure for prolonged periods. Dr. Stanislav V. Kasl of the Yale University School of Medicine and Dr. Sidney Cobb of the University of Michigan kept track of several dozen men whose jobs were threatened. Each man was followed through several stages: while he anticipated being fired, when he lost his job, while he was unemployed, during his probationary re-employment, and finally when he achieved stable employment in a new job.

Kasl and Cobb found that the men's blood pressure stayed high while their employment was unstable, dropping only after a new job was secure. Anticipation alone produced as great a rise in pressure as actual unemployment.

The stresses of modern life may particularly produce chronic hypertension in people who by personality are unable to express their frustration and anger. The typical hypertensive patient is unassertive and overcompliant. He seems a remarkably controlled person. Like other heart patients, he is usually overconscientious and overresponsible, often taking on the burdens of others. This makes him feel resentful, but the hypertensive person demands control of these hostile feelings.

Hypertension often occurs in a setting in which an individual has a particularly intense need to express his hostility and assert himself, but circumstances won't permit him to. For example, a man might be required to do more on his job without being paid more. At the same time, he may be threatened with losing his job should he assert himself.

Hypertensive people usually have had a disturbed relationship with their parents. Jules had grown up during the Depression, and his family was very poor. His father was unemployed and became a heavy drinker, often beating his mother.

"In my childhood," Jules recalls, "there was always an unseen fear, either that my father would come home drunk and beat my mother, or that a bill collector would knock on the door, or a car would hit me." Jules believes his blood-pressure problem began between the ages of nine and twelve. By the time he was nineteen, he had a full-blown case of hypertension.

Jules works for a construction company and is constantly moving around the country. He works hard and has risen steadily. "I love to work. I thrive on it," he says. He never takes vacations and has very little recreation. "I can't sit down," Jules says. "I always have to be moving."

Jules is still an exceptionally fearful person. He worries constantly about his health and the possibility of car accidents and tunnels caving in. At forty-two, he has a case of severe hypertension, and he is particularly concerned about having a stroke or a heart attack. "I often feel as if I'd explode inside," he says. He takes it out on his wife, "my personal whipping boy."

Dr. Caroline Thomas of Johns Hopkins Hospital speculates that Jules's early childhood fears "were linked with repressed rage directed toward his drunken, cruel father." This held-in hostility promoted in Jules a state of hypertension.

Downhearted

A heart patient lives with the constant threat of a heart attack —i.e., the sudden blocking of one of the arteries that supply the heart muscle with blood. Technically termed a coronary occlusion, coronary thrombosis or myocardial infarction, a heart attack can range from the barely perceptible to the suddenly fatal.

Often, anxiety and depression about the possibility of a heart attack can make an invalid of a person without severe heart disease. Joan, a forty-three-year-old married woman without children, began to suffer from chest pain, sleeplessness, and weight loss. Her physician diagnosed a mild heart condition and suggested she stop doing heavy housework and give up her job as teacher in a nursery school.

Joan cut down on her teaching, but didn't want to give it up entirely because "this is all I have left." She became more and more depressed about her "lost life" and began to dwell on thoughts of death. She thought a lot about her father, who had died of a heart attack in his mid-fifties. Her chest pain began to bother her more. Her childlessness began to weigh on her, making her feel barren, powerless, and weak.

She began to lose control of the children in the nursery school, and her classroom became chaotic. Even the minimal household chores which her doctor allowed her became too much for her. Her favorite hobby, cooking, became "too much of an effort." Her sex life, never satisfactory, dwindled to nonexistence.

Joan was treated with antidepressant medications and psychotherapy. Within two months her depression was relieved and her heart symptoms decreased sharply.

Emotional factors can notoriously precipitate a heart attack in heart patients. In a recent study 23 of 41 patients with heart attacks had experienced severe anxiety just before the attack.

There is some evidence that extreme anxiety, in the form of panic and terror, can be fatal. Eighty-five per cent of the people who die from snakebite don't have enough venom in their bloodstream to account for their sudden deaths. Then how do they die? Researchers suggest that the *terror* felt by a person who receives a potentially fatal snakebite may cause heart failure.

In Queens, New York, a fifty-three-year-old toolmaker watched as a passing car went out of control, roared across his lawn, and headed toward where he was standing. The car veered into a pole at the last moment. Forty-five minutes later the toolmaker, untouched, died of a heart attack. The case was a medicolegal landmark, since his widow charged that the heart attack was the result of shock and fright, and sought damages from the owner of the car. A court ruled that the toolmaker was literally frightened to death—perhaps the first such ruling in law. The widow was awarded $740,000.

Depression is another state of mind frequently associated with the occurrence of heart attacks. Dr. F. Dreyfuss and his associates have reported that almost all heart attacks observed at the Talbieh Psychiatric Hospital in Jerusalem throughout many years occurred in patients with depression. Most of the victims had been depressed for several years; many had attempted suicide. They were literally "downhearted."

One of Dr. Dreyfuss's patients illustrates the psychosomatic shift that can occur between depression and heart attack. Forty-seven-year-old Simon had always suffered from a feeling that he did not fulfill his duties to other people. Driven by guilt, he used to burden himself with work.

At the age of forty, Simon had suffered a mild depression after a fight with his employer. He had an episode of heart pain and fainting. His despondency worsened when his only son failed in his studies.

The time finally arrived when he could benefit from accumulated savings and move to a new and more comfortable apartment. But he wouldn't let himself enjoy this situation. He took upon himself the burden of a great amount of additional work, and his obligations increased beyond his ability. When his condition became unbearable, he attempted to drown himself in the sea. For several hours one night he immersed himself in the cold water, imagining that a strong current would eventually drag him away. He was hospitalized in a state of extreme agitation.

At the psychiatric hospital Simon's general physical condition was found to be good. His blood pressure and electrocardiogram were normal. But during the next few weeks he'd often say that he wished for a heart attack that would occur "like a supreme act of justice" and decide whether he was to live or die. Having a depression did not seem to him like a respectable disease, whereas he looked upon heart disease as a "prestige illness."

One day, while sitting on a chair, Simon was struck by the severe pain of an acute heart attack. Almost immediately the deep depression he'd been suffering from disappeared. Two days after the attack, Simon was elated. "Now for me everything is over and I have nothing to worry about," he said.

When he recovered, Simon returned to work in a mood which he described as "equanimity toward the problems of life since I now have this thing." He pointed to his heart.

Conflict and Punishment

The typical heart-attack victim won't accept help from others, even as he burdens himself with hard work and increasing responsibility. He likes to dominate in his family, his work, his community. He is extremely loathe to reveal his shortcomings or weaknesses. "Fine" is his response to "How are things going?"— even if he is involved in a crisis. At the same time, he has a great need for love and recognition.

Dr. J. M. Van Der Valk of Wilhelmina Hospital in Amsterdam and Dr. J. J. Groen of Hadassah Hebrew University Hospital and Medical School in Jerusalem have observed that many patients have heart attacks when they are frustrated in their need to dominate and at the same time feel lack of love and recognition. "The frustration seems to be worst," say Van Der Valk and Groen, "if the very person whom the individual expected to submit to him dominates him or puts him in a position in which he has to submit to him": a nagging or interrupting wife, for instance, or an independent son or aggressive business associate.

The attack-prone person does not react with overt anger and aggression. He may instead turn the aggression toward himself, much as if to say: "Here I am with all my efforts, and nobody sees them. I might as well drop dead!"

Conversely, of course, many heart attack victims die, not of turning their anger in, but in a rage.

But Van Der Valk and Groen most often find that the immediate precipitating event of a heart attack is a strong repressed emotion (such as anger or frustration), combined with a conflict between a need to express aggression and a longing for passivity. If these emotions coincide with an unusual physical exertion, a heart attack may result.

They cite the dramatic example of forty-year-old Irwin, who went to the doctor complaining of heart pain. The doctor advised him to avoid physical exertion. When he went home, his wife asked him to lift a heavy washtub to the table. Irwin told his wife about his visit to the doctor.

"So," said his wife, "I'll have to work me to death, while you sit and look!"

"That I cannot take," said Irwin. He lifted the tub to the table and fell down dead.

CHAPTER 23

A Cancer Personality?

Studies link despair and suggestibility to development of some malignant growths

Some years ago Dr. Helen Flanders Dunbar was to give a paper on aspects of psychosomatic medicine before the Royal College of Surgeons. A colleague who read the paper suggested that she leave out the section dealing with cancer, since he was skeptical about the effect of emotions on cancer. But later, reports Dr. Dunbar, "he encountered enough cases of cancer to be convinced that personality traits play an important role in this illness."

One of the most striking cases he came across involved a woman who repeatedly dreamed that she bit her mother in the breast and made lumps. She also began to dream that she made a lump in her own breast. Concerned, she went to the doctor. He examined her and, finding no evidence of a lump, assumed she was suffering from cancerphobia—extreme fear of cancer. But before long she did indeed develop a cancerous growth in her breast.

The evidence linking psychological factors to the development of cancer is still far from conclusive. But it is mounting, and it seems to suggest, as Dr. Dunbar says, "that only certain types of people succumb to cancer."

"The Mountain Has No Top"

"It's as if all my life I'd been climbing a very steep mountain. It's very hard work. Every now and then there are ledges I can rest on for a little bit and maybe even enjoy myself a little, but I've got to keep climbing, and the mountain has no top."

Such a view of life, studies have shown, is typical of a large number of cancer-prone people. They feel hopeless and inadequate, as if they'll never have the opportunity or the courage to do as they'd like and be what they want to be. Says another cancer patient:

"You know how it is with a house with no insulation and with cracks in the walls? The more heat you put in, the more leaks out. You can never get it warm. I always knew that was how it was with me in life. I had to keep putting and putting out and there was never any reflection back toward me. If I was going to get warm inside, I'd have to do it alone, and no matter how much you do, you can't do that."

Often cancer patients have had a hard-luck orientation toward life. One patient had a favorite saying: "If the rock drops on the egg—poor egg. If the egg drops on the rock—poor egg."

The hopelessness some cancer victims have felt throughout most of their lives sometimes borders on despair. As one victim expresses it: "I go on and I'm very efficient and I function very adequately, but this has nothing to do with the real me. Inside, none of this matters. All I've ever really wanted is just to be left alone, and since you never really can have that, all I wanted is to be dead."

In a study of cancer patients, psychologist Lawrence LeShan of the Institute of Applied Biology in New York City found that about 3 out of 4 shared this feeling of "bleak hopelessness about ever achieving any real feelings or meaning or enjoyment of life." The cancer victims he studied deeply believed that all their efforts in life would ultimately fail. Although these patients were interviewed after they had developed cancer, this feeling of despair did not first appear with the onset of the disease. Rather, the patients said, "This is how I've always felt."

The cancer patients in LeShan's study generally followed the same life pattern. As a child, the typical cancer patient was isolated and lonely. He may have had a traumatic loss, such as the death of a parent or a sibling. He learned to feel that emotional relationships brought pain and desertion. He may also have come to feel guilty and self-condemning, as if the loss were due to some fault of his own.

In the second part of his life, usually as a young adult, he developed a meaningful relationship and enjoyed a sense of acceptance by others and a full life. This may have continued for many years.

Then the blow fell. Something brought an end to the good life —the death of a spouse, job retirement, children leaving home. Suddenly, observes LeShan, "there was no more meaning and hope to their lives. . . . It seemed to them as though the thing they had expected and feared all their lives—utter desolation and rejection—was now their eternal doom. The only way out was to cease existing."

From six months to eight years after this traumatic event, the victims developed the first symptoms of cancer. Investigators emphasize that the experience of hopelessness, in and of itself, does not predispose a person to cancer. Rather, another type of vulnerability, such as a biochemical defect or predisposition, must be present.

Researchers have observed that cancer can be induced in laboratory animals by injecting hormones into susceptible tissues, thereby upsetting the animal's endocrine balance. Hormones may play a similar role in the development of cancerous growths in human beings. Since psychological attitudes can affect the production of hormones, investigators deem it likely that particular states of mind may set the stage for the growth of some kinds of cancer.

Dr. Arthur Schmale, Jr., and Dr. Howard Iker of the University of Rochester Medical Center studied 51 women admitted to the hospital because of a suspicion that they were suffering from cancer of the cervix. The women were to undergo biopsies to determine if the cell changes were malignant or benign. Experience showed that there was a better than even chance that the women did *not* have cancer.

Schmale and Iker were among the researchers who had observed that many cancer patients experienced feelings of hopelessness for some time before their symptoms appeared. Now, without knowing the biopsy results, Schmale and Iker set about trying to predict which of the 51 women actually had cervical cancer. The main determinant was if the woman had undergone a sustained period of feeling hopeless.

Some of the women had experienced profound feelings of doom. "This is the end," they would say. Or, "I'm finished." They felt responsible for their failings and felt that nothing could be done to reclaim any happiness they might have had. No one else could help them, either.

Many of the women followed a particular personality pattern: They'd left school early in order to help their fathers or to help support their families because their fathers had died. Typically they married men who were older and either ill or immature. They'd worked most of their married lives. In general, they had an overconscientious, religious, self-sacrificing approach to life.

Schmale and Iker predicted that the women with these traits would have cancer. To an astonishing extent, they were right. In all, they predicted correctly in 36 out of 51 cases, a degree of accuracy that could be credited only to the linking of cancer and personality.

Running Out of Resources

A middle-aged woman went to a diagnostic clinic for chest disorders. For the past thirty years she had lived in a quiet country area, free of air pollution. She had never smoked. But she had lung cancer.

In talking to her, Dr. David M. Kissen of Southern General

Hospital in Glasgow, Scotland, was struck with her apparent lack of anxieties and worries. But more searching discussions revealed conflicts in her relationship with her aged and ailing parents. It was only in talking with Kissen that she first realized she had these conflicts.

This woman's history, says Kissen, first sparked his "interest in the possibility that psychological factors might play a part in the etiology of lung cancer." What he found significant about this woman was her inability to acknowledge emotional conflict and deal adequately with it. Over the years, Kissen has observed that a large number of lung cancer patients seem to have the same problem. "Poor outlets for emotional discharge," he terms it.

Kissen has interviewed almost 1000 patients who came to three chest units for diagnosis and treatment. Most of those with cancer had a similar life pattern. Before his fifteenth birthday the typical patient with lung cancer had some kind of separation from his parents: one parent died or was away from home for prolonged periods, or the parents were chronically unhappy and argumentative. As an adult, the lung cancer victim had marital difficulties for many years, and frustration in his professional life.

The adverse life situations of lung cancer patients, however, are probably no greater than those of the general population. What Kissen feels is significant is the way in which many cancer victims deal with these situations. Characteristically, they hold in emotional expression and deny conflicts.

Dr. William Greene, Jr., of the University of Rochester Medical Center has come up with similar findings in his studies of patients with leukemia, cancer of the blood.

A large number of patients, he found, had suffered a significant loss, such as a job loss or the death of a spouse or a parent. Because a malignancy may develop slowly—or lie dormant for several years before developing—he took into account all losses occurring within four years of the first symptoms. About half the losses occurred within a year of the onset.

Some patients were dealing with several sorts of losses at the same time. Seventeen-year-old Mike suffered two emotional blows in the spring. His twin brother developed an interest in a girl and spent all his evenings with her, leaving Mike to mope around the house. At the same time, his mother started divorce proceedings against his father. Mike became depressed. By late summer he had developed leukemia.

Joe was a fifty-six-year-old man whose mother had died four years before. Two years before, he had separated from his girl friend of many years. Recently he had developed a hernia which might require surgery, and he had made a change in jobs. For the past five months he had been suffering from weakness and dizziness. Doctors diagnosed leukemia.

Many of the patients in Greene's study had suffered a severe loss many years before and had apparently pulled through both physically and emotionally. It is often a much less severe event —at least on the surface—that seems associated with the onset of illness.

Clara's husband had died suddenly many years before, leaving her with the care of their four children. Displaying no grief or self-pity, Clara resolutely set out to be both mother and father to her children. She not only maintained the home and supported the family, but also participated in the sports and outdoor activities which had been her husband's realm.

When her husband died, Clara had felt particularly sorry for her baby, the only boy. She had identified with him, and in comforting him had gained relief from her own sorrow. When her son left home for college, Clara developed leukemia. As Dr. Greene sees it, her son's departure represented to her the loss of not only her last child but also the mechanisms that had enabled her to bear her earlier misfortune. At that point she became unable to cope.

What struck Dr. Greene in many of his patients was that "it was not so much a matter of a person's running into psychological conflicts as a matter of his running out of psychological resources."

Investigators interested in the relationship between emotions and cancer also take into account the role of suggestibility in the development of the disease. The children of cancer victims frequently develop the disease at the same age as their parents did, the so-called anniversary syndrome.

Might not premonition play a similar role in susceptible people? Dr. John Lion and Dr. Thomas Hackett of the Harvard Medical School interviewed 100 cancer patients at a tumor clinic and asked if they had ever had any kind of hunch they might develop cancer.

Four patients had had distinct premonitions of illness. They repeatedly sought medical help, even after their doctors became irritated with them and assured them they were well. Finally cancer was diagnosed. All four believed that their premonitions had something to do with the illness.

Seven other patients told the researchers that someone had predicted they would develop the disease. Two additional patients had been "cursed." The researchers were particularly struck with the fact that all the patients recalled the incidents with unusual promptness and clarity, even though they had taken place many years before.

One of the cursed patients was William, an intelligent twenty-nine-year-old man with Hodgkin's disease, cancer of the lymph glands. Ten years before, William had gone to a Coney Island amusement park with a group of friends. They watched a fortuneteller making predictions about people's lives. "This is all a lot of nonsense," William said in a loud voice.

The fortuneteller overheard him. "You come up here," she called to William. When he began to walk away, she called angrily after him, "Evil will befall you—you will see an illness that will change your ways and your life will be shot. It will happen in ten years!"

William laughed it off at the time and soon forgot the incident. Eight years later he discovered a swelling on his neck which was diagnosed as Hodgkin's disease. William's thoughts turned to the fortuneteller. In the two years since the beginning of his illness, William's life indeed had become drastically changed. He lost all interest in athletics, previously a large part of his life. He broke his engagement and began to gamble heavily.

This curse and the other foreshadowings may have had no bearing on the development of the illnesses. Yet, Lion and Hackett conclude, there remains the distinct possibility that the emotions associated with such events may in some way trigger a latent vulnerability to cancer.

Rate of Growth

Cancer was induced in two groups of mice. The first group had laboratory-induced neuroses. The second group was free of neuroses. Experimenters noted that the growth of the tumors was faster in the neurotic mice.

Researchers in cancer are finding that much the same may be true of human beings: that emotions may affect not only the start of cancer but also its rate of growth. Studies show that cancer patients with certain personality traits have slow-growing tumors. In patients with other traits, the disease will quickly prove fatal.

One group of investigators administered psychological tests to cancer patients. The findings: Those patients with fast progression of the illness tended to be defensive and depressed. They had a high degree of anxiety, which they had abnormal difficulty in relieving.

Another study shows personality differences between patients with poorer and more favorable outcomes of the disease. Dr. Kathleen M. Stavraky and her associates at the Ontario Cancer Treatment and Research Foundation Clinic gave several types of personality tests to 204 cancer patients.

They found that patients with the most favorable outcome tended to be more hostile and to have above-average intelligence. "An individual who has a favorable prognosis," say the researchers, "would appear . . . to be a well-integrated person with strong hostile drives [yet] without loss of emotional control."

Particularly noteworthy, they found, is the fact that the cancer patients with the most favorable prognosis had not given up. They were not hopeless and helpless. They were still fighting back.

PART X

Overcoming Resistance

Many physicians ignore—or are ignorant

of—psychosomatic principles, often to the patient's harm.

Here is what's in prospect for psychosomatics—and

what's needed to incorporate the psychosomatic

approach into medicine.

CHAPTER 24

"They Are Ignorant of the Whole"

*Many physicians overlook psychosomatic principles,
often to the harm of the patient*

"The cure of many diseases is unknown to the physicians of
Hellas," observed Plato, "because they are ignorant of the whole.
. . . For the part can never be well unless the whole is well.
. . . This . . . is the great error of our day in the treatment
of the human body."

Plato's statement is largely true in our day as well. More than
2000 years after Plato substantially the same sentiments have
been echoed by Dr. Leonard P. Caccamo, an internist in Youngs-
town, Ohio. "You have to take care of the whole person," says
Dr. Caccamo. "You can't treat the heart to the total exclusion of
the problems that bother the soul. To give your patients good
comprehensive care, you have to take care of their problems
with their mothers, daughters, husbands, wives. If you don't,
you're going to allow their condition to worsen."

And yet, despite the growing body of evidence linking emotions to physical illness, acceptance, while increasing, is slow.
Physicians still widely overlook the psychosomatic component of
disease, often to the detriment of the patient. Dr. George L. Engel of the University of Rochester Medical Center says that most
physicians are guilty of "paying lip service" to the notion that
psychological factors are important in bodily illness, yet make

"no corresponding effort" to gain skill in understanding psychosomatic relationships.

Most physicians, Dr. Engel adds, are able to resolve what conflict they have on this score by noting that their colleagues are regarded as successful doctors without having such skills either. Observes Engel wryly: "Shared ignorance is always a good protection."

Merely a Cliché

Doctors who wish to learn more about psychosomatic medicine find that very few training programs exist.

"In the vast majority of medical schools and residency training programs," says Dr. Engel, "psychosomatic medicine represents merely a cliché to which lip service and no more is paid. In general, the level of understanding by the physician hardly exceeds that of the intelligent layman, and it is more likely to be the subject of a dinner table conversation than of a serious scientific meeting."

The schools rarely relate behavioral sciences to medicine. In most medical schools psychiatry is given limited study, and then only as a separate field unrelated to the patient's broader health picture. Psychosomatics requires an integrated approach. But most medical schools are highly compartmentalized into specialized departments which function virtually independently of the rest of the school. As a rule there is little cooperation between departments, and much competition.

Dr. P. C. Anderson of the University of Missouri School of Medicine likens the typical medical school to the African nation of Nigeria, which is "troubled by a citizenry which speaks over two hundred different languages, each backed up by strong territorial, cultural, and political arguments." At medical schools, observes Dr. Anderson, the fifteen or twenty departments have not only "different 'tribal' languages, but also approximately the same disputes as to territory, inherent privileges, and the status of the chief." Such tribalism—with psychiatry staked out here, the other specialties elsewhere—is fatal to the study of psychosomatics.

Increased specialization among doctors tends to fragment patient care still further. A gastroenterologist may see an ulcer case chiefly as a column of barium with an opening at two ends. A cardiologist may concern himself mainly with a hypertensive's heartbeat, not with the emotional torment that is worsening the condition. The specialist tends to become more and more involved with the organ of his specialty, less and less involved with the whole person.

As a consequence of such specialism, observes Dr. David T. Graham of the University of Wisconsin Medical School, patients are separated according to whether their illnesses are "mental" or "physical." They are sent to different clinics and seen by different specialists. "Nothing could be more destructive of efforts to understand the reactions of people to the events in their lives and the ways in which they make adaptive efforts," says Dr. Graham.

The average medical school graduate has had so little training in psychiatry to begin with that he is "virtually incapable of eliciting, much less recognizing, any but the most blatant examples of psychological distress," bemoans Dr. George L. Engel. Little in the typical physician's training after medical school serves to correct this deficiency. Hence many physicians enter practice without ever having experience in the operation of psychological factors in bodily disease.

One medical educator, Dr. Robert Platt, has called it "incredible" that medical education fails to emphasize the emotional aspects of illness. "Although most universities give some lectures in psychology to their medical students," Dr. Platt adds, "academic departments of psychology are all too often concerned with precise methods of measuring the irrelevant rather than with exploring the origin of human emotion."

One reason psychosomatic medicine gets scant attention in medical schools is as follows: To a great extent, the schools regard it as their mission to conduct laboratory investigation and train medical scientists, *not* to teach students how to care for human beings. The schools' emphasis is generally on research rather than on patient care. Observes Dr. C. H. William Ruhe, director of the American Medical Association's Division of Medical Education: "Glory, laud, and honor have resided in scientific investigation"—not in clinical work, i.e., in the diagnosis and treatment of individual cases. The heavy funding available for research from such sources as foundations and government agencies has tended to perpetuate the schools' concentration on laboratory investigation. There has been no comparable support to upgrade clinical training, much less psychosomatic understanding.

Medical school programs tend to be long on lab work and lectures but short on contact with patients. The typical medical student has small exposure to family medicine, which ideally is heavily psychosomatic in approach, and almost no continuing contacts with patients. He has little opportunity to follow the course of a chronic illness or become familiar with family health problems, many of which are emotional in origin.

Against Psychiatry

Many practicing physicians distrust psychiatrists and are hostile toward psychiatry. In a survey of more than 2500 physicians, 86 per cent were critical of psychiatrists, including 9 per cent who were highly critical. "There have been complaints," report the authors of the survey, "that other physicians cannot communicate with psychiatrists, that they do not know them as people, and that they do not understand their terminology." Observations by psychiatrists about psychosomatic concepts thus fall on many deaf ears throughout the profession.

Psychiatrist Z. J. Lipowski of McGill University comments: "Many physicians have little interest in and appreciation of the psychosocial factors in illness and even less conviction that psychiatry has something useful to contribute to the practice of medicine."

In practice, psychiatrists and their nonpsychiatrist colleagues
—internists, general practitioners, pediatricians, and the like—
typically have little to do with each other. "In many general hos-
pitals," notes Dr. Elliot D. Luby of Wayne University College of
Medicine, "internists and psychiatrists rarely meet, other than to
exchange indifferent glances." When a medical man does re-
quest a psychiatric consultation, adds Dr. Luby, "it is usually in
order to 'get that crazy patient off my ward.' "

A study of medical students' attitudes toward patients with
psychosomatic problems found that one type of student ac-
knowledges the existence of patients with psychosomatic disorders but doesn't want to treat them. Another type is primarily
interested in research, science, and technical proficiency, and
has no interest in psychosomatic medicine. A third type is actively hostile to patients with psychosomatic disorders.

One reason that psychiatry in general—and psychosomatic
medicine in particular—gets short shrift in many medical cir-
cles is that physicians widely regard the field as "unscientific."
Physicians (and laymen as well) tend to think of a disease as
having a single physiological cause. This belief is a carryover
from the age of the great microbe hunters, such as Jenner, Pas-
teur, and Koch. These investigators searched for *the* particular
microbe which was the causative agent for a given disease. Iso-
lating the germ responsible for an illness was a great medical
breakthrough, and has resulted through the years in cures for
many diseases.

Accordingly, the overwhelming thrust of modern medicine is
to search for the origin of a disease within the framework of
Koch's postulates governing scientific investigation—i.e., to find
a specific "cause" for each disease that will be unique for that
particular malady and sufficient to explain the patient's entire
disease picture. Medicine has been very successful in this research. Cholera germs always cause cholera, never typhoid.

In psychiatry, however, it is not so simple. Many things can
cause or instigate a depression, for example. The factors that are
significant forerunners of psychiatric and psychosomatic disor-

ders—namely, repressed hostility, dependency, anxiety, guilt, feelings of inadequacy, and isolation, to mention only a few— are common to *all* emotional disturbances, though they may differ in degree and duration. Moreover, multiple disease states may coexist. A person may suffer from two or more psychosomatic diseases, or a psychiatric and a psychosomatic disease, or an organic and a psychosomatic disease. Psychological factors in illness are therefore more complex and subtle than the general medical model of disease.

Such multiple causation makes many physicians, used to thinking in terms of a single cause for illness, resist psychosomatic concepts. Dr. Philip Pinkerton of Alder Hey Children's Hospital in Liverpool points out that medical trainees have trouble accepting an integrated view of medicine. "They are accustomed to clear-cut formulations of disease processes which they can understand and apply objectively," Dr. Pinkerton notes. "They find it . . . difficult to adjust their thinking to include psychodynamic principles."

Most doctors tend to think of body on the one hand and mind on the other. Realize it or not, they believe in mind-body independence, sometimes expressing it with a remark like, "There's nothing physically wrong with you. It's all mental." Alternatively, many physicians—sometimes the same ones—espouse what Dr. David T. Graham calls "interactionism." If asked to state his position about psychosomatic medicine, he might say, "The body influences the mind, and the mind influences the body." This, of course, reflects a belief in two separate entities— body and mind—and is thus far afield from psychosomatic medicine's "monistic" view that emotions and physiology are integrated into one unified whole.

If a disturbance is classified as being primarily "psychological," the typical physician's reasoning, Dr. Graham feels, might follow these lines: "The mind is a vague and insubstantial thing. Therefore it can alter the body's function to some extent, but certainly cannot make any structural changes. ('I don't see how a thought can produce a hole in the duodenum.') The only diseases that are really serious are structural. Therefore, if a disease is caused by psychic forces, it is not worth while trying to understand what is going on in the body, because it isn't important anyway."

Doctors often avoid becoming involved in the emotional aspects of their patients' lives. They often tend to view a patient's feelings and emotional problems as outside the realm of their professional responsibility. "Most of us run like deer," from a patient's emotional difficulties, observes Dr. Lewis M. Fraad, professor of child health at Albert Einstein College of Medicine.

Dr. Fraad is aware of how much his patients need a doctor's understanding and interest. He tells of a high-school boy, John, who had a kidney disease. After performing some tests, Dr. Fraad asked John, "How are you getting along in school? Have you gotten into the social whirl in high school?"

John bridled. "What are you interested in that for?"

"Well, don't you think it's as important as how many red cells you have, since I'm interested in you, John?"

John, it turned out, wanted so much to talk to an adult who was "interested in more than just those damned red cells" that Dr. Fraad practically had to push him out of his office half an hour later.

In a presidential address before the American Psychosomatic Society, Dr. Stanley Cobb declared: "Few [physicians] have disciplined themselves to the point where they have actually stopped thinking dualistically. . . . Psychosomatic medicine . . . will have served its purpose when physicians stop thinking of diseases as having specific causes, when they really conceive of both health and disease as reactions of the human organism to a complex internal and external environment."

"Go Home and Lead a Normal Life"

Some years ago there was a movie called *The Cat Woman* in which a psychiatrist advised a deeply troubled patient to "go home and lead a normal life." The physician who dismisses a patient with the opinion that his illness is "purely psychosomatic" is essentially telling him the same thing.

The unspoken message is: "There's nothing really wrong with you. You can get better if you really want to. You're wasting my time." Both physicians and laymen are often prey to the notion that a psychosomatic complaint is imaginary and under the patient's control. Yet anyone suffering from, say, psychogenic pain knows that it is as real as a fractured leg, and as unlikely to be cured without help.

In many cases, people with disorders for which no organic cause can be found are shunted from one doctor to another, subjected again and again to laboratory tests, given numerous prescriptions. The patient's anxiety about his condition is frequently overlooked by the doctor. Indeed, observes Dr. William A. Steiger of Temple University School of Medicine, since the patients' anxiety is often caught by the physician, the doctor may seek to relieve his own discomfort. He can, for example, refer the patient to another physician, which Dr. Steiger feels is tantamount to a rejection. Or he can get angry with the patient, telling him, "It's all in your head."

Such a patient is likely to be labeled a "crock," which Dr. David Bender of the University of California at Los Angeles defines as a person with symptoms out of proportion to objective findings, and who is burdensome to his doctor. "For the doctor treating this type of patient," says Dr. Bender, "too often the unhappy outcome is frustration followed by disinterest or anger and avoidance." Trusting as he does in medical science, the physician may be angered at a patient who doesn't respond to medication. He may perceive this as a threat to his competence.

Often, says Dr. Bender, the crock has a medical history of "dismissal rather than treatment or referral following identification of a psychological basis." The patient is thus effectively abandoned because of the doctor's lack of understanding of how emotions can affect health. His symptoms are likely to become more severe.

The patient, for his part, often craves just the warmth and

understanding the doctor is withholding. He senses that there is a stigma attached to psychosomatic illness, and that this has led to his rejection by the doctor.

He is insulted by a diagnosis of "psychosomatic," associating it with such charged words as "mental," "imaginary," "nerves," "in the mind." Dr. W. A. Norton of the University of British Columbia observes that patients "tend rather uncritically to accept some of the ill-considered phrases . . . with which they are plied." These include "emotional sickness," "mental illness," "nervous disorder."

The patient may thus be desperate for doctors to find a *physical* complaint to account for his symptoms. He intuits that troubled emotions earn disdain and rejection, whereas troubled organs gain respect and sympathy.

Owen, for example, belches frequently, has a bloated feeling and a burning sensation in his abdomen. He insists that he has an ulcer, and numerous tests are performed by various specialists.

But, says the psychiatrist who interviewed him—Dr. Samuel Silverman of Harvard—Owen "does not have organic disease. Yet he ascribes his physical symptoms to an ulcer." He *needs* to have a diagnosis of organic illness. Dr. Silverman remarks that Owen shares the problem of many patients "who have physical symptoms but no organic illness [and] find it difficult to accept emotional disturbance as the most likely basis for these manifestations." This is due, he says, to the stigma attached to emotional illness, and to "the misconception that physical symptoms due to physical disease are real, and those which are not are imaginary."

Making Patients Sick

"Every day . . . we doctors find in our patients troubles, disturbances, or even severe pathology produced by us," says Dr. Carlos Guerrero of Mexico City.

People are extremely vulnerable to their doctors when ill. "A sick person is always a child, so to speak, in his relation to the physician," comments Dr. Sydney Margolin, a former president of the American Psychosomatic Society. Many physicians are alert to the fact that some patients are easily upset by the doctor's mood. Dr. Peter Bonadero, a practitioner in Fredericktown, Pennsylvania, places a red circle or the initials H. W. C. (Handle With Care) on the charts of unusually sensitive patients.

But, unaware of the extent to which feelings can affect physical changes, a doctor may make an ill-considered remark which has unexpected repercussions. Dr. Guerrero has found, for example, that some cases of psychosomatic infertility are traceable to misinformation received from a doctor.

In one such case, a woman with hirsutism (excessive body hair) had been told by a doctor that it was a masculine manifestation and would be followed by sterility. The woman had a perfect endocrine balance and a good sexual life with her husband. But she was unable to conceive, and no organic cause could be found. Dr. Guerrero explained to the woman that hirsutism should not in any way keep her from having a baby, and it was not long before she became pregnant.

A husband was distressed that his wife's hymen did not bleed on their wedding night. With her premarital chastity in question, they consulted a doctor the next morning. "Believe it or not," says Dr. Guerrero, the doctor did not give them the logical explanation they so urgently desired—that the hymen can be broken in ways other than through sexual intercourse. They felt their marriage was spoiled from then on and were unable to have any children. Their misunderstandings and the infertility problem disappeared after receiving clear and honest information from Dr. Guerrero.

In such inadvertent ways can a doctor's ignorance of psychosomatic principles actually harm a patient. Comments Dr. Charles William Wahl of the University of California at Los Angeles: "It is disquieting to us, as physicians, to learn that often, unbeknownst to ourselves, we have by some commission or omission done definite and often serious harm to one of our patients. . . . We learn that some small thing . . . had great and far-reaching significance for the patient."

Perhaps it was a word said or unsaid, a facial expression, an explanation omitted or misconstrued. Imagine what would go through your mind if a doctor, while listening to your chest through a stethoscope, suddenly shook his head and said, "Uh oh." It may have just occurred to him that he had left his keys in his car—but what would occur to *you*? Psychiatrist Jules H. Masserman of Northwestern University Medical School warns his colleagues that: "A dolorous shake of the head as we fold the stethoscope after listening to his chest—no matter what is said afterward—may mean to him that our all-perceiving ears have heard the footsteps of approaching death."

One common type of iatrogenic (doctor-produced) ailment is the "cardiac neurosis." An estimated twenty million people in the United States are cardiac patients *without* heart disease. One study found that close to half the patients referred to a cardiac clinic did not have an organic heart condition. Another researcher says that 60 per cent of the people who consult a heart specialist do so because of anxiety engendered by the remarks of another physician.

How do these people come to believe they have heart disease? Often a person consults a doctor with symptoms he believes are common in heart disease, such as palpitations, shortness of breath, exhaustion after slight effort, chest pain. More than likely these are stress reactions; his heart is completely normal.

But the doctor, whose training is largely based on the belief that physical symptoms are the result of organic changes, may be reluctant to tell the patient there is no evidence of heart disease. The doctor, wary of a potential malpractice suit, may also want to play it safe. Every physician has heard of colleagues who dismiss a patient as healthy, only to have him suddenly die of a heart attack the following day. Therefore, the doctor may interpret these symptoms as "possible disease." This can produce still more anxiety in the patient, often followed by increased physical distress.

There are more than thirty other common reasons for chest pain besides heart disease. The physician's overcaution may make an invalid of the patient.

A cardiac neurosis is sometimes produced by a doctor's using technical terms without an explanation to put the condition into perspective. Says Dr. Wahl: "I have seen severe states of anxiety precipitated in patients who were told, without the necessary simplification and elaboration, that they had functional murmurs." This condition need never bother the patient. But it sounds serious, and the patient is often too terrified to ask what it means in terms of his life.

In many cases the patient may have a psychological need for a heart condition, perhaps to gain sympathy or justify his failures. Some people manipulate their families and friends through their presumed weak hearts. They may seize upon and use to the utmost any corroboration from the doctor that their problems are possibly due to heart disease. One man, who has been out of work for years, greets visitors to his apartment with X rays of his heart. He once had a suspected heart problem, never confirmed. Now, showing the X rays, he tells visitors, "This is why I can't work."

Physicians often don't realize that every patient is anxious to some degree and is carefully scrutinizing the doctor for clues to the severity of his condition. He may notice when the doctor frowns or hesitates or when he raises an eyebrow or clears his throat. Apprehensive about the possibility of a heart condition, he may imbue every gesture of the doctor's with significance.

Dr. Wahl tells of a man who was greatly concerned about his heart. He watched suspiciously as his physician listened through the stethoscope. The doctor had an intent look. His brows were knit and his lips pursed. He was silent. When the doctor told the man, "Your heart's all right," the patient didn't believe him. He'd been convinced from the doctor's expression that he was suffering from a fatal heart condition. Feeling doomed, he took to his bed for more than a year.

Much later he said: "If the doctor had only talked more, I

think I would have concluded that it was an intent rather than a worried expression he was wearing."

If a patient actually has had a heart attack, the physician may overreact, throwing the patient into a state of panic. Dr. H. E. Pelser of Amsterdam attributes such dire warnings to the doctor's anxiety in the face of his responsibility, of his own impotence in avoiding a fatal outcome for the patient. Dr. Pelser tells of a physician who was leaving the bedside of a patient who had suffered a heart attack. The patient raised his hand from the blanket to motion a good-by. The doctor spun around and snapped: "You are supposed to keep absolutely quiet!"

Another time, an internist was asked by a patient after a heart attack, "When may I go back to work, Doctor?" The internist replied: "Never! You are not allowed to lift any object. You are not allowed to bend down. You are not allowed to go into a cold room, and you are not allowed to eat a heavy meal." Not surprisingly, notes Dr. Pelser, this kind of alarming statement can prompt the patient to develop anxiety reactions which complicate recovery, even produce organic disturbances and paralysis.

CHAPTER 25

Toward the Fullest Flowering of Medicine

What is in prospect for psychosomatics—and what needs to be done

Twenty-five hundred years ago in ancient Greece, Melampus, who was a seer and physician, was called upon to cure the impotence of Iphiclus, prince of Thessalia.

Melampus, a shrewd investigator, learned that when Iphiclus was a child he once watched his father, the king, castrate rams and was frightened by the blood. To tease him, his father threw the knife close to him, and it happened to fall near the child's genitals. Thoroughly terrified, Iphiclus ran away. The king then stuck the knife into a tree, and the bark grew over it.

Now Melampus found the knife and showed it to Iphiclus, who suddenly remembered the forgotten event. Within a few years he was the father of two sons.

Taking into account such buried knives is at the heart of the psychosomatic approach. Psychotherapy needs to be increasingly included in medical treatment. For without a practical understanding of how emotions can injure health, physcians will treat only a fragment of the person.

Bridging the Gap

Psychosomatics, says Dr. George L. Engel of the University of Rochester School of Medicine and Dentistry, is *"the* most complex field in all of medicine. There is no other field which must include under its aegis every aspect of life and living. . . ."

Psychosomatic medicine bridges the gap between psychiatry and medicine. To give a patient effective, comprehensive treatment, the physician needs to be aware of both the emotional and the physiological components of his condition, and how they work together. Dr. Wilfred Dorfman, editor of the journal *Psychosomatics,* believes that it is "mandatory for all physicians, regardless of their specialty or lack of it, to practice comprehensive medicine. . . . Each physician who remains worthy of his title must remain acutely aware that his patient has both a body and a mind and that they are inseparable and absolutely incapable of segregation."

Eventually, Dr. Dorfman believes, all medicine will be comprehensive, since it necessarily deals with people whose minds and bodies are firmly integrated. Doctors, he feels, will have to learn to integrate the disciplines of psychiatry and medicine if they are to provide truly effective treatment.

The physician's acquaintance with psychosomatic medicine ought to begin in medical school. In recent years researchers in psychosomatics have begun to press for the reorientation of the medical curriculum to include the psychosomatic approach. They emphasize the importance of teaching students more about the role of their own personalities, the doctor-patient relationship, and the role of stress and personality factors in illness.

The University of Rochester has pioneered a curriculum that incorporates the psychosomatic viewpoint. Students are systematically oriented toward seeing the patient as a whole, rather than as a collection of potentially diseased organs. Whereas most medical schools delay psychiatry courses until the student's third year, Rochester gives psychiatric training as early as the first and second year. The courses are considered a general preparation for clinical medicine, indeed the main vehicle whereby the student is introduced to the patient as an integrated organism.

Rochester also offers a graduate program for M.D.s interested in the psychological 'aspects of internal medicine. These young doctors are trained primarily in internal medicine, and hold appointments both in the department of psychiatry and the department of medicine.

New physicians need practice in dealing with patients from a psychosomatic standpoint. The U. S. Naval Hospital in Oakland, California, has taken a step in this direction. Interns there are encouraged to make use of the "psychosomatic conference." If an intern has a patient with a problem which seems related to his emotional state, he brings his case before such a meeting.

The conference is attended by a resident, the officer in charge of psychiatric training, and several psychiatrists and internists. The goal of the psychosomatic conference is to examine the doctor-patient relationship and to show that the patient's illness is related to his life pattern and is not an isolated event. A major purpose, says Dr. S. M. Blair, who is in charge of psychiatric training at the hospital, is "to show the intern how to care for patients himself rather than . . . refer patients to a psychiatrist."

It is also important for other medical personnel, such as nurses and doctors' aides, to be aware of the psychic factors that can contribute to illness. An ill-considered remark or a cold manner can undo the work of the most sensitive of doctors.

Dr. Francis J. Gerty, a former president of the American Board of Psychiatry and Neurology, reminds his fellow physicians that doctors cannot escape giving patients psychotherapy because all medical treatment contains good or bad psychotherapy. This is in reply to physicians who protest that they are too busy in their regular practice to add psychiatric counseling to their burdens. Alleviating patients' emotional discomfort need not take much time. Psychiatrists Leonard T. Maholick of Columbus, Georgia, and John Warkentin of Atlanta, who had provided short, inexpensive counseling sessions with emotionally troubled patients, point out that brief interviews can be a "most valuable adjunct in any doctor's office." Maholick and Warkentin advise family physicians to set aside two hours a week specifically for counseling interviews, scheduling from ten to fifteen minutes per patient.

Dr. Robert I. Daugherty, a general practitioner in Lebanon, Georgia, has commented: "Family counseling is just as important as spending an hour and a half taking out somebody's gall bladder, so I'm perfectly willing to adjust my schedule to it. I think it is appropriate for the family physician to organize his office practice and his schedule to spend a significant amount of time with a family that is having trouble."

An awareness of psychosomatics can be incorporated into every patient visit. If a physical examination shows no organic cause for the patient's symptoms, the physician will not need more than a few minutes to explain that this does not mean that the symptoms are less real or that the patient is faking. Dr. William A. Steiger of Temple University School of Medicine advises physicians to point out that emotional problems can cause physical symptoms which are fully as important to the doctor as those produced in other ways. A few such words can help diminish the stigma that patients widely attach to psychogenic illness.

Dr. Steiger urges that physicians encourage patients to talk about their feelings. "Tell me about it," a doctor might say. Or, "How do you feel about what's happened?" The doctor might tell a patient what he senses the patient is experiencing: "I get the feeling that you're upset and hopeless."

"Such questions make the patient an active, adult part of the relationship," says Dr. Steiger. "They show respect for the patient as a person with ideas and feelings, and they encourage his cooperation."

A doctor needs to be sensitive to the reason a patient asks a particular question. A diabetic couple consulted a physician about the advisability of having a child. The doctor simply quoted to them the bleak statistics about childbearing in diabetics. The woman began to cry. She was already three months pregnant.

It is also important to determine what a specific procedure might mean to a patient. One woman refused to have a liver biopsy even after two doctors had painstakingly detailed the need for it. A third doctor finally thought to ask her why she wasn't going to let them do it.

"It *is* a minor operation, isn't it?"

"Yes, it is," the doctor replied. "Does that have a special meaning for you?"

"Well, my mother went to the hospital for a minor operation, and she died."

The physician needs to take into account the impact a disease may have on the patient's family. For example, Dr. Henry Dolger of Mount Sinai Hospital in New York finds family stress is a problem that can worsen the condition of diabetic children. The brothers and sisters of a diabetic child are apt to be jealous of the attention he receives. The parents are likely to feel guilty, sensing that they are somehow responsible for the child's illness. The child himself may resist dietary restrictions and insulin injections.

"The physician must exhibit an all-pervasive interest in the many problems of his patient beyond the chemical test of diabetes," says Dr. Dolger. Ideally, for any condition the physician regards it as an important part of the treatment to cause the least disruption possible of family life.

It is important also for doctors to explore their own attitudes toward particular patients. A doctor may find that he is irritated, angry, impatient, often because the "difficult" patient fails to "improve." The feelings are often communicated to the patient, to the detriment of the treatment. Observes Dr. Wilfred Dorfman: "Self-examination may then generate a greater tolerance and understanding . . . leading to a better relationship." If the physician continues to be irked, advises Dr. Dorfman, the patient should be referred to another doctor.

Helping Yourself

A researcher studied more than 2000 people who lived past ninety. How did they differ from the rest of mankind? In general, they were calm and placid. They rarely worried.

Yet how can you avoid stresses in your life? And once emotional conflicts have contributed to illness, how can you help yourself recover? You may need to re-evaluate much of what you now do. Without belaboring the obvious, physicians experienced with psychosomatic illness offer these pointers:

• *Simplify your life.* Realize that everyone is prone to psychosomatic problems when life stresses accumulate. Avoid making several great changes in your life within the same period, for your adaptive processes may not be able to accommodate them all. The fewer changes at a time, the healthier you're likely to be.

• *Keep adversity in perspective.* Missing a green light is not worth a churning stomach or a pounding heart. Psychologist Albert Ellis advises that you tell yourself, "Tough shit," when troubles get you down. The attitude behind the expression is: "There's more to my life than these instances of hard luck. And I can live with them."

• *Accept responsibility for getting well.* Dr. Helen Flanders Dunbar tells of two men hospitalized with heart disease. The first said, "It's up to you now, Doc." The second said, "I've got to do something to get well." The first died, the second recovered. He saw his illness as part of himself, not an object he was handing over to the doctor. He knew he would have to work at recovering, and he retained hope.

• *Speak up to your doctor.* Help him help you by asking any questions you may have about your condition. Be sure to tell him about any emotional problems that may be contributing to your illness.

• *Keep an open mind about psychotherapy.* It can help you work out the conflicts and stresses that may be involved in your condition, and thus reduce the possibility of subsequent illness. Dr. Heinz H. Wolff of Maudsley Hospital in London remarks that the patient with a physical illness brought on by emotional conflicts "can pretend to himself and others that he himself, and particularly his mind, is healthy, but that some particular part of his body is . . . functioning badly, and that he is in no way responsible for his illness." Thus, the aim of psychotherapy in psychosomatic illness is "to redirect the patient's attention to his personal problems, to make him see what they are and make him realize that his inability to face and tolerate these conflicts are responsible for his illness."

Group therapy has been of particular value in the treatment of psychosomatic patients, and it is usually less expensive than individual therapy. Say internist William Schwartz and psychologist Aris T. Papas, who practice group therapy with psychosomatic patients: "The main objective in small discussion groups is in helping patients minimize the anxiety associated with medical problems . . . to help the patients understand their feelings, modify their behavior . . . and achieve better health and comfort."

What's Ahead

Research in psychosomatics is still in its infancy. In the years ahead, many more studies will explore the linking of psyche and soma. Experimenters are enlarging the scope of endocrine research to determine under what circumstances different hormone systems react to stress. Much promise lies in the field of psychopharmacology, the study of drugs that affect emotional states. Tranquilizers, antidepressants, and the like already have proved useful, and research may well bring drugs of particular value in the treatment of psychosomatic conditions.

The gap between general psychiatry and general medicine is being closed on several fronts. Following the lead of the University of Rochester, training in psychiatry and psychosomatic medicine is being given earlier and more intensively by some medical schools. At the University of North Carolina some medical *pre*freshmen are given a six-week clinical experience with psychiatric patients during the summer before their first medical-school year. The prefreshmen are assigned specific patients and participate in rounds, conferences, and treatment activities.

Dr. Bernard R. Shochet and Dr. Ephraim T. Lisansky of the University of Maryland School of Medicine look to the day when physicians will make a "double diagnosis," entailing both an "organic diagnosis" and a "personality diagnosis" in order to treat a patient more "rationally and successfully." They argue that a doctor needs to know not only what disease the patient is suffering from, but also what kind of person he is, what factors lie behind the choice of a particular illness, why he became ill at this particular time. The physician, say Shochet and Lisansky, must try to understand the patient's "basic assumptions about himself" in order to help him properly.

In an attempt to bring psychotherapy to more patients, Dr. Pietro Castelnuovo-Tedesco of the University of California School of Medicine has experimented with the 20-minute psychiatric "hour." Working with trainees inexperienced in psychiatry, he found that most patients improved if the young physicians merely made the tenor of the doctor-patient relationship one of encouragement and support.

Perhaps the most intriguing psychosomatic experiments involve the discovery that you can regulate your internal organs. It had long been thought that the autonomic nervous system, which controls such responses as brain waves, heart rate, digestion, was completely involuntary and beyond conscious control.

Recent experiments, however, have shown that some people can be taught to direct their internal organs and processes. Dr. Joe Kamiya and his associates at the University of California Medical Center in San Francisco have trained people to control their brain waves. Subjects are asked to try to get into a state in which their electroencephalograms (EEG, which indicates the brain's electrical activity) will reproduce the alpha wave. The alpha impulses denote a pleasurable, relaxed wakefulness, the kind of state some people achieve during meditation. A humming sound informs the person when he succeeds. With practice, some people have become proficient at keeping their EEGs on the alpha wave, maintaining at will the peaceful, meditative frame of mind.

In other experiments of this nature, people are learning to control their heart rhythms and degree of blood flow through various areas of the body. In each case the subject is informed of his success; often colored lights indicate when he's achieving the desired result.

Learning such responses can help some people stay alive. In a study at the National Institute of Child Health and Human Development, half the patients with a dangerous disturbance in heart rhythms have learned to reduce their heart's premature contractions through conscious regulation.

The implications for psychosomatic medicine may be equally dramatic. There is the possibility, for example, that some people may be trained to avoid the physical disturbances that accompany stress and may lead to illness. People might someday learn consciously to prevent their bronchial tubes from contracting, their gastric juices from oversecreting, their blood pressure from rising.

When psychosomatic principles are at last so put to use, medicine will reach its fullest flowering.

NOTES

Prologue

PAGE

xv. Stunted children: POWELL, G. F.; BRASEL, J. A.; and BLIZ-ZARD, R. M. "Emotional Deprivation and Growth Retardation Simulating Idiopathic Hypopituitarism. I. Clinical Evaluation of the Syndrome." *New England Journal of Medicine*, 276:1271, 1967.

Chapter 1: Body, Mind, and Illness

4. Mallett: MALLETT, B. L. "Psychosomatic Pathology." *Journal of Psychosomatic Research*, 9:5, 1965.

4. Lewis: LEWIS, B. I. *JAMA*, 150:776, 1952.

Chapter 2: The Unity of You

9. Levi: LEVI, L. "The Urinary Output of Adrenalin and Noradrenalin during Pleasant and Unpleasant Emotional States." *Psychosomatic Medicine*, 27:80, 1965.

10. Bleuler: Quoted in: DUNBAR, F. *Emotions and Bodily Changes.* New York: Columbia University Press, 1954.

10. Graham: GRAHAM, D. T. "Health, Disease and the Mind-body Problem: Linguistic Parallelism." *Psychosomatic Medicine*, 29:52, 1967.

11. Spink: SPINK, W. W. "Brucellosis." In: BEESON, P. B., and McDERMOTT, W. *Textbook of Medicine.* Philadelphia: W. B. Saunders, 1967.

12. Abrams: ABRAMS, W. B. "Somatopsychic Conditions: Classification and Clinical Orientation." In: NODINE, J. H., and MOYER, J. H., eds. *Psychosomatic Medicine.* Philadelphia: Lea and Febiger, 1962.

12. Churchill: MARTIN, R. G. *Jennie: The Life of Lady Randolph Churchill.* Englewood Cliffs, N.J.: Prentice-Hall, 1969.

16. James-Lange: JAMES, W. In: *The Emotions.* Psychology Classics. Baltimore: Williams & Wilkins, 1922.

17. MacLean: MacLEAN, P. D. "Studies on Limbic Systems ('Visceral Brain') and Their Bearing on Psychosomatic Problems." In: WITTKOWER, E. D., and CLEGHORN, R. A. *Recent Developments in Psychosomatic Medicine.* Philadelphia: J. B. Lippincott, 1954.

PAGE

18. Olds: OLDS, J. "Pleasure Centers in the Brain." *Scientific American*, October 1956.

Chapter 3: Your Emotional Chemistry

23. Cannon: CANNON, W. B. "The Emergency Function of the Adrenal Medulla in Pain and the Major Emotions." *American Journal of Physiology*, 33:356, 1914. Also: *Wisdom of the Body*. New York: W. W. Norton, 1939.

25. Cannon and De La Paz: CANNON, W. B., and DE LA PAZ, D. "Emotional Stimulation of Adrenal Secretion." *American Journal of Physiology*, 27:64, 1911.

26. Military air transport: EULER, U. S. VON, and LUNDBERG, U. "Effect of Flying on the Epinephrine Excretion in Air Force Personnel." *Journal of Appied Physiology*, 6:551, 1954.

26. Flight-training emergency: ULVEDAL, F.; SMITH, W. R.; and WELCH, B. E. "Steroid and Catecholamine Studies on Pilots during Prolonged Experiments in a Space Cabin Simulation." *Journal of Applied Physiology*, 18:1257, 1963.

26. Centrifuge: GOODALL, McC., and BERMAN, M. L. "Urinary Output of Adrenaline, and 3-Methoxy-4-hydroxymandelic Acid Following Centrifugation and Anticipation of Centrifugation." *Journal of Clinical Investigation*, 39:1533, 1960.

26. Frankenhaeuser and Kareby: FRANKENHAEUSER, M., and KAREBY, S. "Effect of Meprobamate on Catecholamine Excretion during Mental Stress." *Perceptual and Motor Skills*, 15:571, 1962.

26. Steel balls: LEVI, L. "A New Stress Tolerance Test with Simultaneous Study of Physiological and Psychological Variables." *Acta Endocrinologica* (Kobenhavn), 37:38, 1961.

27. Invoice clerks: LEVI, L. "Sympatho-Adrenomedullary Responses to Emotional Stimuli: Methodologic, Physiologic, and Pathologic Considerations." In: BAJUSZ, E., ed. *An Introduction to Clinical Neuroendocrinology*. Basel: Karger; Baltimore: Williams & Wilkins, 1967.

27. Sleep deprivation: METZ, B., SCHAFF, G., and GRIVEL, F. "Psychophysiological Effects of Sleep Loss." (Abstract) XVIth International Congress of Psychology: Symposium on Sleep Loss, Bonn, 1960.

27. Child's death: "Child's Death in London Laid to Fear of Dentist." *The New York Times*, July 26, 1970.

27. African mammals: GOODALL, McC. "Studies of Adrenaline and Noradrenaline in Mammalian Heart and Suprarenals." *Acta Physiologica Scandinavica* 24 (Supplement 85), 1951.

28. Mason: MASON, J. W. "A Review of Psychoendocrine Research

PAGE

on the Pituitary-adrenal Cortical System." *Psychosomatic Medicine,* 30:576, 1968.

30. Uno: UNO, T. "Effect of General Excitement and of Fighting on Some Ductless Glands of Male Albino Rats." *American Journal of Physiology,* 61:203, 1922.

30. Responses in novel experiences: MASON, J. W., BRADY, J. V., and SIDMAN, M. "Plasma 17-Hydroxycorticosteroid Levels and Conditioned Behavior in the Rhesus Monkey." *Endocrinology,* 60:741, 1957; MASON, J. W., HARWOOD, C. T., and ROSENTHAL, N. R. "Influence of Some Environmental Factors on Plasma and Urinary 17-Hydroxycorticosteroid Levels in the Rhesus Monkey." *American Journal of Physiology,* 190:429, 1957; MASON, J. W. "Psychological Influences on the Pituitary-Adrenal Cortical System." *Recent Progress in Hormone Research,* 15:345, 1959; MASON, J. W. "Psychoendocrine Approaches in Stress Research." In: *Symposium on Medical Aspects of Stress in the Military Climate.* p. 375. Washington, D. C.: Walter Reed Army Institute of Research, 1964.

30. Hospital emergency: PINCUS, G. "Studies of the Role of the Adrenal Cortex in the Stress of Human Subjects." *Recent Progress in Hormone Research,* 1:123, 1947.

30. Indianapolis Speedway: FROST, J. W.; DRYER, R. L.; and KOHLSTAEDT, K. G. "Stress Studies on Auto Race Drivers." *Journal of Laboratory and Clinical Medicine,* 38:523, 1951.

30. Parachutists: BASOWITZ, H.; PERSKY, H.; KORCHIN, S. J.; and GRINKER, R. R. Sr. *Anxiety and Stress.* New York: McGraw-Hill, 1955.

30. Final exams: SCHWARTZ, T. B., and SHIELDS, D. R. "Emotional Tension and Excretion of Corticoids and Creatinine." *American Journal of Medicine,* 16:608, 1954; SCHWARTZ, T. B., and SHIELDS, D. R. "Urinary Excretion and Formaldehydrogenic Steroids and Creatinine: A Reflection of Emotional Tension." *Psychosomatic Medicine* 18:159, 1956; VENNING, E. H.; DYRENFURTH, I.; and BECK, J. C. "Effect of Anxiety upon Aldosterone Excretion in Man." *Journal of Clinical Endocrinology,* 17:1005, 1957; MELICK, R. "Changes in Urinary Steroid Excretion during Examinations." *Australian Annals of Medicine,* 9:200, 1960; CONNELL, A. M.; COOPER, J.; and REDFEARN, J. W. "The Contrasting Effects of Emotional Tensions and Physical Exercise on the Excretion of 17-Ketogenic Steroids and 17-Ketosteroids." *Acta Endocrinologica* (Kobenhavn) 27:179, 1958; HODGES, J. R.; JONES, M. T.; and STOCKHAM, M. A. "Effect of Emotion on Blood Corticotrophin and Cortisol Concentrations in Man." *Nature,* 193:1187, 1962.

30. Thorn: RENOLD, A. E.; QUIGLEY, T. B.; KENNARD, H. E.;

PAGE

and THORN, G. W. "Reaction of the Adrenal Cortex to Physical and Emotional Stress in College Oarsmen." *New England Journal of Medicine*, 244:754, 1951; THORN, G. W.; JENKINS, D.; LAIDLAW, J. C.; GOETZ, F. C.; and REDDY, W. "Response of the Adrenal Cortex to Stress in Man." *Transactions of the Association of American Physicians*, 66:48, 1953.

Chapter 4: The Gland of Creation Can Destroy

36. Apley: APLEY, J. "Recurrent Disorders in Children: A Synthesis." *Acta Paediatrica Scandinavia*, Supplement 172, 1967.

36. Brown: BROWN, W. L. "Biology of the Endocrine System." *New York Medicine*, 115:373, 1922.

37. Soldiers: ZIEGLER, L. H., and LEVINE, B. S. "The Influence of Emotional Reactions on Basal Metabolism." *American Journal of Medical Science*, 169:68, 1925.

37. Wittkower: Cited in: MASON, J. W. "A Review of Psychoendocrine Research on the Pituitary-Thyroid System." *Psychosomatic Medicine*, 30:666, 1968.

37. Relationship with father: HETZEL, B. S.; DE LA HABA, D. S., and HINKLE, L. E., JR. "Life Stress and Thyroid Function in Human Subjects." (Abstract) *Journal of Clinical Endocrinology*, 12:941, 1952; HETZEL, B. S.; DE LA HABA, D. S.; and HINKLE, L. E., JR. "Rapid Changes in Plasma PBI in Euthyroid and Hyperthyroid Subjects." In *Transactions of the American Goiter Association*, p. 242. Springfield, Ill.: Charles C. Thomas, 1952.

38. Distressing movie: ALEXANDER, F.; FLAGG, G. W.; FOSTER, S.; CLEMENS, T.; and BLAHD, W. "Experimental Studies of Emotional Stress: I. Hyperthyroidism." *Psychosomatic Medicine*, 23:104, 1961; FLAGG, G. W.; CLEMENS, T. L.; MICHAEL, E. A.; ALEXANDER, F.; and WARK, J. "A Psychophysiological Investigation of Hyperthyroidism." *Psychosomatic Medicine*, 27: 497, 1965.

38. Parry: PARRY, C. H. *Collections from the Unpublished Writings of the Late Caleb Hillier Parry*, Vol. 1. London: Underwoods, 1825.

38. Graves: GRAVES, R. J. "Newly Observed Affection of the Thyroid Gland in Females." *London Medical and Surgical Journal*, 7:516, 1835.

38. 94 per cent: CONRAD, A. "The Psychiatric Study of Hyperthyroid Patients." *Journal of Nervous and Mental Disease*, 79:505, 1934.

38. 85 per cent: BRAM, I. "Psychic Trauma in Pathogenesis of Exophthalmic Goiter." *Endocrinology*, II:106, 1927.

39. Bastenie: BASTENIE, P. A., *Lancet*, 1:789, 1947.

PAGE

39. Cope: COPE, O. *Man, Mind and Medicine: The Doctor's Education.* Philadelphia: J. B. Lippincott, 1968.
39–43. Betty, Harry Daley, dreams, Doris, Darlene, Alexander theories: ALEXANDER, F., *Psychosomatic Medicine: Its Principles and Applications.* New York: W. W. Norton, 1950.
41. Flagg: FLAGG, G. W. "Psychosomatic Aspects of Hyperthyroidism." In: WAHL, C. W. *New Dimensions in Psychosomatic Medicine.* Boston: Little, Brown, 1964.

Chapter 5: Diseases of Stress

46. Interaction of hormones: MASON, J. W. "Over-all Hormone Balance as a Key to Endocrine Organization." *Psychosomatic Medicine,* 30:791, 1968.
46. Houssay: HOUSSAY, B. C. Comment in: *Hormonal Regulation of Energy Metabolism,* p. 27. Springfield, Ill.: Charles C. Thomas, 1957.
47. Von Bertalanffy: VON BERTALANFFY, L. *Modern Theories of Development.* London: Oxford University Press, 1933.
47. Monkey: MASON, J. W.; BRADY, J. V.; and TOLLIVER, G. A. "Plasma and Urinary 17-Hydroxycorticosteroid Responses to 72-Hour Avoidance in the Monkey." *Psychosomatic Medicine,* 30:608, 1968. Also: MASON, J.W. "Organization of the Multiple Endocrine Responses to Avoidance in the Monkey." *Psychosomatic Medicine,* 30:774, 1968.
48. Adolescent girl: NIXON, R.E. "Emotional Problems of the Adolescent Girl." *Pediatrics Clinics of North America,* 789–801, 1958.
49, 51. Swedish Army, Selye: SELYE, H. "Stress: It's a G.A.S." *Psychology Today,* 3:4:24, September 1969; *The Stress of Life.* New York: McGraw-Hill, 1956.
51. Brady: BRADY, J. P.; THORNTON, D. R.; and De FISCHER, D. "Deleterious Effects of Anxiety Elicited by Conditioned Pre-aversive Stimuli in the Rat." *Psychosomatic Medicine,* 24:590, 1962.
54. Tuberculosis in rats: SELYE, H. "The General Adaptation Syndrome and Gastroenterology." Lecture at Gastroenterological Congress, New York, 1952.

Chapter 6: Subject To Change

55. Mabaan: BAASHER, T. A. "Treatment and Prevention of Psychosomatic Disorders: Psychosomatic Diseases in East Africa." *American Journal of Psychiatry,* 121:1095, 1965.
55. Peoples with simple ways of life: WITTKOWER, E. D., and LIPOWSKI, Z. J. "Recent Developments in Psychosomatic Medicine." *Psychosomatic Medicine,* 28:722, 1966.

PAGE

56. Eskimos: EHRSTRÖM, M. C. *Acta Medica Scandinavica.* 140:254, 1951.

56. Rhodesia, Donaldson: DONALDSON, J. F. "Letter to the Editor." *Psychosomatic Medicine,* 27:193, 1965.

56. Halliday: HALLIDAY, J. L. *Psychosocial Medicine: A Study of the Sick Society.* New York: W. W. Norton, 1948.

57. Holmes: JEFFERS, W. N. "Do Big Events in Your Life Mean You'll Be Ill?" *Medical Economics,* March 16, 1970, 225.

58. Widowers: "Symposium Report: Bereavement." *British Medical Journal,* 3:232, 1967.

58. Widows: MADDISON, D., and VIOLA, A. "The Health of Widows in the Year Following Bereavement." *Journal of Psychosomatic Research,* 12:297, 1968.

58. Mutter and Schleifer: MUTTER, A. Z., and SCHLEIFER, M. J. "The Role of Psychological and Social Factors in the Onset of Somatic Illness in Children." *Psychosomatic Medicine,* 28:333, 1966.

59. Hall: HALL, P. "Some Clinical Aspects of Moving House as an Apparent Precipitant of Psychiatric Symptoms." *Journal of Psychosomatic Research,* 10:59, 1966.

60. Smith: SMITH, J. A. "Occupational Stress and Emotional Illness." *JAMA,* 161:1038, 1956.

61. Jaques: JAQUES, E. "Executive Organization and Individual Adjustment." *Journal of Psychosomatic Research,* 10:77, 1966.

62. Overachievers: MARTIN, H. R., and SWENSON, W. W. "Limited Intelligence as Psychodynamic Stress in Patients with Physical Symptoms." *Postgraduate Medicine.* March 1966, 240.

63. Musicians: "Musicians' Stress Likened to Pilots'." *The New York Times.* February 24, 1970, 34.

63. Investors: SEWIL, C. "Those Patients with Wall Street Sickness." *Medical Economics.* November 10, 1969, 102.

64. Workers' health: KAHN, R. L. "Stress: From 9 to 5." *Psychology Today,* 3:3:34, September 1969.

65. Blaw-Knox: BARMASH, I. *Welcome to Our Conglomerate— You're Fired!* New York: Delacorte, 1971.

Chapter 7: Who Gets What

69. Owens: ALEXANDER, F.; FRENCH, T. M.; POLLOCK, G. H. *Psychosomatic Specificity: Volume I: Experimental Study and Results.* Chicago: University of Chicago Press, 1968.

71. Kubie: KUBIE, L. S. "The Problem of Specificity in the Psychosomatic Process." In: DEUTSCH, F. *The Psychosomatic Concept in Psychoanalysis.* New York: International Universities Press, 1953.

PAGE

72. Dunbar quote: DUNBAR, H. F. *Emotions and Bodily Change.* New York: Columbia University Press, 1954.

72. Gildea: GILDEA, E. F. "Special Features of Personality which Are Common to Certain Psychosomatic Disorders." *Psychosomatic Medicine*, 12:273, 1949.

72. Ring: RING, F. O. "Testing the Validity of Personality Profiles in Psychosomatic Illnesses." *American Journal of Psychiatry*, 113:1075–1080, 1957.

75. Dunbar personality profiles, accident proneness: DUNBAR, H. F. *Psychosomatic Diagnosis.* New York: Paul B. Hoeber, 1943.

78. Alexander: ALEXANDER, F. *Psychosomatic Medicine: Its Principles and Applications.* New York: W. W. Norton, 1950.

81. Rochester studies: YAHRAES, H. "Psychological Factors in Organic Disease." Publication of the National Institute of Mental Health.

82. Schmale: SCHMALE, A. H., JR. "Relationship of Separation and Depression to Disease: I. A Report on a Hospitalized Medical Population." *Psychosomatic Medicine*, 22:4, 1958. "A Genetic View of Affects, with Special Reference to the Genesis of Helplessness and Hopelessness." *Psychoanalytic Study of the Child*, 19, 1964.

84. Greene: GREENE, W. A., JR. "The Psychosocial Setting of the Development of Leukemia and Lymphoma. Psychophysiological Aspects of Cancer." *Annals of the New York Academy of Science*, 1966, 125.

Chapter 8: Choosing Your Symptoms

85. Leon: GARMA, A. "The Psychosomatic Shift through Obesity, Migraine, Peptic Ulcer, and Myocardial Infarction in a Homosexual." *International Journal of Psycho-Analysis* 49:2, 1968.

88. Wahl: WAHL, C. W. "Factors which Affect Symptom Choice in Psychosomatic Medicine." In: WAHL, C. W. *New Dimensions in Psychosomatic Medicine.* Boston: Little, Brown, 1964.

92. Hinkle: HINKLE, L. E.; CHRISTENSON, W. N.; KANE, F. D.; OSTFELD, A.; THETFORD, W. N.; and WOLFF, H. G.: "An Investigation of the Relation between Life Experience, Personality Characteristics, and General Susceptibility to Illness." *Psychosomatic Medicine*, 20:278–295, 1958.

92. Parents: WOLF, C. T.; FRIEDMAN, S. B.; HOFER, M. A.; MASON, J. W. "Relationship between Psychological Defenses and Mean Urinary 17-Hydroxycorticosteroid Excretion Rates: I. A Predictive Study of Parents of Fatally Ill Children." *Psychosomatic Medicine*, 26:576, 1964.

PAGE

Chapter 9: The Psychology of Pain

96. Eyeballs: GOODHART, S. P., and SAVITSKY, N. "Self-mutilation in Chronic Encephalitis." *American Journal of Medical Science,* 185: 647, 1933.

97, 105. Grinker; missing leg: GRINKER, R. R., SR., and ROBBINS, F. P. *Psychosomatic Case Book,* New York: Blakiston, 1954.

97. Maruyama: MARUYAMA, M. "The Effect of Oscillating Future Perspective." *Journal of Existentialism,* 7: 27, 1967.

99. Musician: ISCHLONDSKY, N. E. *Brain and Behavior.* St. Louis: Mosby, 1949.

99. Housebound patients: BLITZ, B., and LOWENTHAL, M. "The Role of Sensory Restriction in Problems with Chronic Pain." *Journal of Chronic Diseases,* Vol. 19, April 1966.

99. Spear: SPEAR, F. G. "Pain in Psychiatric Patients." *Journal of Psychosomatic Research,* Vol. II, 1967.

100. Blumer: BLUMER, D. "A Study of Patients with 'Psychogenic' Pain." *Psychosomatic Medicine,* 23: 5, 1965.

100. Engel: ENGEL, G. L. "Psychogenic Pain and the Pain-prone Patient." *American Journal of Medicine,* 26: 399, 1959.

101. Solitary hunters: TINLING, D. C., and KLEIN, R. F. "Psychogenic Pain and Aggression: the Syndrome of the Solitary Hunter." *Psychosomatic Medicine,* 30: 738, 1966.

104. Phantom limb: MELZACK, R. "Phantom Limbs." *Psychology Today,* October 1970.

106. Warts: "Questioning Hypnosis." *Time* magazine, July 13, 1970.

107. Bochnak: BOCHNAK, M. A. "The Effect of an Automatic and Deliberative Process of Nursing Activity on the Relief of Patient's Pain; a Clinical Experiment." New Haven, Yale University School of Nursing, 1961. Abstracted in *Nursing Research,* 12: 191.

107. Patient choice: MOSS, F. T., and MEYER, B. "The Effects of Nursing Interaction upon Pain Relief in Patients." *Nursing Research,* 15: 4, 1966.

108. Sympathetic nursing: McBRIDE, M. A. "Nursing Approach, Pain and Relief: an Exploratory Experiment." *Nursing Research,* 16: 4, 1967.

Chapter 10: The Conversion of Anxiety

114. Parachutists: FENZ, W. D., and EPSTEIN, S. "Gradients of Physiological Arousal in Parachutists as a Function of an Approaching Jump." *Psychosomatic Medicine,* 29: 33, 1967. "Stress: In the Air." *Psychology Today,* 3: 4: 27, September 1960.

PAGE

115. Freud on anxiety: FREUD, S. *The Problem of Anxiety.* New York: W. W. Norton, 1936.

115. Grinker: GRINKER, R. R., SR. "Basic Research on Psychosomatic Illness." National Institute of Mental Health Research Project Seminars.

115. Symptoms: ABSE, W. In: *American Handbook of Psychiatry.* New York: Basic Books, 1959.

116. Girl's appendix: BARRACLOUGH, B. M. "Appendectomy in Women." *Journal of Psychosomatic Research,* 12:231, 1968.

116. Tinnitus: HOOPLE, G. "A Neglected Subject." *Laryngoscope,* 76:1312, 1966.

117. West Point cadet: HAMMER, H. M. "Astasia-abasia: A Report of Two Cases at West Point." *American Journal of Psychiatry,* 124:5, 1967.

117. Johns Hopkins: ZIEGLER, IMBODEN, and MEYER. "Contemporary Conversion Reactions: A Clinical Study." *American Journal of Psychiatry,* 116:901, 1960.

118. Prevalence of conversion reaction: CHERTOK, L. "Psychosomatic Medicine in the West and in Eastern European Countries." *Psychosomatic Medicine,* 31:510, 1969.

118. Dora: FREUD, S. "Fragment of an Analysis of a Case of Hysteria (Vol. VII)." "On Hysterical Attacks (Vol. IX)." *Standard Edition of the Complete Psychological works of Sigmund Freud.* London: Hogarth, 1953.

120. West: WEST, F. H. "Etiology and Mechanisms in the Development of Conversion Reaction." In: NODINE, J. H., and MOYER, J. H. *Psychosomatic Medicine.* Philadelphia: Lea & Febiger, 1962.

Chapter 11: The Hypochondriacs

122. Riemer: RIEMER, M. D. "Disability Determinations of Disorders Based on Emotional Factors." *Industrial Medicine,* May 1967, page 347.

123. Asher: ASHER, R. "Münchhausen's Syndrome." *Lancet* 1:339, 1951.

123. Vail: VAIL, D. J. "Münchhausen Returns: A Case Report." *Psychiatric Quarterly,* 36:317, 1962.

124. Wahl: WAHL, C. W. "Psychodynamics of the Hypochondriacal Patient." In: WAHL, C. W. *New Dimensions in Psychosomatic Medicine.* Boston: Little, Brown, 1964.

125. Smith: SMITH, J. A. "For Some Good Health Is a Hazard." *Medical Times,* September 1964.

128. Mally and Ogston: MALLY, M. A., and OGSTON, W. D.

PAGE

"Treatment of the 'Untreatables.'" *International Journal of Group Psychotherapy*, 14:3, 1964.

132, 134. Lisa, Arthur: ROSNER, B. L. "The Use of Valid Psychological Complaints to Screen, Minimize, or Deny Serious Somatic Illness." *Journal of Nervous and Mental Disease*, 143:3:234, 1966.

133. Denial in brain disease: WEINSTEIN, E. A., and KAHN, R. L. "Denial of Illness." In: ARING, C. D., ed. *American Lectures in Neurology.* Springfield, Ill., Charles C. Thomas, 1955.

133. Macrae: MACRAE, D. "Psychiatric Symptoms and the Neurologist." *Psychosomatics*, 9:1:4, 1968.

133. Faigel: FAIGEL, H. C. "The Adolescent and the Physician." *G.P.*, 32:90, 1965.

134. Seidenberg: SEIDENBERG, R. "Omnipotence, Denial, and Psychosomatic Medicine." *Psychosomatic Medicine*, 25:31, 1963.

Chapter 12: Stomaching the Situation

139, 142, 143. Infant psychology, Vera, Doris. ALEXANDER, F. *Psychosomatic Medicine*, New York: W. W. Norton, 1950.

140. Johnson: JOHNSON, D. E. "Etiology and Mechanisms in Development of Gastrointestinal Reactions." In: NODINE, J. H., and MOYER, J. H., *Psychosomatic Medicine.* Philadelphia: Lea & Febiger, 1962.

140. Tom: WOLF, S., and WOLFF, H. G. "Life Situations, Emotions and Gastric Function: A Summary." In: *Contributions toward Medical Psychology*, Vol. I. New York: The Ronald Press Company, 1953. Also in: WOLF, S. "Stress and the Gut." *Gastroenterology*. 52:2, 1967.

143. Constipation: CHAPMAN, A. H., and LOEB, D. G. "Psychosomatic Gastrointestinal Problems." *A.M.A. Journal of Diseases of Children*, 717:724, 1955. Also: KRAKOWSKI, A. J. "The Role of the Physician in the Management of the Emotionally Disturbed Child." *Psychosomatics*, 215–221, 1963.

144. Boarding school: APLEY, J. "Recurrent Disorders in Children: A Synthesis. *Acta Paediatrica Scandinavica*, Supp. 172, 1967.

144. Susie: OLDS, S. "Say It with a Stomachache." *Today's Health*, November 1970.

145. Paul: SILVERMAN, S. *Psychological Aspects of Physical Symptoms.* "Case 17, Stomach Pain and Depression." New York: Appleton-Century-Crofts, 1968.

146. Richard: GRINKER, R. R., SR., and ROBBINS, F. P. "Brief Therapy of a Psychosomatic Case." *Psychosomatic Case Book.* New York: Blakiston, 1954.

Chapter 13: "It's Eating Away at Me"

148. Andy: SILVERMAN, S. *Psychological Aspects of Physical Symptoms.* New York: Appleton-Century-Crofts, 1968.

150. Johnson: JOHNSON, D. E. "Etiology and Mechanisms in Development of Gastrointestinal Reactions." In: NODINE, J. H., and MOYER, J. H., *Psychosomatic Medicine.* Philadelphia: Lea & Febiger, 1962.

150. Psychology of ulcer patients: ALEXANDER, F.; FRENCH, T. M.; POLLOCK, G. H. *Psychosomatic Specificity: Volume I: Experimental Study and Results.* Chicago: University of Chicago Press, 1968; ALEXANDER, F. *Psychosomatic Medicine.* New York: W. W. Norton, 1950.

152. Peter: CHAPMAN, A. H., and LOEB, D. G. "Psychosomatic Gastrointestinal Problems." *A.M.A. Journal of Diseases of Children,* 717:724, 1955.

153. Three baby boys: GERARD, M. W. "Genesis of Psychosomatic Symptoms in Infancy: the Influence of Infantile Traumata upon Symptom Choice." In: DEUTSCH, F. *The Psychosomatic Concept in Psychoanalysis.* New York: International Universities Press, 1953.

153. Ulcers and school: MILLAR, T. P. "Peptic Ulcers in Children." *Canadian Psychiatric Association Journal,* 10:43–49, 1965.

Chapter 14: Hostile Act

157. Homosexual assault: CASTELNUOVO-TEDESCO, P. "Ulcerative Colitis in an Adolescent Boy Subjected to a Homosexual Assault." *Psychosomatic Medicine,* 24:148–156, 1962.

160. Etiology of ulcerative colitis: WOLF, W. J.; WOLF, S.; and WOLFF, H. G. "Life Situations, Emotions and Chronic Ulcerative Colitis." *JAMA,* 142:1044, 1950.

160. Etiology; Elizabeth: O'CONNOR, J. F. "Psychological Considerations in Ulcerative Colitis." *New York State Journal of Medicine,* April 15, 1968.

161. Characteristics of ulcerative colitis patients: ENGEL, G. L. "Studies of Ulcerative Colitis, III. The Nature of the Psychologic Processes." *American Journal of Medicine,* 19:231, 1955; ENGEL, G. L. "Studies of Ulcerative Colitis. V. Psychological Aspects and Their Implications of Treatment." *American Journal of Digestive Diseases,* 3:315, 1958.

161. 86 per cent with crisis: McKEGNEY, F. P.; GORDON, R. O.; and LEVINE, S. M. "A Psychosomatic Comparison of Patients with Ulcerative Colitis and Crohn's Disease." *Psychosomatic Medicine,* 32:2, March-April 1970.

PAGE

161. Infantile expression of accomplishment: ALEXANDER, F. *Psychosomatic Medicine.* New York: W. W. Norton, 1950.
162. Restricted families: JACKSON, D. D., and YALOM, I. Family Research on the Problem of Ulcerative Colitis. *Archives of General Psychiatry,* 15:410, 1966.
164. Course of ulcerative colitis in children: DAVIDSON, M. "Juvenile Ulcerative Colitis." *New England Journal of Medicine,* 277:26, 1967.
164. Psychodynamics in children: KRAKOWSKI, A. J. "The Role of the Physician in the Management of the Emotionally Disturbed Child." *Psychosomatics,* 215–221, 1963; FINCH, S. M., and HESS, J. H. "Ulcerative Colitis in Children." *American Journal of Psychiatry.* 118:819–826, 1962.

Chapter 15: The People Who Starve Themselves

166. Jason: FULLERTON, D. T. "Infantile Rumination." *Archives of General Psychiatry,* 9:593, 1963.
167. Foster child: LANG, P. J., and MELAMED, B. G. "Case Report: Avoidance Conditioning Therapy of an Infant with Chronic Ruminative Vomiting." *Journal of Abnormal Psychology,* 74(1), 1–8, 1969.
169. Dejerine and Gauckler, ambivalence of adolescent: OFFORD, D. R. "Anorexia Nervosa." *Psychosomatics,* 8:281, September-October 1967.
169. Gull: GULL, W. W. "Anorexia nervosa." *Clinical Society Transactions,* 7:22, 1874; "Anorexia nervosa." *Lancet,* 1:516, 1888.
170. Fear of food: RUSSELL, G. F. M. "The Nutritional Disorder in Anorexia Nervosa." *Journal of Psychosomatic Research,* 2:141, 1967.
170 ff. Blitzer, preoccupation with food, body image, regression, Diane: BLITZER, J. R.; ROLLINS, N.; and BLACKWELL, A. Children Who Starve Themselves: Anorexia Nervosa." *Psychosomatic Medicine,* 5:23, 360–383, 1961.
172, 174. Lesser, Arlene: LESSER, L. I.; ASHENDEN, B. J.; DE-BUSKEY, M.; and EISENBERG, L. "Anorexia Nervosa in Children." *American Journal of Orthopsychiatry,* 30:572–580, 1960.
175. Bulimia: GUIORA, A. Z. "Dysorexia: a Psychopathological Study of Anorexia Nervosa and Bulimia." *American Journal of Psychiatry,* 124:3, September 1967.
175. Wedding cake: DALLY, P. J. "Anorexia Nervosa—Long-term Follow-up and Effects of Treatment." *Journal of Psychosomatic Research,* 8:151–155.
175. Beatrice: EHRENSING, R. H., and WEITZMAN, E. L. "The

PAGE

Mother-daughter Relationship in Anorexia Nervosa." *Psychosomatic Medicine*, 32:2, March-April 1970.

Chapter 16: High Tension

182. Malmo: MALMO, R. B. "Emotions and Muscle Tension: The Story of Anne." *Psychology Today*. March 1970:64.

183. Wilson: WILSON, A. W. "Inability to Open the Mouth: An Unusual Psychosomatic Symptom." *Comprehensive Psychiatry*, 5:4:-271, 1964.

184. Fagg: FAGG, G. "The Role of Habitual Movement and Posture in Psychosomatic Disorder." *Journal of Psychosomatic Research*, 9:165, 1965.

185. Sadger, Alexander: ALEXANDER, F. *Psychosomatic Medicine*. New York: W. W. Norton, 1950.

185. Fenichel: FENICHEL, O. *The Psychoanalytic Theory of Neurosis*. New York: W. W. Norton, 1945.

185. Hoople: HOOPLE, G. "A Neglected Subject." *Laryngoscope*, 76:1312, 1966.

186. Sacks: SACKS, O. *Migraine*. Berkeley: University of California Press, 1971.

186. Friedman: FRIEDMAN, A. "Headache: Differential Diagnosis and Treatment." *Medical Insight*, November 1969.

187. Ralph: MARDER, L., and HOOGERBEETS, J. D. "Psychosomatic Disease as a Masked Depression." *Psychosomatics*, Vol. 8, September-October 1967.

188, 191. Zucker, Bernie: ZUCKER, H. D. "Back Pains Are Real." *Medical Insight*, April 1970.

189. Gottschalk, studies: GOTTSCHALK, L. A. "Psychologic Factors in Backache." *GP*, 33:1:91, 1966.

190. Myrna: BOOTH, G. "The Auspicious Moment in Psychosomatic Medicine." *American Journal of Psychoanalysis*, 29:84, 1969.

190, 192. Halliday, Slaughter: SLAUGHTER, F. G. *Medicine for Moderns*. New York: Messner, 1947.

192. Leopold: LEOPOLD, R. L. "Management of Post-traumatic Neuroses." In: NODINE, J. H., and MOYER, J. H. *Psychosomatic Medicine*. Philadelphia: Lea & Febiger, 1962.

192. Minc: MINC, S. "Psychological Aspects of Backache." *Medical Journal of Australia*, 22:1:964, 1968.

193. Lydia: FORDYCE, W. E.; FOWLER, R. S.; and DeLATEUR, B. "An Application of Behavior-modification Technique to a Problem of Chronic Pain." *Behavior Research and Therapy*, 6:105, 1968.

193. Halberstam: HALBERSTAM, M. J. "Depression in Young Adults." *Medical Insight*, June 1970:39.

PAGE

194. Fatigue in depression: LINDBERG, B. J. "Somatic Complaints in the Depressive Symptomatology." *Acta Psychiatrica Scandinavica*, 41:419, 1965.

194. Shafer: SHAFER, N. "Psychosomatic Diagnosis. *GP*, 33:5:100, May 1966.

194. Riemer: RIEMER, M. D. "Disability Determinations of Disorders Based on Emotional Factors." *Industrial Medicine and Surgery*, May 1967: 347.

196. Alexander and Portis: ALEXANDER, F., and PORTIS, S. A. "A Psychosomatic Study of Hypoglycaemic Fatigue." *Psychosomatic Medicine*, 6:191, 1944.

Chapter 17: Iron Hand

198. Ginny, Ludwig: LUDWIG, A. O. "Rheumatoid Arthritis." In: WITTKOWER, E. D., and CLEGHORN, R. A. *Recent Developments in Psychosomatic Medicine*. Philadelphia: J. B. Lippincott, 1954.

199. Rheumatoid factor: SOLOMON, G. F., and MOOS, R. H. "The Relationship of Personality to the Presence of Rheumatoid Factor in Asymptomatic Relatives of Patients with Rheumatoid Arthritis." *Psychosomatic Medicine*, 27:350, 1965. LAWRENCE, J. S. "Epidemiology of Rheumatoid Arthritis." *Arthritis and Rheumatism*, 6:16, 1963.

199. Meyerowitz: MEYEROWITZ, S.; JACOX, R. F.; and HESS, D. W. "An Investigation of Monozygotic Twins Discordant for Rheumatoid Arthritis." American Psychosomatic Society meeting. San Francisco, April 4, 1964.

201–204, 207. Alexander, anger, Jessica, Sylvia: ALEXANDER, F. *Psychosomatic Medicine*. New York: W. W. Norton, 1950.

201. Josselyn: JOSSELYN, I. M. "Psychosomatic Diseases." *Arizona Medicine*. 22:9:695, 1965.

201–205. Fathers, mothers, anger, duty, personality: MOOS, R. H., and SOLOMON, G. F. "Psychologic Comparisons between Women with Rheumatoid Arthritis and Their Nonarthritic Sisters." *Psychosomatic Medicine*, 27:150, 1965.

202. Fathers: CORMIER, B. M.; WITTKOWER, E. D.; MARCOTTE, V.; and FORGET, F. "Psychological Aspects of Rheumatoid Arthritis." *Canadian Medical Association Journal*, 77:533, 1957.

202. Mothers: CLEVELAND, S. E., and FISHER, S. "Behavior and Unconscious Fantasies of Patients with Rheumatoid Arthritis." *Psychosomatic Medicine*, 16:327, 1954.

202. *"American Gothic"*: GERARD, M. W. "Genesis of Psychosomatic Symptoms in Infancy." In: DEUTSCH, F., ed. *The Psychosomatic Concept in Psychoanalysis*. New York: International Universities Press, 1953.

Chapter 18: Flight from Womanhood

211. Nancy, O'Neill, excessive bleeding: O'NEILL, D. "Psychological Aspects of Gynecology and Obstetrics." In: WITTKOWER, E. D., and CLEGHORN, R. A. *Recent Developments in Psychosomatic Medicine.* Philadelphia: J. B. Lippincott, 1954.

212. Personality types with dysmenorrhea: WITTKOWER, E. D., and WILSON, A. T. M. "Dysmenorrhea and Sterility, Personality Studies." *British Medical Journal,* 2:586, 1940; LEVITT, E. E., and LUBIN, B. "Some Personality Factors Associated with Menstrual Complaints and Menstrual Attitudes." *Journal of Psychosomatic Research,* 2:267, 1967; PAULSON, M. J., and WOOD, K. R. "Perceptions of the Emotional Correlates of Dysmenorrhea." *American Journal of Obstetrics and Gynecology,* August 1, 1966.

212. Eleanor, May: BENEDEK, T. "The Functions of the Sexual Apparatus and Their Disturbances." In: ALEXANDER, F. *Psychosomatic Medicine,* New York: W. W. Norton, 1950.

213. Amenorrhea: SLAP, J. W., and NODINE, J. H. "Etiology and Mechanisms in Development of Genito-urinary Reactions." In: NODINE, J. H., and MOYER, J. H. *Psychosomatic Medicine.* Philadelphia: Lea & Febiger, 1962.

213. Amenorrhea and hypnosis: DUNBAR, H. F. *Mind and Body: Psychosomatic Medicine.* New York: Random House, 1966.

214. Nixon: NIXON, R. E. "Emotional Problems of the Adolescent Girl." *Pediatrics Clinics of North America,* 789, 1958.

214. Kathy, Ann: ENGELS, W. D.; PATTEE, C. J.; and WITTKOWER, E. D. "Emotional Settings of Functional Amenorrhea." *Psychosomatic Medicine,* 26:6, 1964.

215. Andrea: PAGE, E. W. "Psychiatric Problems in Obstetrics and Gynecology. *Psychosomatics.* 8:251, September-October 1966.

216. Study of 36 women: ADAM, G. "Brush Up Your Medicine: Functional Gynaecological Disorders." *Medical Journal of Australia,* July 9, 1966.

216. Irritable bladder: CHERTOK, L. "The Irritable Bladder Syndrome." *Medical Insight,* May 1970.

217. Vaginismus: BENEDEK, T., and ELLISON, C. "Psychosomatic Factors in the Unconsummated Marriage." *Journal of Psychosomatic Research,* 12:61, 1968.

218. Naomi: PADDOCK, R. *Spurious Pregnancy. American Journal of Obstetrics and Gynecology,* 16:845, 1928.

218. Doris: SELZER, J. G. "Pseudocyesis in a Six-year-old Girl." *Journal of the American Academy of Child Psychiatry,* 7:4:693, 1968.

PAGE

220. Farm animals: COPE, O. *Man, Mind and Medicine: The Doctor's Education.* Philadelphia: J. B. Lippincott, 1968.

220. Erickson: ERICKSON, M. T. "Method for Frequent Assessment of Symptomology during Pregnancy." *Psychological Reports,* 20:447, 1967.

220. Complications of pregnancy: WOLFF, H. H. "Psychiatric Disorders of Pregnancy." *Journal of Psychosomatic Research,* 12:95, 1968; McDONALD, R. L. "Personality Characteristics in Patients with 3 Obstetric Complications." *Psychosomatic Medicine,* 27:4, 1965.

221. Prolonged labors: McDONALD, R. L. "The Role of Emotional Factors in Obstetric Complications: A Review." *Psychosomatic Medicine,* 30:2, 1968.

221. Rena: DUNBAR, H. F. *Mind and Body: Psychosomatic Medicine.* New York: Random House, 1966.

222. Claire: NODINE, J. H., and MOYER, J. H. *Psychosomatic Medicine.* Philadelphia: Lea & Febiger, 1962.

222. Personality of infertile woman: SMITH, J. A. "Psychogenic Factors in Infertility and Frigidity." *Southern Medical Journal,* 49:4, 1956.

223. Sandler: SANDLER, B. "Emotional Stress and Infertility." *Journal of Psyschosomatic Research,* 12:51, 1968.

223. Adrenalin and miscarriage: BERLE, B. B., and JAVERT, C. T. "Stress and Habitual Abortion." *American Journal of Obstetrics and Gynecology,* 3:298, 1954.

223. Nine women: VANDEN BERGH, R. L.; TAYLOR, S.; and DROSE, V. "Emotional Illness in Habitual Aborters Following Suturing of the Incompetent Cervical Os." *Psychosomatic Medicine,* 28:3, 1966.

224. Viola: DUNBAR, H. F., *Mind and Body: Psychosomatic Medicine.* New York: Random House, 1966.

224. Quarrel with father-in-law: MICHEL-WOLFROMM, H. "The Psychological Factor in Spontaneous Abortion." *Journal of Psychosomatic Research,* 12:67, 1968.

225. Miscarriage averted: SIMMEL, E. "Significance of Psychoanalysis for Gynecology." *California Medicine,* 63:169, 1945.

Chapter 19: Pursuit of Manhood

226. Couvade syndrome: TRETHOWAN, W. H. "The Couvade Syndrome—Some Further Observations." *Journal of Psychosomatic Research,* 12:107, 1968.

227–230. "Losing my nature," Allan, Eddie, Andre: MANDELL, A. J. "Management of Sexual Impotence." In: WAHL, C. W., *New*

PAGE

Dimensions in Psychosomatic Medicine. Boston: Little, Brown, 1964.

227. Chapman: CHAPMAN, A. H. "Put-offs and Come-ons." New York: G. P. Putnam, 1968.

227. Impotence in the Middle Ages: JOHNSON, J. "Prognosis of Disorders of Sexual Potency in the Male." *Journal of Psychosomatic Research,* 9:195, 1965; ROBBINS, R. H. *Encyclopaedia of Witchcraft and Demonology.* London: Peter Neville, 1960.

227, 232, 233. Impotence, Stan, Fred: DUNBAR, F. *Emotions and Bodily Change.* New York: Columbia University Press, 1954.

229. Penis as destructive organ: BENEDEK, T. "The Functions of the Sexual Apparatus and Their Disturbances." In: ALEXANDER, F. *Psychosomatic Medicine.* New York: W. W. Norton, 1950.

230. Premature ejaculation: MELLGREN, A. "Treatment of Ejaculation Praecox with Thioridazine." *Psychotherapy and Psychosomatics,* 15:454, 1967.

231. Arthur: MENNINGER, K. *Man against Himself.* New York: Harcourt, Brace & World, 1938.

231, 232. Wahl, Roger: WAHL, C. W., and GOLDEN, J. S. "Psychogenic Urinary Retention." In: *New Dimensions in Psychosomatic Medicine.* Boston: Little, Brown, 1964.

234–236. No interest in sex, Edgar, Sam, Homer and Ellen, Chris: RUTHERFORD, R. N. "Psyche and the Problems of Reproduction." *Psychosomatics,* 8:101, March-April 1967.

236. Sperm and emotional stress: MICHAEL, M. "Male Psychogenic Subfertility and Infertility." *Gynecologia,* 141:265, 1956.

235–236. Palti, retrograde ejaculation, Michael: PALTI, Z. "Psychogenic Male Infertility." *Psychosomatic Journal,* 31:4, 1969.

Chapter 20: Out of Breath

239. Katharina: FREUD, S. "The Girl Who Couldn't Breathe." In: BREUER, J., and FREUD, S. *Studies in Hysteria.* New York: Nervous and Mental Disease Publishing Co., 1937.

240. Charles: SILVERMAN, S. *Psychological Aspects of Physical Symptoms.* New York: Appleton-Century-Crofts, 1968.

240. Hyperventilation: PINE, I. "Hyperventilation Syndrome." *Psychosomatic Medicine,* 8:156, May-June 1967.

241. Remarks of hyperventilators: DUDLEY, D. L.; MARTIN, C. J.; and HOLMES, T. H. "Dyspnea: Psychologic and Physiologic Observations." *Journal of Psychosomatic Research,* 2:325, 1968.

241. Colds: CAPPON, D. "Emotional Aspects of the Common Cold." *Canadian Medical Association Journal,* 79:173, August 1, 1958.

242–243. Jacobs, Rob, Alex: JACOBS, M. A.; SPILKEN, A.; and

PAGE

NORMAN, M. "Relationship of Life Change, Maladaptive Aggression, and Upper Respiratory Infection in Male College Students." *Psychosomatic Medicine,* 31:1, 1969.

243. Susan: DUNBAR, H. F. *Mind and Body: Psychosomatic Medicine.* Random House, 1966.

244. Paper rose: WAHL, C. W. *New Dimensions in Psychosomatic Medicine.* Boston: Little, Brown, 1964.

245. Miller and Baruch: MILLER, H., and BARUCH, D. "Emotional Problems of Childhood and Their Relation to Asthma." *American Journal of Diseases of Children,* 93:242, 1957.

245. Situation produces asthma: HERXHEIMER, H. "Induced Asthma in Humans." *International Archives of Allergy,* 3:192, 1953.

246. Luparello: LUPARELLO, T.; LYONS, H. A.; BLEECKER, E. R.; and McFADDEN, E. R. "Influences of Suggestion on Airway Reactivity in Asthmatic Subjects." *Psychosomatic Medicine,* 30:6, 1968; "The Mechanism of Action of Suggestion in the Induction of Acute Asthma Attacks." *Psychosomatic Medicine,* 31:2, 1969.

246. Cry averts attack: ALEXANDER, F. *Psychosomatic Medicine.* New York: W. W. Norton, 1950.

247. Bond with mother: STEIN, M. "Etiology and Mechanisms in the Development of Asthma." In: NODINE, J. H., and MOYER, J. H. *Psychosomatic Medicine.* Philadelphia: Lea & Febiger, 1962.

247. Sperling: SPERLING, M. "Asthma in Children—an Evaluation of Concepts and Therapies." *Journal of the American Academy of Child Psychiatry,* Vol. 7, 1968.

248. Peshkin and parentectomy: PESHKIN, M. M. "Rehabilitation of the Intractable Asthmatic Child by the Institutional Approach." *Quarterly Review of Pediatrics,* 11:7, 1956; "The Treatment of Institutionalized Children with Intractable Asthma." *Connecticut Medicine,* 24:166, 1960.

247–249. Therapy of parents: ABRAMSON, H. A., and PESHKIN, M. M. "Psychosomatic Group Therapy with Parents of Children with Intractable Asthma." *Annals of Allergy,* 18:87, 1960.

Chapter 21: Thin Skin

250. Widowed woman: PURCHARD, P. R. "Some Psychiatric Aspects of Dermatology." *Psychiatric Quarterly,* 41:2, 1967.

251. Musaph: MUSAPH, H. "Psychodynamics in Itching States." *International Journal of Psycho-Analysis,* 49:2, 1968.

251. Eileen: ALEXANDER, F. *Psychosomatic Medicine.* New York: W. W. Norton, 1950.

251. Spitz: SPITZ, R. *The First Year of Life.* New York: International Universities Press, 1965.

PAGE

252. Hair loss and stress: LUBOWE, I. I., and COHEN, I. H. "Can Alopecia Areata Be Psychogenic in Origin?" *JAMA* 205(2), 120, 1968.

252. Cohen, Sarah: COHEN, I. H., and LICHTENBERG, J. D. "Alopecia Areata." *Archives of General Psychiatry,* 17(5), 608, 1967.

253. Mehlman: MEHLMAN, R. D., and GRIESEMER, R. D. "Alopecia Areata in the Very Young." *American Journal of Psychiatry,* 125(5), 605, 1968.

253. Gardner and Diamond: GARDNER, F. H., and DIAMOND, L. E. "Autoerythrocyte Sensitization: A Form of Purpura Producing Painful Bruising Following Autosensitization to Red Cells in Certain Women." *Blood,* 10:675, July 1955.

254. Agle: AGLE, D. P.; RATNOFF, O. D.; and WASMAN, M. "Conversion Reactions in Autoerythrocyte Sensitization: Their Relationship to the Production of Ecchymoses." *Archives of General Psychiatry,* 20:4:438, 1969; "Studies in Autoerythrocyte Sensitization: The Induction of Purpuric Lesions by Hypnotic Suggestion." *Psychosomatic Medicine,* 29:5, 1967.

254. Stigmata: HILDENBRAND, B. "Stigmata: a Matter of Mind or Miracle?" *Today's Health,* August 1970.

256. Richter: RICHTER, C. P. "On the Phenomenon of Sudden Death in Animals and Man." *Psychosomatic Medicine,* 19:3, May-June 1957.

256–257. Basedow, Warner, Cannon, primitive deaths: CANNON, W. B. " 'Voodoo' death." *Psychosomatic Medicine,* 19:3, May-June 1957.

257. Mathis, Robert: MATHIS, J. L. "A Sophisticated Version of Voodoo Death." *Psychosomatic Medicine,* 26:2, 1964.

Chapter 22: Heartfelt Emotions

261. Don: RAHE, R. H., and CHRIST, A. E. "An Unusual Cardiac (Ventricular) Arrhythmia in a Child: Psychiatric and Psychophysiologic Aspects." *Psychosomatic Medicine,* 28:2, 1966.

261. Stress and heart changes: WITTKOWER, E. D., and CLEGHORN, R. A. *Recent Developments in Psychosomatic Medicine.* Philadelphia: J. B. Lippincott, 1954.

263. Electrocardiagram and personal matters: STEVENSON, I. P.; DUNCAN, C. H.; and WOLFF, H. G. "Circulatory Dynamics before and after Exercise in Subjects with and without Structural Heart Disease during Anxiety and Relaxation." *Journal of Clinical Investigation,* 28:1534, 1949.

264. Personality of heart patients: MAI, F. M. M. "Personality and Stress in Coronary Disease." *Journal of Psychosomatic Research,* 12:275, 1968.

PAGE

264. Hard-driving men: FRIEDMAN, M.; ROSENMAN, R. H.; and CARROLL, V. "Changes in Serum Cholesterol and Blood Clotting in Men Subjected to Cyclic Variations of Occupational Stress." *Circulation*, 17:852, 1958.

265. Job loss: KASL, S. V., and COBB, S. "Blood Pressure Changes in Men Undergoing Job Loss: A Preliminary Report." *Psychosomatic Medicine*, 32:1, 1970.

266. Jules: THOMAS, C. "Psychophysiologic Aspects of Blood Pressure Regulations: The Clinician's View." *Psychosomatic Medicine*, 26:4, 1964.

267. Joan: MANDELL, A. J. "Psychological Management of Coronary Artery Disease." In: WAHL, C. W., ed. *New Dimensions in Psychosomatic Medicine*. Boston: Little, Brown, 1964.

268. Death from snakebite: WOLF, S. "Cardiovascular Reactions to Symbolic Stimuli." *Circulation*, 18:288, 1958.

268. Medicolegal landmark: "Cause of Death: Fright," *Newsweek*, December 27, 1965.

268. Heart attack and depression, Simon: DREYFUSS, F.; DASBERG, H.; and ASSAEL, M. I. "The Relationship of Myocardial Infarction to Depressive Illness." *Psychotherapy and Psychosomatics* 17:73, 1969.

270. Van Der Valk and Groen, Irwin: VAN DER VALK, J. M., and GROEN, J. J. "Personality Structure and Conflict Situation in Patients with Myocardial Infarction." *Journal of Psychosomatic Research*, 11:41, 1967.

Chapter 23: A Cancer Personality?

271. Dunbar: DUNBAR, H. F. *Emotions and Bodily Changes*. New York: Columbia University Press, 1954.

272. LeShan, hopeless statements: LeSHAN, L. "An Emotional Life-history Pattern Associated with Neoplastic Disease." *Annals of the New York Academy of Science*, Vol. 125, January 1966.

273. Endocrines and cancer: RAKOFF, A. F. "Discussion of the Papers." *Annals of the New York Academy of Science*, Vol. 125, January 1966.

274. Cervical cancer: SCHMALE, A. H., JR., and IKER, H. P. "The Affect of Hopelessness and the Development of Cancer." *Psychosomatic Medicine*, 28:5, 1966; SCHMALE, A. H., JR., and IKER, H. P. "The Psychological Setting of Uterine Cervical Cancer." *Annals of the New York Academy of Science*, Vol. 125, January 1966.

274–275. Kissen, lung cancer: KISSEN, D. M. "Psychological Factors, Personality and Lung Cancer in Men Aged 55–64." *British Journal of Medical Psychology*, 40:29, 1967; KISSEN, D. M. "The

Significance of Personality in Lung Cancer in Men." *Annals of the New York Academy of Science,* Vol. 125, January 1966.

275–276. Greene, Mike, Joe, Clara, leukemia: GREENE, W. A. "The Psychological Setting of the Development of Leukemia and Lymphoma." *Annals of the New York Academy of Science,* Vol. 125, January 1966; GREENE, W. A. "Psychological Factors and the Development of Reticuloendothelial Disease." *Psychosomatic Medicine,* 16:3, 1954.

277. Lion and Hackett, William, premonitions: LION, J. R., and HACKETT, T. P. "Forewarnings of Illness: Predictions and Premonitions in Cancer Patients." *American Journal of Psychiatry,* 125:1, July 1968.

278. Neurotic mice: BOVARD, E. W. A., and NEWTON, D. G. "Systematic Early Handling and Prolonged Experience with the Mother as Developmental Variables in the Male Albino Rat." In: BREWER, N. R., ed. *Proceedings of the Animal Care Panel,* 1955, 67–74. Chicago, Ill., 1956.

278. Progression of illness: BLUMBERG, A. M.; WEST, P. M.; and ELLIS, F. W. "A Possible Relationship between Psychological Factors and Human Cancer." *Psychosomatic Medicine,* 16:277, 1954.

278. Stavraky: STAVRAKY, K. M. "Psychological Factors in the Outcome of Human Cancer." *Journal of Psychosomatic Research,* 12:251, 1968.

Chapter 24: "They Are Ignorant of the Whole

283. Engel: ENGEL, G. L. "Medical Education and the Psychosomatic Approach: A Report on the Rochester Experience 1946–1966." *Journal of Psychosomatic Research,* 11:77, 1967.

284. Anderson: ANDERSON, P. C. "Obstacles to Change in Medical Education." *Journal of Medical Education,* 45:139, 1970.

285. Graham: GRAHAM, D. T. "Health, Disease, and the Mind-Body Problem: Linguistic Parallelism." *Psychosomatic Medicine,* 29:1, 1967.

285. Platt: PLATT, R. "Thoughts on Teaching Medicine." *British Medical Journal,* 2:551, 1965.

286. Ruhe: RUHE, C. H. W. "The Educator." *Journal of Medical Education,* 45:473, 1970.

286–287. Survey of medical students: WALTON, H. J., DREWERY, J., and PHILLIP, A. E. "Typical Medical Students." *British Medical Journal,* 2:744, 1964.

286. Lipowski: LIPOWSKI, Z. J. "Review of Consultation Psychiatry and Psychosomatic Medicine. I. General Principles." *Psychosomatic Medicine,* 29:153, 1967.

PAGE

286. Distrust of psychiatrists: SMITH, J. A.; WITTSON, C. L.; RUDY, L. H. "What the Nonpsychiatrist Physician Apparently Does Not Want in Psychiatric Postgraduate Courses." APA colloquium for postgraduate teaching of psychiatry, Los Angeles, Calif., February 16, 1963.

287. Luby: LUBY, E. D. "An Overview of Psychosomatic Disease." In: FRANK, I., and POWELL, M., eds. *Psychosomatic Illness in Childhood and Adolescence.* Springfield, Ill.: Charles C. Thomas, 1967.

288. Pinkerton: PINKERTON, P. "Demonstrating Pitfalls in Insight Promotion with Recorded Case Abstracts." *Journal of Psychosomatic Research,* 11:95, 1967.

289. Cobb: COBB, S. "Monism and Psychosomatic Medicine." *Psychosomatic Medicine,* 19:117, 1957.

290. Steiger: STEIGER, W. A. "The Management of Anxiety Reaction." In: NODINE, J. H., and MOYER, J. H. *Psychosomatic Medicine.* Philadelphia: Lea & Febiger, 1962.

290. Bender: BENDER, D. "A Reexamination of the Crock." In: WAHL, C. W. *New Dimensions in Psychosomatic Medicine.* Boston: Little, Brown, 1964.

291. Owen, Silverman: SILVERMAN, S. *Psychological Aspects of Physical Symptoms.* New York: Appleton-Century-Crofts, 1968.

291. Guerrero: GUERRERO, C. D. "Psychosomatic Iatrogenic Infertility." *Pacific Medicine and Surgery,* May–June 1966.

292. Margolin: MARGOLIN, S. G. "Genetic and Dynamic Psychophysiological Determinants of Pathophysiological Processes." In: DEUTSCH, F., ed. *The Psychosomatic Concept in Psychoanalysis.* New York: International Universities Press, 1953.

292. Bonadero: BONADERO, P. "Nervous-Patient Reminder." *Medical Economics,* May 3, 1965, 47.

292. Wahl: WAHL, C. W. *New Dimensions in Psychosomatic Medicine.* Boston: Little, Brown, 1964.

293. Masserman: MASSERMAN, J. H. "The Office Therapy of Psychosomatic Disorders." *Archives of General Psychiatry,* 3:320, 1960.

294. Cardiac neurotics: WHITEHOUSE, F. A. "Cardiacs without Heart Disease." *Journal of Rehabilitation,* September-October 1967.

295. Pelser: PELSER, H. E. "Psychological Aspects of the Treatment of Patients with Coronary Infarct." *Journal of Psychosomatic Research,* 11:47, 1967.

Chapter 25: Toward The Fullest Flowering of Medicine

296. Melampus: PAPAGEORGIOUS, M. G. "Forms of Psychotherapy in Use in Ancient Greece and among the Population of Mod-

ern Greece." *Psychotherapy and Psychosomatics,* 17:114–118, 1969.

297. Engel, Rochester: ENGEL, G. L. "Medical Education and the Psychosomatic Approach: A Report on the Rochester Experience 1946–1966." *Journal of Psychosomatic Research,* 11:77, 1967. "The Concept of Psychosomatic Disorder." *Journal of Psychosomatic Research,* 11:3–9, 1967.

297. Dorfman: DORFMAN, W. "Role of the Practitioner in the Comprehensive Management of the Patient: Psychosomatic and Somatopsychic Implications of Medical Practice." *Psychosomatics,* Vol. IX, January-February 1968. *Closing the Gap between Medicine and Psychiatry.* Springfield, Ill.: Charles C. Thomas, 1966.

298. Psychosomatic conference: BLAIR, S. M. "A Psychosomatic Conference for Interns." *Military Medicine,* February 1968.

298. Gerty: GERTY, F. J. "Psychiatry—Office Problems, IV: Treatment of Psychoneuroses in the Office." *American Practitioner and Digest of Treatment,* 11:990, 1960.

298–299. Maholick and Warkentin: MAHOLICK, L. T., and WARKENTIN, J. "The Five-dollar Interview with the Older Neurotic Patient." *Journal of the Medical Association of Georgia,* 49:496, 1960.

299. Daugherty: Special issue on family conflicts. *Patient Care,* October 31, 1969, 53.

299. Steiger: STEIGER, W. A. "It's the Little Things That Count." *Psychosomatics,* 8:261, September-October 1967. "Managing Difficult Patients." *Psychosomatics,* 8:6, November-December 1967.

300. Dolger: DOLGER, H. "The Young Diabetic and Family Stress." *Medical Insight.* May 1970.

301. Live longer without worry: FUDERFER, M. "The Concept of Action as a Measure of Living Phenomena." *Science,* 110, 1949.

302. Wolff: WOLFF, H. H. "The Psychotherapeutic Approach." In: HOPKINS, P., and WOLFF, H. H., eds. *Principles of Treatments of Psychosomatic Disorders.* Oxford: Pergamon Press, 1965.

302. Group therapy: SCHWARTZ, W., and PAPAS, A. T. "Verbal Communication in Therapy." *Psychosomatics,* Vol. IX, March-April 1968.

303. Double diagnosis: SHOCHET, B. R., and LISANSKY, E. T. "Making the 'Double Diagnosis': Technique of Comprehensive Medical Diagnosis." *Psychosomatics.* Vol. IX, January-February 1968.

303. Twenty-minute hour: CASTELNUOVO-TEDESCO, P. "The Twenty-Minute 'Hour': An Experiment in Medical Education." In: WAHL, C. W., ed. *New Dimensions in Psychosomatic Medicine.* Boston: Little, Brown, 1964.

303. Research areas: MASON, J. W. "The Scope of Psychoendocrine Research." *Psychosomatic Medicine,* 30:5, 1968. WITT-

PAGE

KOWER, E. D., and LIPOWSKI, Z. J. "Recent Developments in Psychosomatic Medicine." *Psychosomatic Medicine*, 28:5, 1966.

303. Control of autonomic responses: SCHMECK, H. M., JR. "Control by Brain Studies as Way to Curb Body Ills." *The New York Times*, January 10, 1971. MILLER, N. E. "Learning of Visceral and Glandular Responses." *Science*, Vol. 163, January 31, 1969. MILLER, N. E.; DiCARA, L.; SOLOMON, H.; WEISS, J. M.; and DWORKIN, B. "Psychological Aspects of Hypertension; Learned Modifications of Autonomic Functions: A Review and Some New Data." *Supplement I to Circulation Research*. Vols. 26 and 27, July 1970.

INDEX

A Final Judgment

A Final Judgment

A Ron Shade Novel

Michael A. Black

Five Star • Waterville, Maine

This novel is a work of fiction. Names, characters, places and incidents are either the product of the author's imagination, or, if real, used fictitiously.

First Edition
First Printing: September 2006

Published in 2006 in conjunction with Tekno Books and Ed Gorman.

Set in 11 pt. Plantin by Myrna S. Raven

Printed in the United States on permanent paper.

Library of Congress Cataloging-in-Publication Data

Black, Michael A., 1949–
    A final judgment : a Ron Shade novel / Michael A. Black
—1st ed.
        p. cm.
    ISBN 1-59414-426-5 (hc : alk. paper)
    1. Shade, Ron (Fictitious character)—Fiction.   2. Private
investigators—Illinois—Chicago—Fiction.   3. Chicago (Ill.)
—fiction.   I. Title.
    PS3602.L325F56 2006
    813'.6—dc22   2006013785

To Andrew Vachss

Thanks, Brother.

Acknowledgments

Once again, there are many people to whom I owe a debt of gratitude. I would like to thank my "big brother," Andrew Vachss, for pushing me to be the best writer I could be, and for telling me, in his own inimitable style, that I'd better do another Shade novel. (The two other members of our "Chicago Wolf Pack," Mike McNamara and Zak Mucha, are included in this.) A special thanks to Debbie (D.C.) Brod, who agreed to come out of "editing retirement" to edit this book and find out if Shade does fight for the title this time. Another special thanks to Julie A. Hyzy, my special friend and writing partner, who helped me build this one, step by step, and always told me when I was going wrong. Thanks to my buddies and peerless first readers, J. Michael Major and Len Jellema, both of whom are talented writers in their own right. Thanks to Ray Lovato, my brother and best friend since we both ran up that dirt hill so many years ago. Thanks to my cop-writer buddies, who never let me down when I needed support or advice, Jim Born, Dave Case, Paul Doyle, John Lamb, and Rick McMahan. Thanks to Mr. Stephen Marlowe, whose work inspired me and whose kind words of support gave me faith in myself. Thanks to Tiffany Schofield, Mary Smith, Myrna Raven, and all the rest of the wonderful people at Five Star who had faith in my ability as a writer. Thanks to Martin Greenberg and the great staff at Tekno Books, John Helfers and Denise Little, for their faith in me as well. Thanks to the members of my writers' groups who listened and gave me their honest opinions. There are so many more, too numerous to mention, who have helped me realize my dream of being a writer, who may not be mentioned here, but hold a special place in my heart. Thanks to you all.

Chapter 1

I usually try to avoid lawyers unless it becomes a case of absolute necessity. This one wasn't, but it had all the earmarks of coming real close. It started with a message from my service that Rick Walters wanted me to call him as soon as possible. I'd known Rick from the days when he was an Assistant State's Attorney, and I was a cop. He'd always impressed me as an honest and likeable guy. I often wondered if he had too many of those qualities to be a really effective lawyer.

I looked out the plate-glass window of the restaurant, swallowed a bit of my coffee, and took out my cell phone. Outside, the traffic was backing up along Western Avenue, and my buddy George, who was supposed to be meeting me here this morning, still hadn't shown up. Yet it was a beautiful spring day, full of bright sunshine, cool temperatures, and the promise of things to come. In a few hours I'd be enjoying an afternoon run before my workout. The message from my service loomed in my memory again.

I dialed the number and got connected to his secretary.

"This is Ron Shade," I said, "returning Mr. Walters's call."

"Oh, yes, Mr. Shade, hold on, please."

She'd called me "mister." Always a positive sign.

I waited about thirty seconds, and Rick came on the line.

"Ron, thanks for calling back."

"My pleasure," I said. Mentally I conjured up how he'd looked when I'd last seen him. Curly brown hair, fleshy cheeks, solid build.

"Are you available?" he asked. "I mean for hire. You still have your private investigating business, don't you?"

"Unless the state's planning on revoking my license. And hopefully that won't happen anytime soon."

"Good, good," he said, adding a nervous-sounding chuckle. "When could you come over to talk? I want to hire you."

A red flag went up. Now that Rick was in private practice, that meant I'd be working for the defense. Something I wasn't sure I really wanted to do if the client was some scumbag. He must have sensed my hesitation when I asked about it, because he sprang in with all kinds of assurances.

"This isn't a criminal case, Ron," he said. "In fact, it's just the opposite. A wrongful death suit. The family's hired me to go after the guy the state couldn't put away."

"I see. What are the circumstances?"

"An ugly divorce," he said. "Got real ugly when the wife turned up dead. Husband was arrested and charged, but acquitted. Now we got one last shot to try and get some justice."

"That's in short supply these days." I glanced at my watch. "Okay, I'll drop by this afternoon, if that's all right."

"That'd be great," he said. There was something else; I could tell in his tone. When he spoke again his words were rapid. "There's a little more to it than that, but we can go over it when you get here, okay?"

I told him it was, and that I'd be there at one-thirty. But after we hung up, I couldn't shake the vague uneasiness I was feeling in the pit of my stomach.

Suddenly I saw George's big form passing in front of the window. His head swiveled and our eyes met. He grinned and gave a small wave. I figured he was on his way into work from the way he was dressed: a gray sports jacket that looked like it'd barely made it out of the last century intact, and dark slacks. I could see the outline of his gun, in its pancake holster on his hip, and his shining Chicago star right in front of it. His white shirt was tight around his gut, and made me realize he'd gained weight, which worried me. He was in his early fifties, and spent way too much time sitting behind a desk, drinking way too much coffee, and eating way too much greasy food.

He pulled open the door and headed over toward my table. There seemed to be a bit more gray in his dark hair, too. Like he'd had it frosted, or something. And that wasn't likely.

"Hiya," he said, sliding into the booth opposite me. "Sorry I'm late."

"You seem out of breath," I said. "You had a physical lately?"

"Huh?" His mouth stayed open, and bundles of crow's feet gathered at the corners of his eyes. "What are you talking about?"

"A physical. You know, been checked out by a doctor lately?"

His mouth closed, drawing into a semi-scowl.

"Yeah, right. Who the hell has the time?" He took a deep breath, and looked out the window. "It's a great-looking morning, ain't it?"

The waitress came over with a second cup and the pot of coffee. She set the cup in front of George and asked if he wanted some.

"Absolutely," he said.

"Maybe you should switch to tea," I said.

"Tea?" His brow furrowed, and when the waitress stepped away, he added, "What the fuck is wrong with you today?"

"With me? Nothing. I'm just . . ." I let the sentence dangle. "Concerned that you're not taking good enough care of yourself, that's all."

He snorted as he brought the cup to his lips.

"You trying to make me choke, or what?" he asked. After a long sip, he set it down and looked across the table at me.

I'd always thought George looked like a young Robert Mitchum, but recently he'd begun to take on the more pouchy look that Mitch had developed in his later years. Still, he was a big guy and carried the extra weight well.

"Anyway," he said, "if you're through insulting me, I got some very interesting news for you."

His smile, from across the table, was damn near infectious. Almost gleeful.

"What might that be?" I asked, cocking my head. This could be either real good, or real bad. From his grin, I figured it must be good.

"I got a job for you," he said.

"A job?"

He nodded. "And you'll never guess who the client is."

"Then there's no sense trying."

He smirked again, like a teenager who could barely conceal news of his first sexual conquest.

"Lieutenant Bielmaster," he said.

I felt my jaw drop. The name stunned me. Bielmaster had made it very clear that he had no use for me on many occasions. In fact, he'd made official complaints to the state licensing committee several times, trying to get my PI license revoked.

George sat across from me, watching my reaction, with that Cheshire cat's smile still plastered on his face.

"You're kidding, right?" I said.

He shook his head and waved for the waitress.

"Come on," I said. "This is the same Lieutenant Bielmaster that I've known and loved for so long?"

"The one and only." He took another sip of coffee and turned to the waitress, keeping me in suspense while he ordered his customary eggs sunny-side up, bacon, toast, and orange juice. She turned to me.

"Scrambled," I said weakly. "Skip the bacon, and make my toast whole wheat, no butter."

When she left, I stared at him.

"Suppose you tell me what this is all about?"

The grin again. "Of course, but let me at least have a little fun first."

I stared directly at him.

"The lieutenant wants to hire your services," he said.

"Bullshit."

That got another smirk out of him.

"No, it's true." A furrow appeared between his eyebrows. "You heard he's in the hospital, right?"

I hadn't. I asked what the problem was.

"Ticker," he said, pointing to his own chest. "Gotta have a bypass."

I raised my eyebrows. "That sounds serious. Any idea what he wants from me?"

George took a swig of his coffee.

"Just that he made a point of calling me last night and being real secretive about it." He set the cup down. "And, he said something else that you might find interesting."

The wide grin again. He was either enjoying this more than he should, or what he was about to tell me was extremely shocking.

"He mentioned that if you help him," George said, still grinning, "that he might be able to speak to somebody to get you reinstated on the PD."

I was stunned. I'd lost my job with the police department after a botched HBT/SWAT operation, and my appeal had evolved into an endless series of continuances. Bielmaster himself had always taken a hard line with me, giving George a lot of grief because we were close friends.

"You're kidding, right?" I asked.

He shook his head slowly, still grinning.

I looked down at the table, unsure of what to think.

George reached over and tapped my hand with his fingers.

"Hey, Ron, this is your big chance here. You could get back on the job, full pay and bennies, not to mention back pay." He paused. "Then you could take the detective exam . . . Hell, we could be working together in no time."

"I don't know," I said slowly, shaking my head.

"You don't know what? You want back in, don't you?"

I took a deep breath, uncertain of the answer. Sure, it was something I'd sought for several years, but I'd been able to build up my own business fairly well, and wasn't handcuffed by a lot of rules. Still, I'd be working for the right side, and not have to worry about owing loyalty to some unsavory client. But regardless, it would have been nice to leave on my own terms.

"How come you ain't saying something?" he asked, the lines appearing between his brows again.

"I'm just kind of used to working for myself. Being my own boss . . ."

The waitress came carrying a tray with our plates. George moved his cup and smiled at me.

"Yeah," he said, chuckling, "but remember what you always tell me. If you work for yourself, you got no one to blame if your boss is an asshole."

14

dants to rearrange our seating so that I could stretch out without a seat in front of me. And the whole way back he kept asking how I was, and saying, "Lordy, I shoulda never let you fight that dude."

"What are you talking about?" I asked him. "I knocked him out, didn't I?"

His dark eyes looked solemn, and his shaved mahogany head glistened under the dome lights.

"Yeah, you did," he said. "But sometimes you can win, and still lose."

Yeah, I thought as I shifted into gear and pulled out of the space, seeing Bielmaster's smug expression in my mind's eye. Sometimes you can.

Chapter 2

Rick Walters's office was nicely furnished, the way most suburban law offices are. The carpeting was functional brown, capable of hiding the overt winter dirt until the annual spring cleaning, and the furniture was slightly above what could crassly be called cheap. Even Rick's secretary looked harried and overworked, although I did have to admit, she was a babe. She looked to be in her mid-twenties with dark hair and a bronze-colored complexion. Her smile was dazzling as I told her who I was and that I had an appointment to see Mr. Walters.

Rick came out of his office to greet me, extending his open hand from a rolled-up shirtsleeve.

"Ron, thanks for coming," he said, making me feel extra welcome and a bit uneasy at the same time.

Inside, I checked out the certificates and pictures on his wall. John Marshall Law School, Northern Illinois University, an academy graduation picture of him in uniform shaking hands with the Chicago Police Superintendent, and a final eight-by-ten of him receiving the medal of valor after being wounded in the line of duty. Pictures of his mother and father sat in a gold frame on the front of his desk, which was awash with papers.

He gestured toward the chair in front and leaned over to stretch his back. When he turned and sat down, I automatically looked for the small, star-shaped scar on his left temple left by the bullet that had almost ended his life. The scar was still there, like a small, reddish jewel.